Roblox Lua Scripting Essentials

A Step-by-Step Guide

Christopher Coutinho

Apress®

Roblox Lua Scripting Essentials: A Step-by-Step Guide

Christopher Coutinho
Mumbai, Maharashtra, India

ISBN-13 (pbk): 979-8-8688-0025-2   ISBN-13 (electronic): 979-8-8688-0026-9
https://doi.org/10.1007/979-8-8688-0026-9

Managing Director, Apress Media LLC: Welmoed Spahr
Acquisitions Editor: Spandana Chatterjee
Development Editor: James Markham
Project Manager: Jessica Vakili

Cover image designed by rawpixel.com on Freepik

Distributed to the book trade worldwide by Springer Science+Business Media New York, 1 New York Plaza, Suite 4600, New York, NY 10004-1562, USA. Phone 1-800-SPRINGER, fax (201) 348-4505, e-mail orders-ny@ springer-sbm.com, or visit www.springeronline.com. Apress Media, LLC is a California LLC and the sole member (owner) is Springer Science + Business Media Finance Inc (SSBM Finance Inc). SSBM Finance Inc is a **Delaware** corporation.

For information on translations, please e-mail booktranslations@springernature.com; for reprint, paperback, or audio rights, please e-mail bookpermissions@springernature.com.

Apress titles may be purchased in bulk for academic, corporate, or promotional use. eBook versions and licenses are also available for most titles. For more information, reference our Print and eBook Bulk Sales web page at http://www.apress.com/bulk-sales.

Any source code or other supplementary material referenced by the author in this book is available to readers on GitHub (https://github.com/Apress/Roblox-Lua-Scripting-Essentials). For more detailed information, please visit https://www.apress.com/gp/services/source-code.

Paper in this product is recyclable

To my unwavering pillars of support and inspiration, this book is dedicated to my beloved parents, wife, and daughter whose unwavering encouragement and boundless love have been the guiding stars of my journey into the world of Roblox scripting. Your belief in my dreams has been the foundation upon which I've built my passion for game development.

In the world of Roblox scripting, where lines of code become adventures, and virtual worlds come to life, your love and support have been the ultimate power-up.

With all my love and appreciation,

Christopher Coutinho

Table of Contents

About the Author

Christopher Coutinho is a game developer with an impressive seven-year track record in the domain of virtual reality (VR) development. As the visionary founder of Game Works, a cutting-edge game development studio based in Mumbai, he has honed his expertise in creating immersive virtual reality experiences.

His contributions extend beyond the commercial sphere; he has also played a pivotal role in shaping the next generation of game developers. He has been an instrumental educator, sharing his knowledge and insights in video game development through platforms like iDTech, a division of Emeritus. His teachings span popular game engines such as Unity and Roblox. Additionally, Christopher has taught a specialized program on augmented/virtual reality (AR/VR) design created by the NYU – Tandon School of Engineering, for iDTech. His blend of hands-on experience and pedagogical prowess positions him as a leading figure in the contemporary gaming landscape.

About the Technical Reviewer

Dr. Tiow Wee Tan is an Associate Professor at the Game School, Inland Norway University of Applied Science (INN), Norway. He also serves as the Course Leader for the Augmented and Virtual Reality Add-On Program at the Game School.

Before joining Game School at INN in 2019, Tiow Wee received his BSc (Hons.) in Computer Science (Software Engineering) from the University of Greenwich, UK, an MSc in Computer Vision, Visual, and Virtual Environments from the University of Leeds, UK, and a PhD in Bi-manual Interaction within Virtual Environments from the University of Salford, UK. After completing his PhD, he worked as a Post-Doctoral Research Assistant at the Materials Science Center, University of Manchester, UK, and later pursued a career as a Senior Lecturer and Course Leader for the Computer Games Technology course at Manchester Metropolitan University, UK.

Tiow Wee's research interests encompass the development of XR (extended reality) for cross-disciplinary enterprise applications. In the past, he has also been involved in neural networks and artificial intelligence (AI) for gaming. Currently, his research focuses on emotion and personality AI, with an emphasis on representing emotion traits through facial expressions for digital learning in VR. Additionally, Tiow Wee is conducting research on realistic interactions with physical objects within VR environments.

His primary research areas of focus include

1. Use of AR and VR technology in game engines

2. Development of hybrid versions of augmented and virtual reality for applications in healthcare, art, and tourism

3. Utilization of deep learning algorithms for predicting micro-facial expressions and their integration into simulations and games

4. Exploration of human cognitive issues integrated into neural network systems in the context of human-computer interaction environments

Acknowledgments

Writing a book is never a solitary endeavor. It takes the collective efforts, encouragement, and support of many individuals to bring a project like this to fruition. I would like to express my heartfelt gratitude to those who have played a pivotal role in making *Roblox Lua Scripting Essentials: A Step-by-Step Guide* a reality.

First and foremost, I want to extend my deepest appreciation to the Roblox community. Your passion for game development and Lua scripting has been a constant source of inspiration. Your questions, feedback, and enthusiasm have shaped the content of this book.

I am immensely thankful to the talented Roblox developers whose work has enriched the platform and provided valuable insights for this book. Your contributions to the Roblox ecosystem are truly remarkable.

To my dedicated editor and the publishing team, thank you for your guidance, patience, and expertise in helping me refine and polish this manuscript. Your commitment to excellence has made this book a better resource for readers.

I want to acknowledge the mentors and teachers who have shared their knowledge and expertise in Lua scripting and game development. Your guidance has been instrumental in shaping my own understanding and skills, which I now pass on to others through this book.

To my family and friends, thank you for your unwavering support and understanding during the long hours of writing and research. Your encouragement has kept me motivated throughout this journey.

Last, but certainly not least, I want to thank the readers of this book. Your interest in learning and mastering Lua scripting for Roblox has driven me to create a resource that I hope will help you achieve your game development goals.

Writing this book has been a rewarding experience, and I am grateful to everyone who has been a part of it. I hope *Roblox Lua Scripting Essentials: A Step-by-Step Guide* serves as a valuable companion on your journey to becoming a skilled Roblox developer.

With deep appreciation,

Christopher Coutinho

Introduction

Prologue

In the boundless universe of digital creation, game development is one of the most vibrant and exciting frontiers. It is a realm where imagination meets reality, where pixels and code blend to create worlds as real as our dreams. And in this world, the Roblox platform shines like a beacon, inviting creators from all walks of life to embark on an extraordinary journey.

The joy of creating, the thrill of problem-solving, and the satisfaction of sharing one's creation with others are no longer confined to the experienced few. Roblox opens the gates to everyone, regardless of age or experience, and within these pages lies the map to navigate this wondrous landscape.

Who Is This Book Written For?

Whether a hobbyist, an educator, a student, or simply curious, this guide is for anyone eager to step into the universe of Roblox development. It's a tool, a mentor, and a friend for those who have the spark to create, imagine, and explore virtual worlds. You don't have to be an expert; all you need is the will to learn.

What You'll Learn

This guide is your compass as you

- Dive into Lua: Explore the foundational concepts that power Roblox Lua scripting.

- Master Roblox Studio: Unlock the capabilities of this incredible creative tool.

- Hone your skills: Learn to write scripts that breathe life into your games.

- Design with purpose: Learn the principles to make your game resonate with players.

What Is Required for This Book?

Embark on this adventure with:

- A computer: The vessel to navigate the Roblox universe.

- Internet connection: Your gateway to resources, updates, and community.

- A Roblox account: Your passport to creation and publication.

- A thirst for knowledge: Experience is not required, only a passion for learning.

How to Use This Book

Travel at your pace, starting at the very beginning, or leap to sections that intrigue you. This book adapts to your journey, providing a comprehensive guide to your success. In the realm of programming, hands-on practice is often the most effective path to mastery. Engaging directly with the code, experimenting with each listing, and applying what you've learned through practical exercises are central to this book's approach. *Roblox Lua Scripting Essentials: A Step-by-Step Guide* is designed as a hands-on resource to enrich your learning experience, allowing you to read about and actively practice and internalize the essential concepts of Lua scripting within Roblox. Your journey through these pages will be an interactive exploration, providing a tangible and immersive understanding of the subject.

Downloadable Content

Enhance your ease of learning with the downloadable scripts available at the Apress GitHub link for this book [https://github.com/Apress/Roblox-Lua-Scripting-Essentials] – a treasure trove to deepen your understanding and skill.

   Roblox Lua Scripting Essentials: A Step-by-Step Guide is not merely a book; it's a voyage into a universe where your creativity reigns supreme. As you turn these pages, you take the first step on a thrilling journey of creation, learning, and infinite possibility. Welcome aboard, dear developer. Here's to your triumph and joy as you unearth the wonders of Roblox Lua scripting!

CHAPTER 1

Introduction

Welcome to the exciting world of Roblox game development!

Roblox is an unparalleled behemoth in entertainment platforms, offering a unique gaming and game creation fusion. Boasting a staggering user base of over 200 million active monthly participants, Roblox is a fertile ground for aspiring and seasoned developers to breathe life into their visions and craft triumphant games, commonly called experiences. The beauty of this creative platform lies in its accessibility; players worldwide can indulge in these captivating experiences without any financial burden. With a wealth of invaluable resources and an expansive, supportive community of developers from diverse corners of the globe, stepping into the Roblox game development scene unveils unparalleled opportunities that resonate in a league of their own.

In this chapter, you will delve into the fundamental aspects of creating immersive experiences on the Roblox platform. We'll begin by guiding you through the installation process of Roblox Studio, the powerful toolset that enables developers to bring their visions to life. Next, we'll explore the convenience of Roblox Studio Templates, which provide a solid foundation for your projects. As you become familiar with the Roblox Studio Editor, I will demonstrate how to navigate and utilize its various features effectively. Discover the art of camera movement using the W, A, S, D, E, Q, and F keys and right mouse button to enhance your editor interactions. Embrace the heart of Roblox development as you delve into the world of Lua, a powerful and extensible scripting language. To ensure a smooth workflow, I will help you set up your coding workspace, empowering you to write your first simple Lua script and bring interactivity to your creations. Finally, I will guide you through saving and publishing your projects, enabling you to share your future creations with the vast Roblox community. Embark on this journey, and soon you'll craft engaging experiences that captivate players worldwide. Let's begin!

C. Coutinho, *Roblox Lua Scripting Essentials*, https://doi.org/10.1007/979-8-8688-0026-9_1

What Does This Book Require?

To follow along with this book and learn the art of creating Roblox experiences, you'll need to have Roblox Studio running on either a MacBook or a Windows machine. Once your game experience is published, it can be enjoyed across many platforms, including IOS, Android, Mac, Windows, and Chrome.

About Lua

Lua is a versatile and efficient procedural scripting language known for its lightweight nature and high performance. The core of Lua, including the virtual machine and interpreter, is implemented in C, providing a solid foundation for the fast execution required by gaming experiences.

Lua boasts an approachable and concise syntax as a programming language, making it relatively simple for developers of various skill levels. With just 21 keywords, Lua maintains a compact and straightforward structure, contributing to its readability and ease of understanding. Its syntax bears a resemblance to natural language, which further enhances its user-friendliness.

One notable implementation of Lua can be found in the game development platform Roblox, where it is employed as "Luau." Luau is an evolved version of Lua, originating from Lua 5.1, and enriched with additional functionalities specific to the Roblox ecosystem. This adaptation provides developers with enhanced capabilities and tools for crafting immersive gaming experiences.

Lua's true strength, however, lies in its extensibility. Programmers can leverage Lua's flexible design to introduce various programming paradigms, such as object-oriented programming (OOP), despite the language's lack of built-in object support. This adaptability empowers developers to tailor Lua to their needs, making it an ideal choice for various applications.

This scripting language offers a powerful yet accessible platform for various projects, while its extensibility unlocks a wealth of creative possibilities. With its C-based implementation, user-friendly syntax, and adaptability, Lua stands out as a compelling language choice for developers seeking efficiency and versatility in their software endeavors.

Installing Roblox Studio

Evolved by the burgeoning concept of the metaverse, Roblox transcended its roots as a gaming platform and embraced a more expansive vision. This transformative shift redefined the very essence of the Roblox experience: games evolved into encompassing "experiences," and players morphed into empowered "users." In the ensuing sections, you shall delve into the realms of Roblox Studio dedicated to forging these wondrous experiences.

To embark on your creative journey with Roblox Studio (the application where you will create all your experiences), you must first download and install it.

First, visit the official Roblox website at `www.roblox.com/develop`, and create an account or log in if you already have one.

Once you're logged in, navigate to the "RESOURCES" section on the left (Figure 1-1), and click "Download Studio." This will prompt you to download the Roblox Studio executable to your hard drive. After downloading, run the installer and follow the on-screen instructions to complete the installation process. Once installed, Roblox Studio should automatically launch.

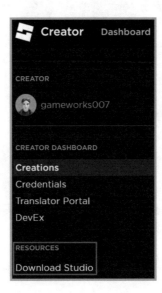

Figure 1-1. *Dashboard*

Roblox Studio Templates

With Roblox Studio launched and the Roblox Studio Home Screen (Figure 1-2) open, click the "New" button to access the "All Templates" tab, which serves as the starting point for creating your game experiences. If you already have a primary theme in mind for your game experience, check the "Theme" tab for predefined templates that align with your vision. For instance, the Castle template could be a suitable starting point if you create a game set in the "Medieval" era. The "Gameplay" tab lists interactive templates like "Combat," allowing players to wield pistols and swords. These templates provide valuable insights into object creation, script implementation, and overall game experience design.

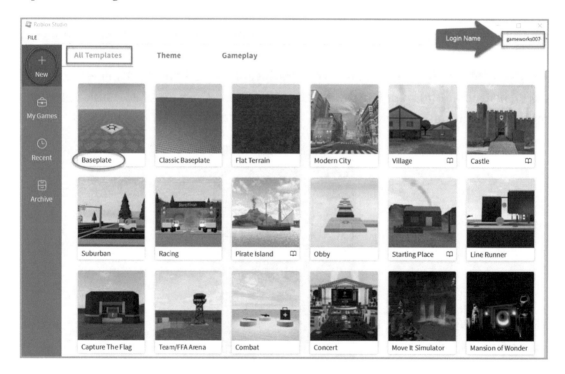

Figure 1-2. *Roblox Studio Home Screen*

For learning Roblox Lua scripting in this book, the "Baseplate" template is sufficient. It includes a spawn point for the player and a flat floor base. Select the "All Templates" tab, and click the "Baseplate" Template to launch the Roblox Studio Editor (Figure 1-3). The Roblox Studio editor allows you to create, modify, and test your game experience.

Exploring Roblox Studio's Editor

You will notice several menu tabs at the top of the Roblox Studio Editor, with the "VIEW" tab currently selected. The Toolbar ribbon changes based on the selected tab.

The "Explorer" window on the right side provides access to every object and system within your game. Objects introduced into your world, such as the "Spawnlocation" depicted within the 3D view of your world, all reside within the "Explorer" window as children of the "Workspace" object. The Baseplate represents the floor in your 3D world and can also be found within the "Explorer" window as a child of the "Workspace" object. All these entities, "Baseplate," "Spawnlocation," "Workspace," "Camera," "Terrain," etc., are referred to as objects within your game. The "Workspace" that holds these objects is referred to as the Parent object, and the objects, "Baseplate," "Spawnlocation," "Camera," and "Terrain" that are all contained within this "Workspace" object, are referred to as children of the "Workspace" object.

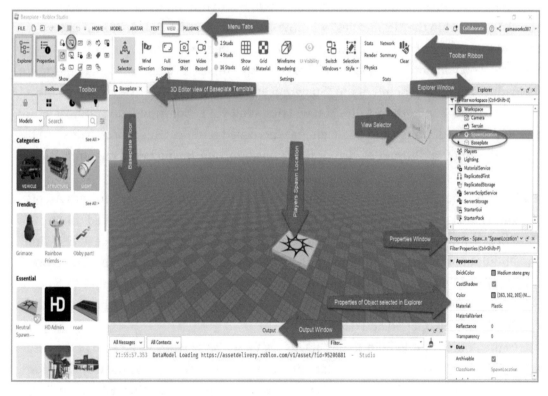

Figure 1-3. *Roblox Studio Editor*

The "Spawnlocation" object (Figure 1-3) is the position in the world at which the player character starts at – (spawns at) when your game is launched.

Beneath the "Explorer" window is the "Properties" window, which allows you to modify the properties of selected objects. For example, selecting the "Spawnlocation" game object in the "Explorer" window lets you manipulate its properties, such as "BrickColor," "Size," etc. From the following figure, you will note that within the "Explorer" window, the "Spawnlocation" game object has been selected (highlighted), so it's this "Spawnlocation" game object properties that are now available for you to manipulate within the "Properties" window. You can change the behavior or look of an object by manipulating its properties. With the "Spawnlocation" game object selected in the hierarchy, locate its "BrickColor" property within the "Appearance" category of the "Properties" window. Click the "BrickColor" property name within the "Properties" window, and a color picker dialog appears. Hover your mouse over the hexagonal grid of colors and note that within the 3D view of your world, the "Spawnlocation" object changes color. Select a color by clicking it to assign it to the "Spawnlocation" object. Scroll down within the "Properties" window until you locate the "Transform" category. Expand this category using the chevron, should you need to, so that the "Size" property is visible. You will note that this "Size" property comprises X, Y, and Z, which determine the width, height, and depth of the "Spawnlocation" object, respectively. Change the X and Z values to 24 and the Y to 10. You will note that your "Spawnlocation" object width and depth have doubled, and its height has increased tenfold. Object properties can be adjusted using the "Properties" window or Lua code, offering powerful customization options.

The "Toolbox" window on the left-hand side of the editor provides you with Assets (free and paid) that you could add to your game experience. You won't need this "Toolbox" window currently, so you can click on its "Close" button to close it, allowing you additional screen space within the 3D view of your world. Should you want to open the "Toolbox" window or any other window you may have closed accidentally, you can do so by selecting the "VIEW" tab, and within its "Show" section, locate the icon of the window you want opened and click it.

In the Roblox Studio Editor, the "3D Editor View" is the window located at the center, accessible through the "Baseplate" tab (Figure 1-3). It offers a view of the world under construction, which I will call the "Scene View" or "Scene." Navigating within the "Scene View" involves using the W, A, S, D, E, Q, and F keys and the right mouse button to reposition the camera. The following section discusses how these key presses and mouse actions facilitate camera movement within the Scene View.

Scene View: Camera Movement

The camera movement within the Scene View can be controlled using the mouse and the W, A, S, D, E, Q, and F keys on the keyboard, allowing you to navigate and explore the 3D environment. I advise you to try out each key press.

1) W or ↑ key: Pressing the W or ↑ key moves the camera forward, allowing you to move toward objects or explore different areas within the scene.

2) S or ↓ key: Pressing the S or ↓ key moves the camera backward, letting you move away from objects or change your position within the scene.

3) A or ← key: Pressing the A or ← key moves the camera to the left, enabling you to strafe leftward and change your viewpoint.

4) D or → key: Pressing the D or → key moves the camera to the right, allowing you to strafe rightward and alter your perspective.

5) E key: Pressing the E key moves the camera upward, enabling you to gain a higher viewpoint or explore elevated areas.

6) Q key: Pressing the Q key moves the camera downward, allowing you to lower your viewpoint or explore lower areas within the scene.

7) F key: Pressing the F key focuses the camera on a selected object or model within the scene. When you select an object or model in the "Scene View" using the mouse or other selection tools, pressing the "F" key automatically centers the camera on the selected item, ensuring it becomes the focal point of your view. To focus the camera on the "Spawnlocation" game object within the scene, select it by clicking it within the "Scene View" window or in Explorer. Once selected, a blue outline will indicate its selection. Pressing the "F" key with the "Spawnlocation" game object selected will center the camera on it, making it the focal point within the "Scene View."

This feature is helpful when working on a specific object within your world that you want to zoom in and center the camera on quickly. It saves time and provides a more convenient way to inspect and edit specific objects within a complex scene without having to manually move and pan around within the scene to locate the particular object, especially when there are several similar-looking objects, as you could have several spawn locations within your game that all look alike.

Mouse actions provide essential ways for navigating, selecting, and manipulating elements while building and designing game experiences.

Here are the key mouse actions available within "Scene View" of the Roblox Editor, and I advise you to try each one:

1) Left-click: Left-clicking an object in "Scene View" or within the "Explorer" window selects the object. Once selected, you can move, rotate, or scale the object using the appropriate tools.

2) Right-click: Right-clicking an object in "Scene View" or the "Explorer" window opens a context menu with various options related to the selected object, such as copying, pasting, duplicating, deleting, Zoom, etc.

3) Click and drag: Clicking and dragging an object in "Scene View" allows you to move it to a different location within your 3D world.

4) Scroll wheel: Using the scroll wheel on your mouse enables you to zoom in and out within "Scene View." Scrolling forward zooms in, while scrolling backward zooms out.

5) Shift + left-click: Holding down the Shift key while left-clicking multiple objects allows you to select multiple items simultaneously. This is useful for grouping objects or applying changes to various elements simultaneously, such as changing property values common to these multiple selected objects.

6) Ctrl+ left-click (Cmd + left-click on Mac): Holding down the Ctrl (Cmd on Mac) key while left-clicking allows you to add or remove individual objects from the current selection.

7) Ctrl + A (Cmd + A on Mac): Pressing Ctrl + A (Cmd + A on Mac) selects all objects within the "Scene View."

8) Click and drag with right mouse button: Clicking and dragging with the right mouse button held down lets you rotate the camera around the scene, providing a different viewing perspective.

9) Click and drag with middle mouse button (mouse wheel): Clicking and dragging with the middle mouse button (mouse wheel) held down lets you pan the camera in "Scene View," shifting the view horizontally and vertically without changing the camera's distance from the objects.

Using these keys and mouse action combinations allows you to freely navigate your 3D world in the Roblox Editor, providing you with better control and flexibility while building and exploring your game world.

View Selector

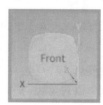

Figure 1-4. *View Selector Gizmo*

The "View Selector" available within the "Scene View" of the Roblox Studio Editor (Figure 1-4) is a user interface element that provides quick access to different views and perspectives of the 3D environment. It is located at the top-right corner of the "Scene View" and is represented by icons.

The "View Selector" aims to allow developers and designers to switch between different viewing modes and camera perspectives, providing flexibility and convenience during the creation and editing process. Listed as follows are the different views accessible through the "View Selector" and their uses:

1. Perspective view: This is the default viewing mode and provides a realistic 3D perspective of the scene, allowing you to naturally navigate and interact with objects. Should you want to return to "Perspective View" from any other views, rotate the camera around within "Scene View" by clicking and dragging the mouse with its right mouse button held down.

2. Top view: Clicking the chevron icon for the "Top View" switches the camera to a top-down view, allowing you to look directly down on the scene and at the upper surface of objects within the scene. This view is helpful for precisely positioning objects on the ground plane and getting an overall scene layout.

3. Bottom view: Clicking the chevron icon for the "Bottom View" changes the camera to a view looking up from the ground plane. It is useful for precisely positioning objects on the ground or on top of other objects and inspecting their underside surface.

4. Front view: Clicking the chevron icon for the "Front View" changes the camera's perspective to face the front of the scene. It helps align objects along a specific axis or to obtain a front-facing view of the scene, allowing you to view the frontal surface of objects in the scene.

5. Back view: Clicking the chevron icon for the "Back View" switches the camera's perspective to face the back of the scene. It helps view objects from behind, resulting in a rear-facing view.

6. Right view: Clicking the chevron icon for the "Right View" sets the camera to view the scene from the right side. This view is valuable for aligning objects along the right-left axis or for a side view of the scene, where you can view the right surface of objects.

7. Left view: Clicking the chevron icon for the "Left View" sets the camera to view the scene from the left side. This view helps align objects along the right-left axis or for a side view from the opposite direction, where you can view the left surface of objects in the scene.

The "View Selector" gizmo streamlines the workflow in Roblox Studio by providing quick access to different camera perspectives, which is especially valuable when positioning and aligning objects, adjusting the layout, and inspecting the scene from various angles. It allows creators to work efficiently and ensures they have the flexibility to visualize their 3D world from different viewpoints during the development phase.

Setting Up the Coding Workspace

To begin coding, you need access to the "Script Editor" and the "Output Window" within Roblox Studio. In this section, you will set up the "Output" Window, and in the next section, you will look at a "Script Object" and the "Script Editor."

The "Output Window" lets you view messages and any errors plaguing your code. This output window is not open by default, so you need to explicitly open it within Roblox Studio by following the steps listed:

1) Click the "VIEW" tab (Figure 1-3). If you accidentally closed any window and need to reopen it, you can do so from the "VIEW" tab. This "VIEW" tab is used to manage open or closed windows.

2) You will find a whole list of icons in the "Show" section of the "VIEW" tab. Hover over each icon until you locate the icon titled "Output." It should ideally be the second icon within the first row of icons in the "Show" section. Click this icon to have the "Output" window display itself at the bottom of the 3D Editors – "Scene View" window (Figure 1-8). This icon works as a toggle, so clicking it again will cause the "Output" window to disappear.

Creating Your First Lua Script

Within Roblox, your Lua code must reside within a "Script," an object like other objects you have encountered in the Roblox Editor. Scripts can be inserted directly into objects within your world, becoming a child of the concerned object. By attaching scripts to Parts (a type of object), creators can create interactive objects, trigger events, and gameplay mechanics. Roblox's basic primitive building block is called a "Part." A Part is fundamental to constructing a 3D environment in Roblox games and experiences.

The primary and most common type of primitive "Part" (object) is the standard "Block" part. It is a simple cuboid shape with six faces (front, back, top, bottom, left, and right). Developers can resize and scale it to build various complex objects and structures within the game world. The other different primitive "Part" (object) types that provide unique visual and physical characteristics are the following:

1) The "Sphere" is a "Part" (object) that represents a circular shape. Developers can adjust their radius to create spheres or round objects in the game world.

2) The "Wedge" is a "Part" (object) that has a triangular cross-section, forming a wedge-like shape. It helps create slanted surfaces, ramps, steps, and other angular objects.

3) The Corner "Wedge" "Part" (object) is like the "Wedge" part but is specifically designed for creating corner pieces or angles in structures.

4) The "Cylinder" is a "Part" (object) with a circular cross-section, forming a cylindrical shape. Developers can adjust their height and radius to create objects like pillars, tubes, and rounded surfaces.

Roblox also has some non-primitive parts (objects) such as a Seat, Vehicle Seat, Union, etc. In this section, you will create a new basic standard cuboid "Part" (object) and insert a "Script" object into it as its child.

Select either the "HOME" tab or the "MODEL" tab within the Roblox Editor. Locate the "Part" button, which on the "HOME" tab is located within the "Insert" section, and the "MODEL" tab is located within the "Parts" section. Click the chevron at the bottom of the "Part" button to expand it. You will note that it contains all the primitive objects we discussed above. From this drop-down, select "Block," you will note that a cuboid block has been dropped into the center of the world, most likely on top of your "Spawnlocation" object. Select this "Block" part in the "Scene View," and drag it to either the left or the right side of the "Spawnlocation" object to ensure that it's not sitting atop your "Spawnlocation" object. In the "Explorer," you will notice that a new "Part" object has been added as a child of the "Workspace" object. With the "Part" object selected, either right-click it and select "Rename" from the context menu that pops up, or press the "F2" key on your keyboard to rename this block part. Rename it to "Cuboid" (Figure 1-5). It is essential to rename objects appropriately within your world so that you may access them easily when you need to.

With the "Cuboid" object selected in the "Explorer" window, hover over it with your mouse pointer until you notice a plus icon. Click this plus icon (Figure 1-5), and from the menu that pops up, select "Script" to add a "Script" object as a child of the "Cuboid" object. You will note that a new "Script" tab has now opened in the Roblox Editor besides the "Baseplate" tab and has been populated with a single line of Lua code, the print function. Select the "Script" object in the hierarchy and press the "F2" key to rename this "Script" object. Rename it to "Cuboid_Script" (Figure 1-6).

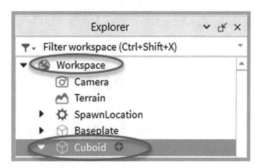

Figure 1-5. *Cuboid object – plus icon*

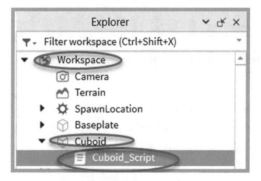

Figure 1-6. *Renamed Cuboid Script object*

Tip   If you close the Script Editor tab, you can reopen it by double-clicking the concerned Script object (Cuboid_Script) within the Explorer window.

The "Cuboid_Script" tab has been populated with the default Roblox script "print" function (Figure 1-7) that will print the string "Hello World" to the "Output Window" when this script runs. To run this script, select the "HOME" tab, and locate the "Test" section that contains the blue triangular "Play" button. Click the chevron situated at the bottom of the "Play" button to expand it and select "Run," which could also be executed by pressing the "F8" function key on your keyboard. Within the "Output" window, you will notice that the string "Hello World!" has been printed with the name of the script that contained the print function displayed (Figure 1-8). Click the red "Stop" button to stop playing the experience. You can return to the "Script" code by clicking on the Cuboid_Script tab.

Figure 1-7. *Print function*

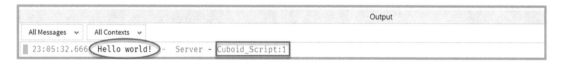

Figure 1-8. *String "Hello World!" displayed in the Output window*

The "Run" button allows you to test your code without loading your character avatar, while the "Play" button would have loaded your character avatar into the world.

Congratulations on creating your very first Lua script!

Note   Any changes made to objects in your world during play testing using "Run" mode won't persist when you stop playtesting. By default, when you exit "Run" mode, the changes you made during runtime will not be saved to the game experience.

A "string" is a data type representing a sequence of characters. It can hold any combination of alphabets, numbers, and symbols, making it a versatile data type for handling text-based information. Chapter 3 will teach you about the "string" data type.

A "function" is a chunk of code that can be referred to by a name (such as "print") and can be executed at any time. In Chapter 4, you will learn about functions.

Saving and Publishing Your Project

As Roblox doesn't auto-save your projects, you must save your progress regularly to avoid losing your work. When your game experience is ready for the world, you can publish your creation for others to enjoy.

Within the Roblox Editor, on its menu bar, click "File," which is located at the top left corner. From the menu that pops up, you will note four different "Save to" menu items (Figure 1-9). Selecting either "Save to File" or "Save to File As…" allows you to save your Roblox experience to your local drive as a ".rbxl" file. The "Save to File" menu item allows you to retain the template name when you save your Project to your local drive, while the "Save to File As…" menu item allows you to rename your Project, giving it the name of your liking. Of course, you could always overwrite the default template name provided within the "Save As" dialog when using the "Save to File" menu item selection.

The menu items "Save to Roblox" or "Save to Roblox As…" (Figure 1-9) allow you to save your Roblox experience to Roblox Servers in the cloud. Your Project is saved to a secure place on a Roblox Server and is not accessible to the public.

Once you are satisfied with the game experience you have created, you would want to make it available to the public, for which you need to publish your Project to Roblox. The menu items "Publish to Roblox" or "Publish to Roblox As…" (Figure 1-9) allow you to publish your creation to the Roblox community. Selecting "Publish to Roblox" brings up the "Publish Game – Basic Info" window (Figure 1-10), where you need to provide your game experience with a Title, Description, Genre, and list of devices on which your experience can be played. Once these details are complete, click the "Create" button.

You can finally close your Roblox experience by selecting the menu item File – Close Place (Figure 1-9), which closes the Roblox Editor and returns you to the main Roblox Studio Home Screen.

Figure 1-9. *Saving, publishing, and closing the project*

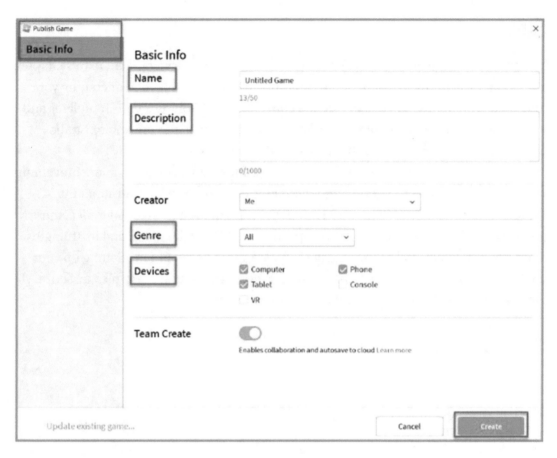

Figure 1-10. *Publish Game – Basic Info window*

Reopening Your Project

To reopen the Project you have been working on, locate it within Roblox Studio's Home Screen (Figure 1-2) by clicking "Recent" within the sidebar and then clicking your projects thumbnail available within the "Recent Games" tab. If you publish your experience to Roblox, it will be available by clicking on "My Games" within the sidebar.

Summary

You embarked on an exhilarating journey into Roblox game development in this chapter. You began by learning to install Roblox Studio, the indispensable tool for crafting your imaginative creations. You discovered the convenience of Roblox Studio Templates and found a solid starting point for your projects. You then dived into the Roblox Studio Editor, exploring its features to shape your learning effectively.

You learned how to interact with the Roblox editor with a grasp of camera movement using the W, A, S, D, E, and Q keys and right mouse button. You learned about the View Selector available in Roblox and how it provides quick access to different camera perspectives. You learned about the compactness of the Lua language and its strengths and flexibility, which make it a language suited to game development. Setting up your coding workspace ensured a smooth workflow for writing your first simple Lua script. Finally, we learned how to save and publish our projects.

CHAPTER 2

Working with Parts

In this chapter, you will equip yourself with the essential building blocks of Roblox development and begin by delving into "Primitive Part Creation," where you will uncover the power of using basic geometric shapes to craft 3D structures. Understanding the "Transform" component of "Part objects" is crucial to enabling precise positioning, alignment, sizing, and rotation of your objects. You will also demystify the concepts of "Pitch, Yaw, and Roll Rotation of Part objects," essential for giving life to objects by allowing them to move and orient in three-dimensional space. Diving into the distinction between "Local space versus Global coordinate space of Part objects," you will learn how to control the reference point for transformations, providing flexibility and efficiency in object manipulation. Moreover, you will uncover the art of "Translating, Scaling, and Rotating a Part," essential skills for molding objects to fit your vision. As you venture further, you will familiarize yourself with "Studs," Roblox's unit of measurement, which underpins the dimensions and precision of your creations. The "Translation and Rotation Snapping" concept will enable you to align objects seamlessly, ensuring a polished and professional touch to your projects. Additionally, you will explore "Part Collisions," a vital aspect of object interaction and physics simulation responsible for adding depth and realism to your games and experiences. Finally, you will delve into the concept of "Anchoring Parts," which allows you to decide whether objects can have gravity applied to them within the game world.

Part Primitives

Primitive Parts are a collection of basic geometric shapes that are the foundation for constructing various objects and structures in Roblox. They include cubes, spheres, cylinders, wedges, and more. These simple shapes provide a starting point for developers, allowing them to unleash their creativity and build complex designs quickly. Using primitives, creators can shape and manipulate objects, combining them to form

© Christopher Coutinho 2023

C. Coutinho, *Roblox Lua Scripting Essentials*, https://doi.org/10.1007/979-8-8688-0026-9_2

more complex designs. These basic shapes can be resized, rotated, and textured to create custom models and props for games and experiences in the Roblox universe. Primitives are particularly helpful for beginners as they offer a straightforward way to begin building without the need for more complex 3D modeling software.

As seen in Chapter 1, creating a primitive part is straightforward. You created the primary and most common type of primitive "Part" (Object), the standard "Block" part.

Let's create a "Wedge" part. Select either the "HOME" tab or the "MODEL" tab within the Roblox Editor. Locate the "Part" button, which on the "HOME" tab is located within the "Insert" section, and on the "MODEL" tab is located within the "Parts" section.

Click the chevron at the bottom of the "Part" button to expand it. You will note that it contains several primitive objects.

From this drop-down, select "Wedge," and you will note that a "Wedge" part has been dropped into the center of the World and most likely on top of your "Spawnlocation" object. Select this "Wedge" part in the "Scene View" and drag it to either the left or the right side of the "Spawnlocation" object to ensure that it's not sitting atop your "Spawnlocation" object. In the "Explorer," you will notice that a new "Part" object has been added as a child of the "Workspace" object. Rename it to Wedge. As discussed in Chapter 1, a "Part" is an object that has properties associated with it, such as size, color, material, position, orientation, etc., that can be accessed via the "Properties" window and changed, thereby providing you the ability to manipulate the look and behavior of the "Part."

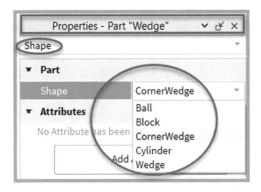

Figure 2-1. *Filter properties search box*

Some of the most utilized properties of primitive "Part" objects are listed as follows:

1) Shape: With the "Wedge" part selected in the "Explorer" window, within the "Properties" window, use the Filter properties search box to locate the Shape property (Figure 2-1). Note that from within the drop-down for this property, you can change the shape of your "Part" by selecting a new desired shape (e.g., ball, cylinder, corner wedge, etc.).

2) Anchoring and CanCollide: The "Anchored" property determines whether the part remains stationary or is affected by forces like gravity. Anchoring is essential for creating stable structures and ensuring objects stay in their intended positions. The "CanCollide" property available within the "Collision" category governs whether a part can collide with other objects or players, affecting the physical interactions within the game world.

3) Material: The "Material" property in the "Appearance" category determines the look and feel the part should have. Some commonly used material types are plastic, pebble, mud, ice, metal, limestone, marble, etc.

4) Attributes: The "Attributes" property is a feature used to customize and extend the behavior of objects within the game world. It allows developers to add custom key-value pairs (Dictionary) to objects, making it possible to store and retrieve additional data or settings specific to those objects. For example, you could create an "Activated" Boolean attribute for a part and have it activated/deactivated via code.

The Transform

In Roblox, the "Transform" represents the position, orientation, and scale of an object or part in three-dimensional space. It encapsulates all the information needed to define the Object's transformation, allowing developers to precisely manipulate its position, rotation, and size. The "Transform" contains several sub-categories, each representing a different aspect of the Object's transformation (Figure 2-2):

1) Size: The "Size" property (Figure 2-2) determines the Object's size in each dimension. It is a Vector3 with three components, "X," "Y," and "Z," representing the Object's width, height, and depth, respectively. The "Size" property enables dynamic scaling of the Object, essential for creating objects of varying dimensions, from tiny props to massive landscapes.

2) Origin: The "Origin" property contains two sub-properties: Position and Orientation (Figure 2-2). The "Position" property defines the position of the Object in the 3D space, based on its Pivot point and relative to its parent (if it has one) or the "Workspace" if it is the parent object. It is a Vector3 with three components, "X," "Y," and "Z," where "X" represents the position of the Object along the horizontal "X-axis" (red axis), "Y" represents the position of the Object along the vertical "Y-axis" (green axis), and "Z" represents the position of the Object along the forward/backward "Z-axis" (blue axis). By manipulating the "Position" property, developers can move objects to the desired location in the game world. This is crucial for creating dynamic environments, moving platforms, or objects affected by physics and animations.

   The "Orientation" property represented by a Vector3 with three components, "X," "Y," and "Z," corresponds to the "Pitch," "Yaw," and "Roll" of the Object's rotation. It represents the Object's orientation (rotation) relative to its parent's coordinate frame. This will be discussed in depth in a separate section in this chapter. Changing these orientation values allows you to animate, turn, or have the Object face specific directions in the game, allowing you to craft interactive gameplay elements like rotating platforms or doors.

3) CFrame: The "CFrame" property is a critical and powerful feature used to represent the transformation of an object in 3D space. "CFrame" stands for "Coordinate Frame," and it combines both position and orientation (rotation) information, making it more compact and efficient for managing object transformations. It comprises both "Position" and "Orientation" sub-properties like the "Origin" property.

Using a "CFrame" is the preferred way to manipulate an object's transform, allowing you to change an object's positional and rotational data in a single expression. A "CFrame" is also more performant. You will learn all about the "CFrame" in an upcoming chapter.

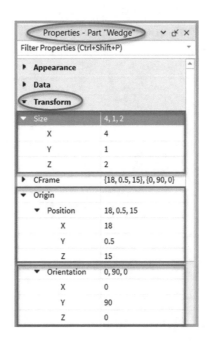

Figure 2-2. *Transform*

Note   A Vector3 structure in Roblox is a data type representing a point or direction in three-dimensional space. It contains three components, "X," "Y," and "Z," which represent the coordinates of the point or the magnitude of the direction along each axis (horizontal, vertical, and depth). Roblox uses Vector3 extensively for position, rotation, and scale operations on objects in the 3D World. It is a versatile and crucial data type for 3D game development in the Roblox game engine.

Pitch, Yaw, and Roll

In 3D space, we commonly refer to three axes, denoted as "X," "Y," and "Z," which are easily understood for positioning and movement, as you'll explore in the section "Translating a Part" later in this chapter. However, these axes are crucial in describing rotations, much like aeronautics. For this reason, programmers working with 3D graphics often borrow terms from aeronautics, namely, Pitch, Yaw, and Roll. Figure 2-3 visually represents these concepts: Pitch involves rotation around the "X" axis, Yaw around the "Y" axis, and Roll around the "Z" axis. With the ability to describe rotation along these axes, Roblox naturally offers the "Orientation" property, a Vector3 comprising "X," "Y," and "Z" components, accepting angle measurements in degrees, ranging between -180 and 180.

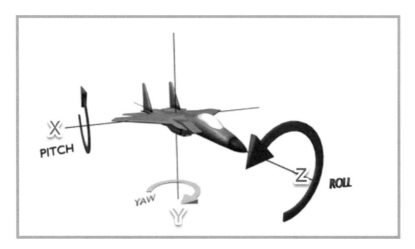

Figure 2-3. *Pitch, Yaw, and Roll rotation*

Global vs. Local Coordinate Space

In Roblox and most 3D worlds, two coordinate spaces are used to define the positions and orientation of objects: Global (World) coordinate space and Local coordinate space. So far, we have been talking about the Global (World) coordinate space, which represents the placement and rotation of objects based on the "X," "Y," and "Z" axes of the 3D World. The Global coordinate space, also known as the World coordinate space, is the absolute reference frame for the entire Roblox game world. In this coordinate space, the origin (0, 0, 0) represents the center of the Roblox world, and all positions and rotations of objects are measured relative to this global origin.

In the Global (World) coordinate space, the X, Y, and Z axes represent the three-dimensional directions in the game world. When viewing the 3D World with the "Back View" selected on the "View Selector," the positive X-axis points to the right, the positive

Y-axis points up, and the positive Z-axis points forward (out of the screen). This Global (World) coordinate space is fixed and does not change regardless of an object's position or orientation.

The Local coordinate space represents how an object is positioned and rotated relative to itself. It turns out that every Object in Roblox has its origin point and direction for the three axes, which is unique to the Object. This Local coordinate space moves around with the Object. Within this Local coordinate space, the Object's position and rotation are defined based on its parent's position and rotation. When an object is not anchored to the game world (the "Anchored" property is set to false), it can move and rotate freely within its parent's Local coordinate space. For example, if a part is placed inside another part (parented to it), its position and rotation are relative to the parent part's Local coordinate space. The "X," "Y," and "Z" axes of an object's Local coordinate space need not align with the Global (World) coordinate space (Figure 2-4). The "X," "Y," and "Z" axes of an object's Local coordinate space will only align with the Global (World) coordinate space axes when the Object's rotation is at its default state (no rotation). As the Object rotates, its Local coordinate space rotates with it, affecting how its "X," "Y," and "Z" axes align with the global axes.

Figure 2-4. *Cuboid part – Local coordinate space*

Figure 2-4 shows that the cuboid part has been rotated with values X=90, Y=45, and Z=0. As a result, the local axes of the cuboid Object now align differently from the Global (World) coordinate axes, which are visible via the "View Selector" gizmo in Figure 2-4. The alphabet "L" enclosed by a red circle in Figure 2-4 indicates that you are in "Local" mode. The key combination "Cmd/Ctrl + L" toggles you in and out of "Local" mode. Upon toggling out of "Local" mode into "Global" (World) mode, you will note that the axes of the cuboid Object are now more closely aligned to the Global (World) coordinate axes.

It would help if you tried out rotating a cuboid object yourself, as detailed above, to understand the distinction between Global (World) coordinate space and Local coordinate space, as it is crucial for proper object positioning, rotation, and movement in Roblox. It allows developers to create complex and dynamic hierarchies of objects, facilitating smooth interactions and animations within the game world.

Translating (Moving) a Part

In Roblox, "Translation" refers to moving an object from one position to another in three-dimensional space. It involves changing the Object's coordinates along the "X," "Y," and "Z" axes to relocate it to a new position. This movement can be relative to the Object's current position or, in absolute terms, relative to the World's origin. Translations are essential for creating interactive gameplay and dynamic environments in Roblox game experiences. By manipulating an object's position, developers can control movement, simulate physics, and create various effects to enhance the player's experience.

Roblox provides various ways to translate a part (Object):

1) Roblox Studio Tools: On the "HOME" tab, within the "Tools" section, Roblox provides you with a "Move" tool that can be used to move any object within the 3D World. This is the tool you will use in this section.

2) Using Vector3: You can use the Vector3 data type to specify the new position and update the Object's position using methods like "SetPrimaryPartCFrame," which sets the position and orientation of a model or part in the World.

3) Relative movement: You can move an object by adding a Vector3 value to its current position. This way, you perform a relative translation based on the Object's position.

4) Tweening: Roblox has built-in functions and libraries for smooth interpolation between two positions, known as tweening. The "TweenService" can create animations that automatically move an object from its current position to a specified destination over time, creating smooth transitions.

To translate a "Wedge" part (Object) using the Move tool in Roblox Studio, follow these steps:

1) Select the part: In Explorer or the "Scene View," select the "Wedge" part you want to translate. Click this "Wedge" part to highlight it.

2) Access the Move tool: On the menu bar, click the "HOME" tab to display the available tools. Click on the "Move" tool icon in the "Tools" section.

3) Alternatively, you can use the hotkey "Q" to activate the "Move" tool.

4) Manipulate the part: Once the "Move" tool is active, you'll see three colored arrows (red, green, and blue) extending from the selected part (Figure 2-5):

    •   Red arrow: Controls the part's movement along the X-axis (left and right)

    •   Green arrow: Controls the part's movement along the Y-axis (up and down)

    •   Blue arrow: Controls the part's movement along the Z-axis (forward and backward)

5) Translate the part: To move the part, click and drag one of the colored arrows in the direction you want to move the part. You can move it freely in any direction.

6) Fine-tune the translation: If you need precise positioning, you can also enter specific values for the part's position in the Properties window. Select the part, go to the "Properties" tab, and locate the "Position" property. Change the "X," "Y," and "Z" values to numerically adjust the part's position.

7) Confirm the translation: After moving the part to the desired location, you can release the mouse button to finalize the translation.

8) Save your work: Remember to save your changes in Roblox Studio to preserve the new position of the part in your game.

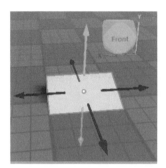

Figure 2-5. *Move tool activated on Wedge part*

Scaling a Part

Scaling refers to resizing an object uniformly or non-uniformly along its three axes (X, Y, and Z) in three-dimensional space. It allows you to adjust the size of a part or model, making it larger or smaller in proportion to its original dimensions. Proper scaling can significantly enhance the visual appeal and overall experience of a Roblox game.

Figure 2-6. *Scale tool activated on a Cylinder part*

Roblox provides different methods to Scale a part (Object):

1) Using the Scale tool: In Roblox Studio, the "Scale" tool can be accessed by selecting the "HOME" tab in the menu bar and then clicking the "Scale" tool icon, available within the "Tools" section. Alternatively, you can use the hotkey "R" to activate the "Scale" tool. Once activated, the selected part will display colored orbs (red, green, and blue) representing scaling along each axis (Figure 2-6).

2) Proportional scaling: If you want to maintain proportions while scaling, you can hold down the "Shift" key by dragging an orb or setting the scale values in the Properties window. This will ensure that the part remains uniformly scaled in all dimensions.

3) Non-uniform scaling along a single axis: To perform disproportionate scaling along a single axis, click and drag one of the orbs of the selected part. You will note that the part scales along just one side of the axis.

4) Uniform scaling along an axis: To achieve uniform scaling along an axis, wherein both sides scale simultaneously even when you click and drag an orb located on any side of the axis, you need to hold down the Ctrl key (on Windows) or Command key (on Mac) while dragging one of the orbs.

5) Pivot point: By default, scaling takes place around the part's pivot point, which is its center. However, you can change the pivot point by selecting a different part (parent part) or changing the pivot settings in the "Properties" window. This allows you to scale the part around a specific point, making it useful for more intricate transformations. The "PivotOffset" property value (both position and orientation) is zero by default.

Add a "Cylinder" part to your World and try scaling it using the abovementioned techniques.

Rotating a Part

In Roblox, "Rotation" refers to changing the orientation or angle of a part (Object) in three-dimensional space. It involves rotating the part around one or more axes (X, Y, and Z) to achieve a new orientation. Rotations can be applied to individual parts, models, or the entire game world. By manipulating an object's rotation, developers can bring life to their game's elements, making them interactive and visually engaging.

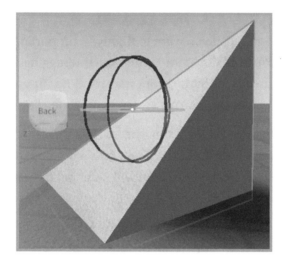

Figure 2-7. *Rotate tool activated on a Corner Wedge part*

Roblox provides different ways to rotate a part (Object):

1) Using the Rotate tool: In Roblox Studio, you can access the "Rotate" tool by selecting the "HOME" tab in the menu bar and then clicking the "Rotate" tool icon. Alternatively, you can use the hotkey "E" to activate the "Rotate" tool. Once activated, the selected Object will display three colored circles (red, green, and blue) representing rotation around each axis. The blue circle allows rotation of the selected Object around its local "Z" axis. The green circle enables the selected Object to rotate around its local "Y" axis. The red circle allows the selected Object to rotate around its local "X" axis (Figure 2-7).

2) Euler angles: Roblox uses Euler angles to represent rotation, which means you can specify the rotation in degrees around each axis individually. By manipulating these angles, you can rotate the Object in any direction.

3) Orientation properties: In the Properties window, you can find properties like "Orientation" or "CFrame," which allow you to set an object's rotation precisely. A "CFrame" is a coordinate frame that combines an object's position, rotation, and scale information.

4) Tweening: Roblox provides functions within its "TweenService" that can create smooth animations to rotate an object from its current orientation to a specified target orientation over time.

5) Relative and absolute rotation: You can apply rotations relative to an object's current orientation (local rotation) or, based on the global axes (World), around a specific point in 3D space, by changing its pivot point.

Add a "CornerWedge" part to your World, and with it selected, click the rotate button to have the circular rotation handles appear. Click and drag one of the circular rotation handles to see the "CornerWedge" part rotate around the specific axis.

Studs: Roblox Unit of Measurement

In Roblox, a "Stud" is the fundamental unit of measurement used in the creation and design of games. It represents a fixed distance within the Roblox world and is a building block for constructing objects, structures, and environments in the game experience. Understanding "Studs" effectively is essential for creating well-proportioned and functional game elements. One stud is equivalent to 0.2 meters or roughly 20 centimeters in the Roblox world.

When building in Roblox Studio, the grid is aligned with Studs, making it easier to align and position objects precisely. The "Baseplate" floor visible within "Scene View" comprises several 4x4 grids. Each square within this grid represents a "Stud" (Figure 2-8).

When inserted into the game world, most objects will automatically snap to the grid, ensuring they align with the Studs. You can move objects by dragging them around the 3D World, and they will snap to the grid as you move them, which helps maintain proper alignment.

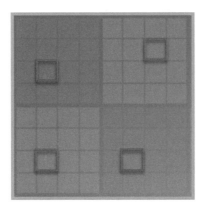

Figure 2-8. *A Stud – within each 4x4 grid*

When resizing objects, Roblox Studio uses Studs as the unit of measurement by default. For example, if you resize a part to be 5x5x5, the dimensions are 5 Studs in width, 5 Studs in height, and 5 Studs in depth.

Using Studs can help maintain a consistent scale in your game, making it visually pleasing for players. It's good practice to align parts and objects to the grid, ensuring they fit together neatly and precisely.

Translation Snapping

Translation snapping in Roblox allows you to move objects precisely along the grid, ensuring they align with the Studs and other game objects in the Roblox world. It helps in creating well-proportioned and neatly arranged structures in your game. To use translation snapping in Roblox, follow these steps:

1) Enable translation snapping: By default, translation snapping is enabled in Roblox Studio. You can check if it's turned on by looking at the "MODEL" tab on the menu bar, where within the "Snap to Grid" section, you will find a "Move" check box. If this "Move" check box is checked (which it should be by default), then

grid snapping has been enabled (Figure 2-9). Besides this check box, a spinner button defaults to the value of 1 stud. This indicates that a part within your World can be moved by about one stud when dragged. Should you want to move in larger increments, increase this value, or decrease it should you wish to move by, say, half a stud.

2) Move the Object using Snap to Grid: Select the Object you want to move by clicking it in the "Scene View" or the "Explorer" window. Ensure that the "Move" tool has been selected. Click and hold the Object with your mouse, then move it to the desired location. Note how the Object moves using the movement value that has been set.

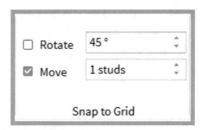

Figure 2-9. *Snap to Grid movement*

3) Move the Object using free movement: To move an object freely within the 3D World, you can turn off the snapping ability by simply unchecking the "Move" check box. This will now allow you to move the Object freely within the World.

Using translation snapping in Roblox Studio helps maintain consistency and alignment within your game environment. It ensures that objects fit together neatly and look visually appealing to players. Take advantage of this feature while building your game to create a well-structured and professional-looking experience.

Rotation Snapping

Rotation snapping in Roblox Studio allows you to rotate objects precisely along the grid, ensuring they align with specific angles or orientations. This feature is handy for creating well-aligned structures, smooth movements, and precise game mechanics. To use rotation snapping in Roblox, follow these steps:

1) Enable rotation snapping: By default, rotation snapping is not enabled in Roblox Studio. You can check if it's turned on by looking at the "MODEL" tab on the menu bar, where within the "Snap to Grid" section, you will find a "Rotate" check box. If this "Rotate" check box is checked, then rotation snapping has been enabled (Figure 2-9). If not, check the "Rotate" check box. Besides this check box, a spinner button defaults to the value of 45 degrees. This indicates that a part within your World can be rotated around 45 degrees about each axis using the "Rotate" tool. Change this value if you want to rotate in larger or smaller increments.

2) Rotate the Object: Select the Object you want to rotate by clicking it in the "Scene View" or the Explorer window. Ensure that the "Rotate" tool has been selected. Hover your mouse cursor over one of the Object's rotation handles (the colored circles that appear around the Object). Click and drag the rotation handle in the direction you want to rotate the Object. As you rotate the Object, you'll notice it snaps to specific angles or orientations. These angles are determined by the rotation snapping value set for the spinner button, ensuring the Object rotates in these degree increments.

3) Rotate the Object using free rotation: To rotate an object freely within the 3D World, turn off the rotation snapping ability by simply unchecking the "Rotate" check box. This will now allow you to rotate the Object freely within the World.

Collisions

Collisions refer to the interaction between two or more objects in the game world. It determines how these objects react when they encounter each other. Understanding collisions is crucial to creating realistic and interactive environments in your games. Roblox provides collision settings that allow developers to control how objects interact and respond to each other during gameplay. In the Roblox physics simulations, when two objects collide, they can either pass through each other (no collision occurs), stop and push each other (collide and interact), or bounce off each other (elastic collision). Objects with collision enabled can block other objects from moving through them, preventing overlapping, and ensuring proper interaction between game objects.

You can access several collision settings when you insert an object into the game world using Roblox Studio. These settings can be adjusted in the "Properties" window of the selected Object:

- CanCollide property: This property determines whether an object participates in collisions. If set to true, the Object will be solid and react with physics to other objects; if set to false, it will become non-physical and not collide with other objects, allowing them to pass through. Most objects have their "CanCollide" property set to true by default.

- CollisionGroup property: This property assigns the Object to a specific collision group. Objects with the same CollisionGroup will not collide with each other. It's commonly used to create custom collision groups for various game mechanics. Collision groups can be created using the Collision Groups Editor, available in the "MODEL" tab in the Advanced section.

- Customizing collisions via scripting: In addition to the collision settings in the "Properties" window, developers can customize object collisions through scripting. The "Touched" event allows you to define custom interactions when two objects come into contact. For example, you can trigger an action when a player touches a specific part within the game environment. You can use the "CanCollide" property and change it dynamically during gameplay to create temporary barriers or allow objects to pass through each other under certain conditions.

Careful consideration of collisions is essential when designing games to ensure that objects interact correctly and deliver a smooth, immersive gameplay experience. Proper collision management is crucial for creating realistic physics simulations and engaging game mechanics.

Anchoring Objects

In Roblox, should you want a part to be immovable, you need to anchor it. Anchoring allows you to fix a part's position relative to its parent (if any) or the World, making it stay in place or move along with other parts as desired. This property is handy for constructing structures and ensuring that parts remain in their intended positions during gameplay.

When a part's "Anchored" property is set to true, it will stay in its current position and will not move, regardless of any external forces or physics. Other parts can still collide with and interact with anchored parts. If a part's Anchored property is set to false, the part behaves like a regular physics object and can be affected by external forces, such as gravity or collisions. If the part is not anchored, it will respond to physics and move according to the game's physics simulation.

To anchor a part in Roblox, follow these steps:

1) Select the part: In the "Scene View" or the Explorer window, click the part you want to anchor to select it.

2) Toggle anchoring: With the part selected from within the "Properties" window, locate the "Anchored" property under the "Part" category, and check its check box, thereby setting its "Anchored" property to true.

3) Test anchoring: After setting the "Anchored" property to true, use the "Move" tool in the Scene View to lift the part in the World, and observe its behavior. When anchored, the part won't respond to physics, so that gravity won't affect it. Playtest your game by pressing "F8" or clicking "Run." If the part stays in place, it is correctly anchored. To test its dynamic behavior, uncheck the "Anchored" property while the game is running, and the part should fall to the ground due to gravity.

Commenting Your Code

Commenting on your code is considered good practice that can provide several benefits:

1) Code documentation: Comments serve as documentation, helping other developers (including your future self) understand the purpose and functionality of specific parts of the code. Remembering the intent behind every line of code can be challenging, especially in large projects, so well-placed comments make the code more readable and maintainable.

2) Communication with other developers: Multiple developers might work on the same codebase in collaborative projects. Comments allow them to communicate with each other about different aspects of the code, such as explaining why a particular approach was chosen or flagging potential issues.

3) Explain complex logic: Sometimes, code might be complex due to optimizations or other reasons. In such cases, comments can help break down the logic, making it easier for others to follow the thought process and understand how it works.

4) Disable code temporarily: When troubleshooting or debugging, you may want to disable certain sections of code temporarily. You can comment instead of deleting the code (which can be risky if you forget to restore it later). This way, the code is still there but not executed until you decide to remove the comments.

5) Regain understanding after time: Codebases can evolve, and you might return to a piece of code you wrote months or even years ago. Comments can serve as a quick refresher and remind you of the code's functionality and purpose.

Lua provides two styles of comments to annotate and document your code:

1) Single-line comments start with a double hyphen (--). Anything written after the double hyphen on the same line is considered a comment and will be ignored by the Lua interpreter. Single-line comments are helpful when you need to add a brief explanation or comment on a specific line of code. Listing 2-1 shows several single-line comments.

Listing 2-1. Leaving single-line comments in code

```
-- This is a single-line comment
-- Assigning the scripts parent object to variable 'part.'
local part = script.Parent
part.Anchored = true              -- Anchor the Part
```

2) Multi-line comments (block comments): Multi-line comments, also known as block comments, are enclosed between a pair of double square brackets ([[and]]). Anything written between the brackets, including new lines, will be treated as a comment and won't be executed by the Lua interpreter. Multi-line comments are helpful when you want to add more extensive explanations or temporarily disable a code block – Listing 2-2 shows examples of multi-line comments.

Listing 2-2. Leaving multi-line comments in code

```
--[[ This is a multi-line comment in Lua.
     It spans multiple lines and can provide
     detailed explanations for complex code.
]]
--[[
     local y = 5
     print(y)
]]
-- Code inside the block comment above won't be executed.
```

Summary

This chapter has provided a concise overview of fundamental Roblox topics for developers. It covered "Primitive Part Creation," where basic shapes serve as building blocks for 3D structures. Understanding the "Transform component" ensures precise positioning and sizing of objects, while "Pitch, Yaw, and Roll Rotation" enables dynamic rotation in 3D space. Differentiating "Global and Local Space" helps control transformations efficiently. Exploring "Translating, Scaling, and Rotating a Part" aids in shaping objects to match your creative vision. "Studs" were introduced as Roblox's unit of measurement, determining object dimensions. The importance of "Translation and Rotation Snapping" for precise alignment and "Part Collisions" was discussed, adding realism to object interactions. The concept of "Anchoring Parts" was explored, shaping object behavior using gravity in the game world. Lastly, you learned about the significance of commenting code for improved clarity and maintainability.

CHAPTER 3

Variables, Scope, Arrays, Operators, and Conditionals

In this chapter, we will explore key concepts that form the foundation of game development within the Roblox environment: Variables, Scope, Arrays, Operators, and Conditionals. These elements serve as the backbone of creating interactive experiences, allowing you to manage data, manipulate information, and guide the flow of your games. Join in as we delve into the practical aspects of coding for Roblox Lua, equipping you with the fundamental skills needed to bring your virtual worlds to life.

Basic Lua Data Types

In programming languages, data types categorize and determine how data or values can be represented and manipulated. Each data type specifies the operations possible on the data and the required memory for storage. Understanding data types is crucial for defining variable behavior and program efficiency. Programmers must know the available data types to ensure code correctness and efficiency.

The native Lua language has the following eight basic data types:

1) nil: The nil type represents the absence of a value, symbolizing literal nothingness. It is often used to indicate the lack of data or to reset a variable. Also, when data is invalid or unknown, using nil is a common practice to signify its state.

© Christopher Coutinho 2023
C. Coutinho, *Roblox Lua Scripting Essentials*, https://doi.org/10.1007/979-8-8688-0026-9_3

2) boolean: The boolean type represents logical values and can have two possible values: true or false. However, it can only be in either one of these two states. Booleans are commonly used in conditional statements and logical operations.

3) number: The number type represents numerical values, including integers and floating-point numbers. Lua automatically converts between integer and floating-point representations as needed.

4) string: A string type represents a sequence of characters, such as text. Strings in Lua can be enclosed in single quotes or double quotes. When declaring a string literal, it must be included in quotation marks.

5) function: A function is a chunk of code referred to by a name (print() function) that can be invoked at any time. In Lua, functions are first-class values, meaning they can be assigned to variables, passed as arguments to other functions, and returned from functions.

6) table: A table is Lua's primary data structure and represents arrays, dictionaries (key-value pairs), objects, and other complex data structures. They are incredibly versatile and can be used for various purposes.

7) Thread: Threads in Lua provide support for coroutines. This programming concept allows you to execute code in parallel (cooperative multi-tasking/concurrency), where your code can run several statements simultaneously. Unlike traditional threads, which are managed by the operating system and run concurrently on multiple CPU cores, coroutines are managed by the program itself.

8) userdata: A userdata type is used to interface with complex data structures or external libraries written in either "C" or other programming languages. You won't be using this data type in your Roblox game experiences.

Variables and Literals

A variable is a named storage location that holds a value or data. They are labels that provide a descriptive name for some data that a program can read or modify. They act as containers that hold different types of information, such as numbers, strings, Booleans, or custom data types (Vector3). You can think of a variable as a label. Suppose you are visiting an ice cream outlet with several containers containing different flavors. How would you know what flavor a specific container has? Hopefully, there is a Label on the container that lists the flavor. This is precisely what a variable is. It is a container that can hold different types of information and can be referred to via a name (label).

Imagine you are building a game experience of a city that requires a weather monitoring system. This system gathers and displays real-time weather information, including temperature, humidity, and wind speed. You'll need variables to store and update this data as it changes. In this example, you would ideally use variables such as "currentTemperature," "currentHumidity," and "currentWindSpeed" to store the real-time weather data of the city whose experience you are simulating. You would then update the values of these variables as the weather changes over time and then use Roblox's "print ()" function to print the current weather information to the "Output" window. Using variables in this weather monitoring system allows you to easily track changing weather conditions and display the latest information to the user.

Some of the key characteristics of variables include

1) Name: Each variable has a unique identifier, known as its name. The name refers to the memory location where the data is stored. It allows developers to access and modify the data associated with that variable.

2) Data type: Variables have a specific data type, defining the data they can store. Common data types include integers (whole numbers), floating-point numbers (decimal numbers), strings (sequences of characters), booleans (true or false), and more complex types like arrays, vectors, and objects. The data type determines the operations that can be performed on the variable and the memory space required to store its value.

3) Value: The value is the actual data stored in the variable. It can be a constant (hard-coded value) or the result of a calculation. The value of a variable can change during the program's execution, making it dynamic and flexible.

4) Declaration: Before using a variable in a program, it needs to be declared. Declaration involves specifying the variable's name and data type. Some programming languages require explicit declaration, like C, C#, C++, etc., while others, like Lua, use dynamic typing, where the data type of a variable is determined at runtime based on the value assigned to it.

5) Assignment: Once a variable is declared, its value can be assigned or updated using the assignment operator (=). The value on the right side of the assignment operator is stored in the variable on the left side.

6) Scope: Variables have a scope that defines where they are accessible in code. A variable can be local, meaning it is limited to a specific block or function, or global, meaning it can be accessed from anywhere in the script. Scoping helps manage the visibility and lifetime of variables, reducing naming conflicts and enhancing code clarity.

Literals in programming refer to the notation used to represent fixed concrete values that help initialize variables, define data structures, and pass data to functions. They make code more readable and understandable by making the data values explicit and self-explanatory.

Some common types of literals in programming are

1) Numeric literals: Numeric literals represent numerical values such as integers or floating-point numbers.

   Examples of numeric literals are

   ```
   25          -- Numeric Integer literal
   3.14159     -- Floating-point (decimal) literal representing
   the value of pi
   ```

2) String literals: String literals are sequences of characters enclosed in single (' ') or double (" ") quotes.

Examples of string literals are

```
"Hello, World"    -- A String literal must be enclosed
in either double or single -- quotes.
```

3) Character literals: Character literals represent single characters
    enclosed in single quotes. In some programming languages,
    character literals are distinct from string literals; however, this is
    not the case in Lua, where character literals in Lua are treated as
    strings with a length of one character.

    Examples of character literals are

```
'Z'    -- Represents the single character(alphabet) 'Z'
```

4) Boolean literals: Boolean literals represent Boolean values, which
    are either true or false.

    Examples of boolean literals are

```
true    -- A Boolean literal which could also indicate
'Yes' or 'On.'
false    -- A Boolean literal which could also indicate
'No' or 'Off.'
```

5) Table (array) literal: In Lua, arrays are implemented using tables.
    A table in Lua is a versatile data structure that can act as an array,
    dictionary, or list. To create a table (array) literal in Lua, you
    use curly braces {} to enclose the elements of the table (array),
    separated by commas.

```
Example of a table (array) literal is
{"apple," "Banana," "orange," "pear"}    -- A Table
(Array) literal
```

Note   In this chapter, you will utilize the "Cuboid_Script" from Chapter 1 to experiment with the Lua code provided in all the code listings starting from the next section. To access the "Cuboid_Script," you created in Chapter 1, expand the "Cuboid" part in the "Explorer" window, and double-click "Cuboid_Script" to launch Roblox's Script Editor. You will observe that this script consists of only one line of code: print ("Hello World!"). It would help if you tried out every upcoming code listing in the Roblox Editor to grasp Roblox Lua coding well.

Naming Variables in Lua

In Lua, variable names must adhere to rules to ensure proper usage and compatibility with the language. Here are the rules for naming variables in Lua:

1) Start with a letter or underscore: Variable names must begin with a letter (uppercase or lowercase) or an underscore (_). A hyphen is not allowed as part of a variable name.

2) Subsequent characters: After the initial letter or underscore, variable names can contain letters, digits, and underscores. They are case-sensitive, meaning myVariable and myvariable are treated as different variables.

3) Reserved words: Variable names cannot be Lua-reserved words with special meanings in the language. For example, you cannot use words like if, while, function, or end as variable names.

4) Digits after the first character: While variable names can contain digits, they cannot start with a digit. For example, myVariable123 is valid, but 123variable is not.

5) Length: There is no strict limit on the size of variable names, but keeping them reasonably concise for readability is recommended.

Examples of some valid variable names in Lua:

- counter
- _myVar
- total_amount

- playerName

- MAX_VALUE

- _123abc

Examples of some invalid variable names in Lua:

- 123variable (Starts with a digit)

- if (Reserved keyword)

- my-variable (Contains a hyphen (not allowed))

Variable Declaration and Initialization

Variables in Lua support dynamic typing. Dynamic typing means that the data type of a variable is determined at runtime based on the value assigned to it. Unlike statically typed languages (C, C++, C#), where you must explicitly declare the data type of a variable before using it, Lua allows you to assign values of any data type to a variable without prior declaration.

The steps to creating a variable involve the following:

- Declaring the variable

- Assigning a value (data) to the variable

Here's an example of creating a variable and illustrating dynamic typing in Lua:

Listing 3-1. Variable declaration and dynamic typing example

```
local playerHealth                      --1) Variable
declaration without
                                        -- specifying a data type.
playerHealth = 100                      -- 2) Assigning an
integer value
print(playerHealth)                     -- 3) Output: 100
print(typeof(playerHealth))             -- 4) Output: number
playerHealth = "Fantastic!"             -- 5) Assigning a string value
print(playerHealth)                     -- 6) Output: Fantastic!
print(typeof(playerHealth))             -- 7) Output: string
```

```
playerHealth = true                        -- 8) Assigning a Boolean value
print(playerHealth)                        -- 9) Output: true
print(typeof(playerHealth))                -- 10) Output: boolean
                                           -- 11) Assigning a table
                                                  (array) literal

local fruits = {"Apple," "Orange," "Pear"}
print(fruits [2])                          -- 12) Output: Orange
print(typeof(fruits))                      -- 13) Output: table
```

1) local playerHealth: When you use the "local" keyword before defining a variable, you create a new variable local to the current block of code (e.g., a function or script). In this case, it's local to your "Script," as your script has no function. It's also important to note that you have created the variable playerHealth without specifying the type of data it will contain.

2) playerHealth = 100: Here, you are assigning the numeric literal integer value 100 to the variable playerHealth (initializing the variable), indicating to Lua that this variable's data type is now a "number" (integer). The "=" operator symbol used here is an assignment operator used to assign a numeric integer literal (100) to the variable playerHealth.

3) print(playerHealth): This is the same print() function you used in Chapter 1 when you wrote your first Lua script. It has now been passed the variable playerHealth, whose value is 100, and this value (100) is printed to the "Output" window.

4) print(typeof(playerHealth)): The print() function doesn't just accept variable or literals only. It can also be passed a function. Here you are passing it the typeof() function and asking it to print out whatever value is returned by the typeof() function. The typeof() function can be passed a variable and will return the data type of that variable. Your playerHealth variable contains the numeric integer value 100, which is represented by Lua's "number" data type, so typeof(playerHealth) will return the string literal "number" to the print() function, which then goes on to print this string literal to the "Output" window.

5) playerHealth = "Fantastic!": Here, you are now assigning the string literal "Fantastic!" to the playerHealth variable, indicating to Lua that this variable's data type is now a "string."

6) print(playerHealth): Here, you are using the print() function to print out the value contained within the variable playerHealth. The string literal "Fantastic!" will be printed to the "Output" window.

7) print(typeof(playerHealth)): Now, at this point, your playerHealth variable contains the value "Fantastic!," which is represented by Lua's "string" data type, so the function typeof(playerHealth) will return the string literal "string" to the print() function, which then goes on to print "string" to the "Output" window.

8) playerHealth = true: You are now assigning the boolean value true to the playerHealth variable, indicating to Lua that this variable's data type is now a "boolean."

9) print(playerHealth): You are now printing out the value contained within the playerHealth variable, which prints out the value true to the "Output" window.

10) print(typeof(playerHealth)): At this point in the code, the playerHealth variable contains the boolean value true, which is represented by Lua's "boolean" data type, so the function typeof(playerHealth) will return the string literal "boolean" to the print() function, which then goes on to print "boolean" to the "Output" window.

11) fruits = {"Apple," "Orange," "Pear"}: Here you are assigning an array (table) (which is a complex Lua data type) to the variable fruits, indicating to Lua that this variables data type is now a "table." A table (array) is assigned to a variable using the same "=" assignment operator.

12) print(fruits [2]): You are printing the value from the fruits variable, which has been assigned an array (table). Since it is an array, Lua recognizes it as a table with three elements indexed from 1 to 3. The first element contains "Apple," the second "Orange," and the third "Pear." When you access fruits[2], you access the second element, and the print() function displays "Orange."

13) print(typeof(fruits)): As this variable fruits has been assigned an
     array (table), Lua identifies it as a table. The function typeof(fruits)
     will return the string literal "table" to the print() function, which
     then goes on to print "table" to the "Output" window.

In Listing 3-1, we declare the variable playerHealth without specifying a data type
explicitly. We assign different values to it, including an integer, a string, a boolean, and
a table (an array). The typeof() function checks the variable's data type at runtime.
Lua's dynamic typing feature allows it to adapt to the data type of the assigned value
automatically, providing flexibility and convenience. However, changing a variable's
data type after assignment is considered bad programming practice and discouraged. It's
recommended to maintain a consistent data type for a variable once it's assigned.

A variable merely represents the underlying data, allowing for changes in its value
over time. For instance, with a variable called "time," one would anticipate updating its
value every second. The assignment operator "=" can assign a fresh value to the variable
at any moment. Additionally, a variable can be assigned the value of another variable,
but you must ensure that the variable's data type remains consistent throughout the
program.

Listing 3-2. Variable declaration and initialization

```
local originalValue = 42 -- Assigning a numeric integer literal
local otherValue = "Hello" -- Assigning a string literal
-- Assigning the value of one variable to another
local copiedValue = originalValue
-- Printing the initial values
print("originalVal:"..originalValue) --Output: originalVal: 42
print("otherValue:".. otherValue) -- Output: otherValue: Hello
print("copiedValue:".. copiedValue) -- Output: copiedValue: 42
--Trying to change the data type of the variable
copiedValue = otherValue
-- Printing the updated values
print("originalVal:"..originalValue) -- Output:originalVal: 42
print("otherVal:".. otherValue)      -- Output: otherVal: Hello
print("copiedVal:".. copiedValue)   -- Output: copiedVal: Hello
```

In Listing 3-2, we have three variables: originalValue, otherValue, and copiedValue. Initially, originalValue is assigned an integer value (42), and otherValue is assigned a string value ("Hello").

Then, we assign the value of originalValue to a new variable copiedValue, using the assignment operator "=." This indicates that a variable can be assigned the value of another variable. At this point, both originalValue and copiedValue have the same value (42), but they are independent variables.

Next, we attempt to assign the value of otherValue to copiedValue, which is bad programming practice as it would change the data type of the variable copiedValue from an integer to a string. However, the code will still execute without error, and copiedValue will now hold the value ("Hello"). This dynamic typing feature is a significant disadvantage of Lua that could easily lead to error-prone code. In statically typed languages, you are required to explicitly declare the data type of a variable before using it, and once declared, only values of that specific data type can be assigned to the variable. The lesson here is to be cautious when assigning the value of one variable to another and to ensure that their data types match to avoid unexpected behavior with your code.

The "local" keyword in Listing 3-2 specifies that the variable is local to the current script, block, or scope. Using "local" is a good practice as it helps manage variable scope and reduces the chance of naming conflicts. You will learn more about the "local" keyword in the Variable Scope section.

The ".." symbol within the print() function in Listing 3-2 is the concatenation operator that allows you to concatenate any combination of variables and literals. Having at least one space on the left and right sides of the ".." concatenation symbol is good practice.

In Lua, the remainder of that line is treated as a comment whenever you encounter the "--" symbol. Comments are solely meant to aid in code readability and comprehension; they do not get executed. Listing 3-1 and 3-2 illustrate the usage of comments.

Variable Scope

Variable scope is a fundamental concept determining where a variable can be accessed or used within the program. The scope of a variable is confined to the chunks they appear in. In Lua, a chunk is essentially a section of code, and it can be considered similar to blocks in other programming languages. Every Lua file that is executed is treated as a chunk. These chunks can contain other smaller chunks, creating a hierarchical relationship among them.

In Lua, the scoping mechanism ensures that variables are accessible only within the specific chunk in which they are defined or within any nested chunks. When the program encounters a new chunk, a new scope is created, and any variables declared within that chunk become visible and usable only within that specific chunk or any of its nested chunks. Essentially, the scope of a variable defines where in the program that variable can be accessed, determining its visibility and usability within different parts of the code.

There are three major types of chunks in Lua that determine the scope of a variable: Global, File, and Local chunks. Global chunks have the broadest scope and are accessible from any loaded Lua file. File chunks represent the scope of a Lua file being executed as a whole, and variables defined in this scope can be accessed anywhere within that file. On the other hand, local chunks have a more limited scope, confined to specific code sections. You can use the "do...end" keywords to create a local chunk within a Lua file. The "if...then...elseif...else...end" statement, which you'll learn about in a later section, also acts as a local chunk. Functions, which you'll learn about in a forthcoming chapter, are also named chunks of code with their own scope, following the same scoping rules as "do...end" chunks. This means that variables defined within a function are only accessible within that function's scope, ensuring encapsulation and preventing unintended interference with other parts of the code.

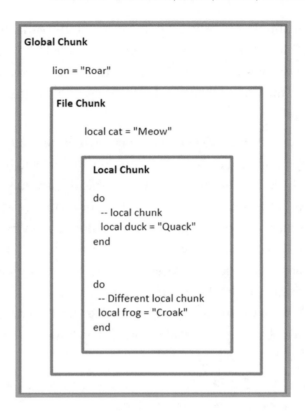

Figure 3-1. *Variable scope – chunks*

You can create a local chunk in a Lua file using the "do...end" block (Figure 3-6). A chunk can access variables declared in its parent chunk but cannot access any variables available in its child chunks. To illustrate this, let's consider the variable declarations in Figure 3-1:

1) Local Scope/Chunk: The "Local Chunk" can access variables within its "Local Chunk," its parent "File Chunk," and those within the "Global Chunk." Hence, the variables lion and cat are accessible within the "Local Chunk." However, this "Local Chunk" comprises two "do...end" blocks, each with its local variables: duck and frog. Attempting to access the duck or frog variable within "Local Chunk" outside their "do...end" block will result in an error. The variable duck can only be accessed within its "do...end" block, as can the frog variable. Listing 3-3 demonstrates this.

2) File Scope/Chunk: The "File Chunk" can access the variables
    within its "File Chunk" and those within the "Global Chunk."
    However, variables within the "Local Chunk" are not accessible.
    Hence, only the variables lion and cat are accessible within the
    "File Chunk."

3) Global Scope/Chunk: You would have noted that we used the
    "local" keyword in Figure 3-1 and Listing 3-3. Should you have
    omitted this "local" keyword from the variable declarations, the
    variable would default to having Global scope, no matter which
    chunk it is in. Note that the "local" keyword does not prefix
    the variable lion and hence has global scope. In Listing 3-3,
    the variable bird has been declared without a "local" keyword
    prefix, so even though it has been declared within the first
    "do...end" block, due to not being declared as "local," it defaults
    to having a global scope. Its value is printed within the second
    "do...end" block.

In Listing 3-3, the lines of code that would cause an error because variables are out of
scope or not declared have been commented in the code.

Variable shadowing considered a bad programming practice, can occur by giving a
local variable in a chunk the same name as a global variable. The local variable's value
will be used when printing the variable inside the chunk. The closest variable in the
current scope takes precedence when using the same variable name in different scopes.
Always ensure that your variables have unique names, as variable shadowing can lead to
debugging nightmares.

Listing 3-3. Variable scope

```
lion = "Roar"
local cat = "Meow"
do
     local duck = "Quack"
     bird = "Chirp" --Not declared as local, has Global Scope
     print("FileChunk: " .. lion .. " ".. cat)
     print(duck)
     print (frog)    -- Error frog variable not yet declared.
```

```
end
print("FileChunk: " .. lion .. " ".. cat)
print (duck)          -- Error duck variable no longer in scope
do
    local frog = "Croak"
    print("FileChunk: " .. lion .. " ".. cat)
    print(frog)
    print (duck)    -- Error duck variable no longer in scope
    print (bird)
end
print("FileChunk: " .. duck .. frog)   -- Error both duck and
                                       -- frog variables are not in scope.
```

Tables, Arrays, and Dictionaries

Lua provides a single data structure called a "table." However, this "table" data structure is highly versatile and can be employed to create various other data structures like lists, queues, or stacks. Essentially tables can represent a dictionary or array. A table is a key-value pair. If the keys to the table are numeric, the table represents an array. If the keys are non-numeric or mixed, the table is a dictionary. Within a table, almost anything can be used as a key except for nil, while values can include anything, including nil.

Creating an Array

An array is a simple and fundamental data structure that stores a collection of elements, all of the same data type, in a linear order. An array in Lua is essentially a sequence of values stored in a table, where each element in the array is accessed by its index, which starts at 1 for the first element. Listing 3-4 demonstrates how you can create an array in Lua.

Listing 3-4. Array creation, element insertion, and deletion

```
-- Creating a numeric array using a table
local numberArray = {10, 20, 30, 40, 50}    -- 1
-- Accessing array elements
print(numberArray[1])          -- 2 Output: 10
print(numberArray[3])          -- 3 Output: 30
-- Inserting array elements
```

```
table.insert(numberArray, 75)   -- 4 Insert item at array end
table.remove(numberArray, 4)    -- 5 Remove fourth item
print(numberArray)              -- prints out all array elements
```

1) local numberArray = {10, 20, 30, 40, 50}: This line declares a local variable named numberArray and assigns it a value, which is a table containing five elements: 10, 20, 30, 40, and 50. This creates an array-like structure since the indices for the array are implicit and numeric.

2) print(numberArray [1]): This line prints the value stored at index 1 in the numberArray table. In this case, it prints "10" because the first element in the array is 10.

3) print(numberArray [3]): This line prints the value stored at index 3 in the numberArray table. It prints "30" because the third element in the array is 30.

4) table.insert(numberArray, 75): Inserts the value 75 as the last element of the array, i.e., element number 6.

5) table.remove(numberArray, 4): Removes the fourth element of the array (i.e., number 40), causing the following two elements (50 and 75) to shift to fill in the gap.

Two-Dimensional Array

A two-dimensional array is a programming data structure designed to arrange and manage information in a grid-like configuration (e.g., a spreadsheet), aligning data elements in rows and columns. Elements within this array are accessed using a pair of indices: one for row and the other for column identification. This arrangement effectively represents and manipulates structured data, encompassing tabular data, matrices, grids, and other organized datasets. Unlike certain languages like C#, Lua lacks inherent support for multidimensional arrays. Instead, you can simulate a multidimensional array by forming an array of arrays, which essentially involves creating a table of tables. This approach necessitates specifying each array element as a distinct row within the two-dimensional matrix.

In a two-dimensional array,

- The first index represents the row number.

- The second index represents the column number.

Two-dimensional arrays prove valuable when data organization involves multiple dimensions. They excel in scenarios requiring depicting elements like game boards, images, screen coordinate points, and similarly structured datasets.

Listing 3-5. A two-dimensional array

```
local grid = {                        -- 1
    {1, 2, 3},                        -- 2
    {4, 5, 6},                        -- 3
    {7, 8, 9}                         -- 4
}
-- Accessing element in row 2, column 3 (value = 6)
local r2c3 = grid[2][3]               -- 5
```

1) local grid = {...}: This initializes a local variable named grid and assigns it a value. The value is a table containing three sub-tables, each representing a row of the 2D array. In other words, a grid is a table (2D array) where each element/row is a table (single-dimensional array).

2) {1, 2, 3}: This is the first element/row of the grid table (2D array), which itself is a table containing the values 1, 2, and 3. This represents the first row of the 2D array.

3) {4, 5, 6}: This is the second element/row of the grid table, another table with values 4, 5, and 6. This is the second row of the 2D array.

4) {7, 8, 9}: This is the third element/row of the grid table, yet another table with values 7, 8, and 9. This represents the third row of the 2D array.

5) local r2c3 = grid[2][3]: This line of code accesses a specific element(cell) of the 2D array. grid[2] refers to the second row (which is itself a table), and grid[2][3] refers to the third element(column) (value 6) within the second row. Therefore, r2c3 will contain the value 6.

Creating a Dictionary

A dictionary is a data structure that stores a collection of key-value pairs. Each key in the dictionary is unique and maps to a specific value. Keys can be of any data type (usually strings) and allow you to retrieve corresponding values quickly. This allows for the efficient retrieval of values based on their corresponding keys. Dictionaries are often used to represent relationships between entities or for storing metadata. Listing 3-6 shows how to create a dictionary using the table data structure.

Listing 3-6. Dictionary creation

```
-- Creating a dictionary using a table
local personDetails = {               -- 1
    name = "John",
    age = 30,
    city = "New York"
}
-- Accessing dictionary values using keys
print(personDetails["name"])   -- 2 Output: John
print(personDetails["age"])    -- 3 Output: 30
print(personDetails["city"])   -- 4 Output: New York
-- 5 Add a key-value pair to an existing dictionary
personDetails["gender"] = "Male"
print(personDetails)
-- 6 Remove a key-value pair from an existing dictionary
personDetails["city"] = nil
print(personDetails)
```

1) local personDetails = {name = "John," age = 30, city = "New York"}:
   This line of code declares a local variable named personalDetails
   and assigns it a value, which is a table containing key-value pairs
   that have been defined within the curly braces. Here, "name"
   is a key with the value "John," "age" is a key with the value 30,
   and "city" is a key with the value "New York." This constructs a
   dictionary-like structure where each key corresponds to a specific
   piece of information.

2) print(personDetails["name"]): This line prints the value associated with the key "name" from the personDetails dictionary (table). It displays "John."

3) print(personDetails["age"]): This line prints the value associated with the key "age" from the personDetails dictionary (table). It displays 30.

4) print(personDetails["city"]): This line prints the value associated with the key "city" from the personDetails (dictionary) table. It displays "New York."

5) personDetails["gender"] = "Male": Here, you are adding a new key-value pair to the existing dictionary, namely, personDetails. Note that the current value will be overwritten if the key already exists.

6) personDetails["city"] = nil: By setting the value of the key you want to be removed from the dictionary to nil, you can remove that key-value pair from the existing dictionary. This essentially deletes the key. If you try accessing this key-value pair after removing it, you will receive a nil value.

Operators (Unary/Binary) and Operands

Operators are symbols or keywords used in programming languages to perform various operations on data or variables. They allow you to manipulate and combine values to produce desired results. Roblox Lua supports a variety of operators.

Operands are the values or variables operators act upon in programming. In other words, operands are the inputs to operators, and they can be of different data types, such as numbers, strings, or booleans. Operators perform various operations on operands to produce a result. For example, in the expression "5 + 3," the operands are "5" and "3," and the operator is the addition operator "+." The addition operator adds these two operands, resulting in "8."

Operators can be classified into two main categories based on the number of operands they take:

- Unary operators: Unary operators are operators that work with a single operand. For example, in the expression y = -x, the unary minus operator "-"negates the variable x's value, resulting in y being assigned the value -x.

- Binary operators: Binary operators are operators that work with two operands. For example, in the expression sum = a + b, the binary addition operator "+" adds variables a and b, assigning the sum the value of a + b.

Assignment Operator

The assignment operator is a fundamental concept in programming. The assignment operator "=" is used to assign a value to a variable. This value could be a literal, another variable, or the result of an expression. Listing 3-7 shows four different assignment operations in Lua.

Listing 3-7. Examples of the assignment operator

```
local age = 25                -- 1
local playerName = "John Doe"  -- 2
local isGameOver = false       -- 3
local oldAge = age + 55        -- 4
```

1) Here, "age" is the variable, and the numeric literal value 25 is assigned to it.

2) Here, "playerName" is the variable, and the string literal value "John Doe" is assigned to it.

3) Here, "isGameOver" is the variable, and the false boolean value is assigned to it.

4) Here, "oldAge" is the variable, and the expression (age + 55) is assigned to it.

The assignment operator works as follows:

1) The assignment operator's left-hand side (LHS) is the variable name. The identifier (label) will access the data (value) stored in memory.

2) The assignment operator's right-hand side (RHS) is the value you want to store in the variable. It can be a literal value (e.g., numbers, strings, booleans) or the result of an expression.

Arithmetic Operators

Arithmetic operators in Lua perform addition, subtraction, multiplication, and division. Lua also provides a modulus operator to compute the remainder of a division and an exponentiation operator to raise a number to a power. Following are Lua's arithmetic operators:

1) Addition (+): Used to add two numbers together.

2) Subtraction (-): Used to subtract one number from another.

3) Multiplication (*): Used to multiply two numbers.

4) Division (/): Used to divide one number by another.

5) Modulus (%): Calculates the remainder after dividing one number by another.

6) Exponentiation (^): The exponentiation operator in Lua is represented by the caret symbol. It calculates the value of a number raised to a specific power.

Listing 3-8. Examples of arithmetic operators

```
local a = 10 + 5              -- Output: 15
local b = 20 – 3              -- Output: 17
local c = 4 * 6              -- Output: 24
local x = 15 / 3              -- Output: 5
local y = 17 % 5              -- Output: 2
local base = 2
local exponent = 3
local result = base ^ exponent    -- Output: 8
```

Compound Assignment Operators

Roblox Lua supports compound assignment operators for arithmetic operations. These operators combine a binary arithmetic operation with the assignment operator (=) to perform an operation and store the result back into the variable in a single step.

These compound assignment operators are convenient shortcuts for performing common arithmetic operations and updating variable values in Roblox Lua code. They help make the code more concise and readable. Listing 3-9 demonstrates the usage of compound assignment operators.

Listing 3-9. Examples of compound assignment operators

```
local age = 25
local oldAge = 55
age += oldAge -- 1 Equivalent to age = age + oldAge (age=80 now)
age -= oldAge -- 2 Equivalent to age = age - oldAge (age=25 now)
age *= 2      -- 3 Equivalent to age = age * 3 (age=75 now)
age /= 4      -- 4 Equivalent to age = age / 4 (age=12.5 now)
age %= 3      -- 5 Equivalent to age = age % 3 (age=0.5 now)
age ^= 3      -- 6 Equivalent to age = age ^ 3 (age=0.125 now)
```

1) Addition Assignment Operator (+=): It adds the right-hand operand to the value of the left-hand operand and assigns the result back to the left-hand operand.

2) Subtraction Assignment Operator (-=): It subtracts the right-hand operand from the value of the left-hand operand and assigns the result back to the left-hand operand.

3) Multiplication Assignment Operator (*=): It multiplies the value of the left-hand operand by the right-hand operand and assigns the result back to the left-hand operand.

4) Division Assignment Operator (/=): It divides the value of the left-hand operand by the right-hand operand and assigns the result back to the left-hand operand.

5) Modulo Assignment Operator (%=): It calculates the remainder of dividing the value of the left-hand operand by the right-hand operand and assigns the result back to the left-hand operand.

6) Exponentiation Assignment Operator (^=): It raises the value of the left-hand operand by the right-hand operand and assigns the result back to the left-hand operand.

Relational Operators

Relational operators in programming are used to compare two values and determine the relationship between them. They always yield a boolean value (true or false) based on the comparison result. These operators are used to address questions like "Is the Player alive?" and "Is 45 > 90?" They test for equality, inequality, and which of the operands on either side of the relational operator is either less than, greater than, or equal to the other. The equality operator (==) checks whether the values of the two operands are equal, returning true if they are equal and false otherwise.

Relational operators are extensively utilized in conditional statements and loops to make decisions and control the program's flow.

Following are the relational operators available to compare values and determine relationships between them:

1) Equal to (==): Checks if the left operand is equal to the right operand.

2) Not equal to (~=): Checks if the left operand is not equal to the right operand.

3) Greater than (>): Checks if the left operand is greater than the right operand.

4) Less than (<): Checks if the left operand is less than the right operand.

5) Greater than or equal to (>=): Checks if the left operand is greater than or equal to the right operand.

6) Less than or equal to (<=): Checks if the left operand is less than or equal to the right operand.

Listing 3-10. Examples of relational operators

```
-- Define variables for the left and right operands
local a = 5
local b = 10
-- Equal to (==)
print(a == b)              -- Output: false
-- Not equal to (~=)
print(a ~= b)              -- Output: true
-- Greater than (>)
print(a > b)               -- Output: false
-- Less than (<)
print(a < b)               -- Output: true
-- Greater than or equal to (>=)
print(a >= b)              -- Output: false

-- Less than or equal to (<=)
print(a <= b)              -- Output: true
```

In Listing 3-10, we have variables a and b with values 5 and 10, respectively. We then use each of the six relational operators to compare these variables and print the results. As relational operators always yield a Boolean value, the output indicates each comparison's boolean value (true or false) based on the specific relational operator used.

Length Unary Operator

In Roblox Lua, the length operator is considered a unary operator. The (#) symbol represents the length operator and determines the length of a string or the number of elements in a table (array). As a unary operator, the length operator works with a single operand and returns a numeric value representing the length of the operand. Listing 3-11 demonstrates the usage of the length unary operator.

Listing 3-11. Length unary operator used with a string

```
local str = "Hello, Lua!"
local len = #str
print(len)-- Output: 11 (length of the string "Hello, Lua!")
```

In Listing 3-10, the "#" (length) operator is applied to the variable str, which returns the length of the string contained within this variable.

Listing 3-12. Length unary operator used with an array (table)

```
local myArray = {1, 2, 3, 4, 5}
local length = #myArray
print(length) -- Output: 5 (number of elements in the array)
```

In Listing 3-12, the "#" (length) operator is applied to the variable myArray, and it returns the number of elements in the array (table).

Concatenation Operator

Concatenation refers to the process of combining any combination of variables and literals. You can combine multiple strings into a single text string or a string with a variable value.

Lua provides a straightforward way to achieve concatenation using the concatenation operator represented by two periods ".".

It is good practice to have at least one space on the left and right of the concatenation ".." symbol. Concatenating two strings results in a new string, which can be stored in a variable or used in place. Listing 3-13 displays examples of various forms of concatenation.

Listing 3-13. Concatenation

```
local str1 = "Hello, "
local str2 = "Lua!"
local result = str1 .. str2
print(result)              -- Output: Hello, Lua!
local dist = 2.5
print("Distance between Cuboid & Cylinder : " .. dist)
-- Output: Distance between Cuboid & Cylinder: 2.5
```

Note   Instead of using the concatenation symbol () you could also use a comma as follows: print("Greeting: ", str1, str2).

String Coercion

String coercion in Lua refers to automatically converting non-string values to strings when a string is expected. This feature allows you to treat non-string values as strings without explicitly converting them using functions like tostring(). Listing 3-14 illustrates examples of string coercion in Lua.

Listing 3-14. String coercion – coercing a number to a string

```
local pi = 3.14159
local str = "The value of Pi is : " .. pi
print(str) -- Output: The value of Pi is : 3.14159
```

In Listing 3-14, the variable pi is of type number. When we use the concatenation operator ".." to combine it with the string "The value of Pi is:", Lua automatically converts the number to a string and performs the concatenation, resulting in the output "The value of Pi is: 3.14159".

Listing 3-15. String interpolation

```
local name = "John Doe"
local age = 45
local message = string.format("Hello, my name is %s and I am %d years
old.", name, age)
print(message)
-- Output: Hello, my name is John Doe and I am 45 years old.
```

In Listing 3-15, we use string.format() to create a formatted string. The placeholders %s and %d are used for string and number values, respectively. When we pass the variables, name and age to the string.format() function, Lua automatically converts the non-string variable age into a string and assigns this newly created "text string" to the variable message, which gets printed out.

Listing 3-16. Printing non-string values

```
local pi = 3.14159
print("The value of Pi  is : " .. pi)
-- Output: The value of Pi is : 3.14159
```

```
local isPlayerAlive = true
print("Is the player alive? " .. isPlayerAlive)
-- Output: Is the player alive? true
```

In Listing 3-16, we concatenate a number and a boolean value with strings inside
the print() function. Lua automatically coerces the non-string variables (pi and
isPlayerAlive) into strings to be combined with the surrounding strings and printed out.

Escape Sequences

In Roblox Lua, escape sequences are special combinations of characters used to
represent certain non-printable or special characters within strings. When you include
an escape sequence in a string, it alters the way the Lua interpreter interprets the string.
Escape sequences start with a backslash () followed by a specific character or code,
determining their special meaning. In Lua, strings need to be enclosed within quotes,
and Lua doesn't care if that string uses single or double quotes so long as the symbol
used at the start and end of the string is the same. As standard practice, double quotes
are typically used to represent a string. Should you need to include a double quote
within a string, the character must be escaped using an escape sequence. To escape a
character, you precede it with backslash, as shown in Listing 3-16.

Listing 3-17. Escape sequences

```
local str = "John Doe said \"Hello !\" to you."      -- 1
print(str)
str = 'This is a single \'quoted\' string.'          -- 2
print(str)
str = "This is a backslash: \\"                       -- 3
print(str)
str= "Line 1\nLine 2"                                 -- 4
print(str)
str = "Column 1\tColumn 2"                            -- 5
print(str)
str = "Text\rNew text"                                -- 6
print(str)
str = "Backspace\b"                                   -- 7
```

```
print(str)
str = "Alert!\a"                              -- 8
print(str)
str = "Line 1\vLine 2"                        -- 9
print(str)
str = "Null terminated string\0"              --10
print(str)
```

1) \": Represents a double quotation mark ("). It is used when you must include a double quote within a string delimited by double quotes.

   Example: "John Doe said \"Hello !\" to you."

2) \': Represents a single quotation mark ('). It is used when you must include a single quote within a string delimited by single quotes.

   Example: 'This is a single \'quoted\' string.'

3) \\: Represents a backslash itself. If you need to include a backslash character in your string, you escape it with another backslash.

   Example: "This is a backslash: \\"

4) \n: Represents a newline character. It is used to insert a line break in a string.

   Example: "Line 1\nLine 2"

5) \t: Represents a horizontal tab character. It is used to insert a horizontal tab in a string.

   Example: "Column 1\tColumn 2"

6) \r: Represents a carriage return character. It is sometimes used to reset the cursor to the beginning of the line.

   Example: "Text\rNew text"

7) \b: Represents a backspace character. It is used to move the cursor one position backward.

   Example: "Backspace\b"

8) \a: Represents an alert (bell) character. It produces a visible alert. A symbol is displayed in the Output window.

Example: "Alert!\a".

9) \v: Represents a vertical tab character. It is less commonly used but can be used to create vertical spacing. A symbol is displayed in the Output window.

Example: "Line 1\vLine 2"

10) \0: Represents a null character. It is used to represent the null terminator in strings. The null escape sequence character is not visible in the string.

Example: "Null terminated string\0"

Escape sequences are beneficial when you want to include special characters or formatting in your strings without disrupting the string's interpretation. You can create more dynamic and informative strings within your Roblox Lua scripts using these sequences.

Conditionals

Conditionals (aka control structures) are fundamental constructs in programming languages that allow you to make decisions and control the flow of your code based on certain conditions or criteria. They enable your program to execute different chunks (blocks) of code depending on whether a given condition is true or false. Conditionals allow your program to react dynamically to changing circumstances or input values. They are crucial for creating flexible, responsive, and intelligent code. Lua provides you with the if statement for this purpose. An if statement is followed by a Boolean condition, followed by a "then...end" chunk (block). The chunk (block) is executed only if the Boolean condition evaluates to true.

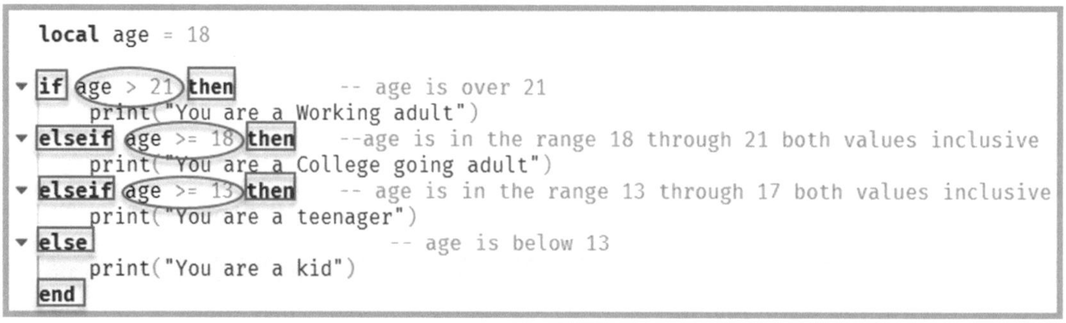

```
local age = 18
if age > 21 then          -- age is over 21
    print("You are a Working adult")
elseif age >= 18 then     --age is in the range 18 through 21 both values inclusive
    print("You are a College going adult")
elseif age >= 13 then     -- age is in the range 13 through 17 both values inclusive
    print("You are a teenager")
else                      -- age is below 13
    print("You are a kid")
end
```

Figure 3-2. *if-elseif-else conditionals*

In Figure 3-2, note the keywords used as depicted by the rectangular shape: "if,"
"then," "elseif," and "end." The ellipse shape defines the boolean conditions, which
revolve around age. The "if…then…elseif," "elseif…then…elseif," "elseif…then…else,"
and "else…end" are blocks (chunks) to which scope rules discussed earlier apply. Here,
the print statement for the block (chunk) whose boolean condition evaluates to true is
executed.

Lua provides a few different conditional structures that you can use:

1) if statement: This is the simplest form of a conditional
   (Figure 3-2). It executes a code block if a given condition is true, as
   illustrated in Listing 3-18. If the boolean condition, temperature
   > 30, evaluates to true, then the statement "It's a hot day!" is
   displayed. As the variable temperature has been initialized to 25,
   which is not greater than 30, the print statement contained within
   the "if…then…end" block (chunk) will never be executed.

Listing 3-18. The if conditional

```
local temperature = 25
if temperature > 30 then
    print("It's a hot day!")
end
```

2) if-else statement: This control structure allows you to execute one block of code if a condition is true and another block if it's false. In Listing 3-19, if the boolean condition, age >= 18, evaluates to true (which it will, as we initialized the variable age to the value 18), the code contained within the "if...then...else" block (chunk) is executed displaying the statement "You are an adult." If you had assigned a value less than 18 to the variable age (e.g., age = 10), then the block (chunk) of code between "else...end" would be executed as the boolean condition, age >= 18, would evaluate to false, resulting in the statement "You are not yet an adult" being displayed.

Listing 3-19. The if-else conditional

```
local age = 18
if age >= 18 then
    print("You are an adult.")
else
    print("You are not yet an adult.")
end
```

3) if-elseif-else statement: This structure lets you check multiple conditions sequentially and execute different code blocks accordingly. Listing 3-20 illustrates this concept.

Listing 3-20. The if-elseif-else conditional

```
local score = 85
if score >= 90 then
    print("You got an A!")
elseif score >= 80 then
    print("You got a B.")
elseif score >= 70 then
    print("You got a C.")
else
    print("You need to improve your grade.")
end
```

In Listing 3-20, the "if-elseif-else" conditional statement in the given code determines the grade associated with a specific score. In this specific case, the code checks the value of the score variable against certain thresholds to determine the grade. The order of the boolean conditions matters because once a condition is satisfied (evaluates to true), the corresponding code block (chunk) is executed, and the rest of the conditions are skipped and will never be checked. It's essential to list the scores in descending order from highest to lowest within this conditional statement to ensure that the correct grade is assigned based on the score range.

The way this chained "if...elseif...elseif...else" control structure works is that if you have "if...elseif...elseif...else" blocks (chunks), and the condition in one of those blocks (chunks) is found to be true, then the rest of the "elseif...elseif" blocks and the "else" block won't be checked or used.

Listing 3-21. The if-elseif-else conditional – listing conditions in ascending order

```
local score = 85
if score >= 70 then
    print("You got a C.")
elseif score >= 80 then
    print("You got a B.")
elseif score >= 90 then
    print("You got an A!")
else
    print("You need to improve your grade.")
end
```

In Listing 3-21, the conditions have been listed in ascending order (from lowest to highest) and would lead to incorrect results. Even though the score is 85, the first condition score >= 70 would be satisfied, and the code would display "You got a C." This is inaccurate because the score of 85 corresponds to a "B," not a "C." If the score is 85, it will fall within the range of score >= 80 and < 90, so "You got a B" should be displayed. Be watchful of these situations, as they can trip your code.

Logical Operators

Logical operators in programming allow you to manipulate and evaluate boolean conditions or expressions. Boolean conditions represent either true or false, and logical operators help you combine or modify these boolean conditions to make decisions, control program flow, and create even more complex conditions. Logical operators are widely used in various programming languages to create conditional statements, loops, and other control structures.

In Lua, we have a unique way of thinking about true and false. Anything that's not false is treated as true. Only two values represent false: one is called "false," and the other is called "nil." Everything else is considered as true. An interesting facet of Lua logical operators is that they do not evaluate to a boolean result but evaluate to one of the provided operands.

There are three primary logical operators:

1) and: The "and" operator returns true if all its operands are true; otherwise, it returns false. It's often used to ensure that multiple conditions are simultaneously satisfied.

2) or: The "or" operator returns true if at least one of its operands is true; if all operands are false, it returns false. It's used when you want to check if at least one out of multiple conditions is true.

3) not: The "not" operator is a unary operator that negates the value of its operand. If the operand is true, "not" makes it false, and if it is false, "not" makes it true.

The "and/or" operators both use shortcut evaluation. This means that the second operand is only evaluated if needed.

Listing 3-22. The logical operator «and»

```
local x = true and true    -- 1 Output: true
x = false and false        -- 2 Output: false
x = true and false         -- 3 Output: false
x = true and nil           -- 4 Output: nil (x evaluates to nil which
                           -- represents false)
x = 1 and 5                -- 5 Output: 5 (x evaluates to value of second
                           -- operand which is neither nil nor false so
```

73

```
                                  -- represents true)
x = 1 and 0                       -- 6 Output: 0 (any number evaluates
                                  -- to true even 0)
local y = "John" and "Doe"        -- 7 Output: Doe (y evaluates to
                                  -- value of second operand
                                  -- which is neither nil or
                                  -- false so represents true)
x = nil and 1                     -- 8 Output: nil (x evaluates to nil
                                  -- which represents false)
```

1) Both operands on either side of the "and" operator are true.
   Lua evaluates the first operand, and as it is true, it evaluates
   the second operand, which is also true, resulting in the overall
   expression being true.

2) Both operands on either side of the "and" operator are false. Here,
   Lua evaluates just the first operand, and the moment it knows
   it's false, it will not bother to evaluate the second operand, as the
   entire expression can never be true. Hence, the resultant output
   is false.

3) Here the first operand is true, and the second operand is false. As
   the first operand is true, Lua must evaluate the second operand
   to determine if all operands in the expression are true. Upon
   evaluating the second operand, it finds it to be false, due to which
   the entire expression now evaluates to false, resulting in the
   output false.

4) Here the first operand is true, and the second operand is nil.
   Remember from an earlier discussion that "nil" represents false.
   As the first operand is true, Lua must evaluate the second operand
   to determine if all operands in the expression are true. Upon
   evaluating the second operand, it finds it to be nil (false). This
   results in the entire expression being false and returns the second
   operand value nil and not false.

5) Here both operands are numbers (1 and 5), which evaluate
    as true. Hence, Lua now returns the second operand value 5,
    resulting in the entire expression evaluating to true.

6) Here both operands are numbers (1 and 0), which evaluate as
    true. Hence, Lua returns the second operand value 0, resulting in
    the entire expression evaluating to true. In certain programming
    languages (e.g., C), the value 0 represents false. However, in Lua,
    this is not the case. Any number, even zero, represents true.

7) Here both operands are string literals, which evaluate as true.
    Hence, Lua returns the second operand value "Doe," resulting in
    the entire expression evaluating to true.

8) Here the first operand is nil, and the second operand is 1. As the
    first operand nil represents false, Lua won't bother to evaluate the
    second operand as both operands can never be true. This results
    in the entire expression being false, and as Lua evaluated just the
    first operand, it returns the value nil.

Listing 3-23. The logical operator «or»

```
local x = true or true    -- 1 Output: true
x = false or false        -- 2 Output: false
x = false or true         -- 3 Output: true
x = nil or true           -- 4 Output: true (x evaluates to true as the
                          -- second operand is true)
x = 1 or 5                -- 5 Output: 1 (both operands represent true
                          -- x evaluates to value of first operand which
                          -- represents true)
x = 0 or 1                -- 6 Output: 0 (any number evaluates to true
                          -- even 0, so x evaluates to the value of the
                          -- first operand)
local y = "John" or "Doe" -- 7 Output: John (y evaluates to
                          -- value of first operand which
                          -- represents true)
x = nil or 1              -- 8 Output: 1 (x evaluates to 1 which
                          -- represents true)
```

1) Both operands on either side of the "or" operator are true. Lua evaluates the first operand, and as it is true, it won't bother evaluating the second operand as the 'or' operator requires only one operand (condition) to evaluate as true for the entire expression to evaluate to true. This results in x being true.

2) Both operands on either side of the "or" operator are false. Here, Lua evaluates the first operand and realizes it is false. As it needs just one operand (condition) to be true, it proceeds further with checking the second operand with the hope of it being true. However, it realizes that the second operand is also false, resulting in the entire expression being false. Hence, the resultant output is false.

3) Here the first operand is false, and the second operand is true. As the first operand is false, Lua must evaluate the second one to determine if it is true. At least one operand in the "or" expression must be true for the entire expression to be true. Upon evaluating the second operand, it finds it to be true, due to which the entire expression now evaluates to true, resulting in the output true.

4) Here the first operand is nil, and the second operand is true. Remember from an earlier discussion that "nil" represents false. As the first operand is false, Lua must evaluate the second operand to determine if it is true. Upon evaluating the second operand, it finds it to be true. This results in the entire expression being true.

5) Both operands are numbers (1 and 5), representing true. Lua evaluates the first operand and finds it to be true. As the first operand (condition) is true, Lua won't bother checking the second operand (condition) and returns the first operand value 1, resulting in the entire expression evaluating to true.

6) Both operands are numbers (0 and 1), representing true. Lua evaluates the first operand (condition) and finds it to be a number that represents true. As the first operand (condition) is true, Lua won't bother checking the second operand (condition) and returns the first operand value 0, resulting in the entire expression evaluating to true. In certain programming languages (e.g., C), the value 0 represents false. However, in Lua, this is not the case. Any number, even zero, represents true.

7) Here both operands are string literals, which represent true. Lua checks the first operand's value "John," which evaluates to true, so it doesn't bother checking the second operand's value "Doe" as one condition in the "or" expression has evaluated to true, resulting in the entire expression evaluating to true.

8) Here the first operand is nil, and the second operand is 1. As the first operand nil represents false, Lua evaluates the second operand as at least one should be true for the entire expression to be true. The second operand, 1, represents a true value, resulting in the entire expression being true, and the value returned is 1.

Listing 3-24. The logical operator «not»

```
local playerDead = false
if not playerDead then
    print("Hurray! Its Game ON")
else
    print("GAME OVER")
end
```

Listing 3-24 checks the status of the playerDead variable. If the player is not dead (playerDead is false), it displays "Hurray! Its Game ON" to indicate the game is ongoing. Otherwise, if the player is dead (playerDead is true), it displays "GAME OVER" to suggest that the game has ended.

You can combine these logical operators to create more intricate conditions. Listing 3-25 demonstrates this.

Listing 3-25. Creating intricate conditions by combining logical operators

```
-- Can the Player Escape the Zombies?
local hasKey = true
local isZombieNearby = false
local isDark = false
if not isZombieNearby and hasKey or not isDark then
    print("You successfully escaped the zombies!")
else
    print("The zombies got you. Game over.")
end
```

In Listing 3-25, the if condition checks to see if you can somehow escape the zombies; the other part is what happens if you can't. In short, you can avoid the zombies by either (zombies not being close and having a key) or (it's not dark), in which case you escape and win. However, if the zombies are close irrespective of you having a key, and it's dark, you cannot escape and lose.

Here's a more straightforward breakdown:

- If there are no zombies nearby and you have a key, or it's not dark, the game says, "You successfully escaped the zombies!" This means you get away safely if you meet any of these conditions: either no zombies are close, you have a key, or it's not dark outside.

- If you don't meet these conditions, the game says, "The zombies got you. Game over." This means if you have zombies nearby, regardless of whether you have a key, but it's dark, you can't escape, and the zombies get you.

In the section on operator precedence and using parentheses, you will learn how to simplify intricate logical conditions by using parentheses.

Operator Precedence and Using Parentheses

In Lua, just as in mathematics, operator precedence plays a crucial role. Like how $10 + 5 * 4$ equals 30 in math due to multiplication taking precedence over addition, Lua operates similarly. Operator precedence in Lua entails a predefined hierarchy that dictates the sequence of operations when an expression contains multiple operators. This hierarchy influences the order in which operators interact with operands. Lua adheres to a defined set of rules that dictate the evaluation order for operators. Operators with higher precedence are assessed before those with lower precedence. If multiple operators share the same precedence, their evaluation follows a left-to-right sequence.

Some common operators and their precedence levels in Lua (from highest to lowest) include

- Exponentiation (^)

- Unary operators (-, not, #)

- Multiplicative operators (*, /, %)

- Additive operators (+, -)

- Concatenation (...)

- Relational operators (<, <=, >, >=, ~=, ==)

- Logical operator (and)

- Logical operator (or)

- Assignment operators (=, +=, -=, etc.)

Understanding operator precedence helps you write expressions that produce the intended results and avoid unexpected behavior. If in doubt, using parentheses to explicitly indicate the desired order of evaluation is a good practice.

Parentheses in Lua play a pivotal role by allowing explicit specification of the evaluation order in expressions. This proves especially valuable when you seek to prioritize specific operations, irrespective of the default precedence. Parentheses control the grouping of operations, ensuring precise execution of calculations according to your intentions. This practice enhances code readability, minimizes ambiguity, and guards against errors stemming from misinterpretation of operation order. Furthermore, Lua's logical operators, such as "and" and "or," can be harnessed with parentheses. This enables tailored management of logical operations and construction of intricate conditions. Using parentheses alongside operators and logical operators in Lua provides a potent mechanism to define operation sequences and logical assessments meticulously. This robust tool effectively governs your program's course and behavior, yielding expressive and resilient code against errors. Listing 3-26 provides examples of using parentheses to clarify precedence when working with math and logical operators.

Listing 3-26. Clarifying precedence using parentheses

```
-- Examples using math expressions
result = 10 + 5 * 2    -- Result: 20 (Multiplication before
                       -- addition)
result = (10 + 5) * 2 -- Result: 30 (Addition before
                       -- multiplication)
area = (length + width) * height -- use of parentheses to
                                 -- enforce addition before
                                 -- multiplication.
-- Examples using parentheses with logical operators
```

```lua
local age = 25
local hasValidLicense = true
if (age >= 18 and age <= 65) or hasValidLicense then
    print("You can drive!")
end
local isWeekend = false
local isHoliday = true
isSpecialEvent = true
isFull = false
if (isWeekend and isHoliday) or (isSpecialEvent and not isFull) then
    print("Discount available!")
end
local isAdmin = false
local isModerator = true
if not (isAdmin or isModerator) then
    print("Access denied.")
else
    print("Access granted.")
end
```

Summary

This chapter has provided a concise yet thorough exploration of crucial Roblox Lua coding concepts, covering Variables, Scope, Arrays, Operators, Operator Precedence, Parentheses, and Conditionals. By comprehending and applying these fundamentals, you can now proficiently control data, manipulate information, make informed decisions, and execute complex operations.

You began by looking at the basic data types provided by Lua and explored the table data structure, learning to create tables, arrays, and dictionaries. You examined variables and literals as well as delved deep into variable scope. You then went on to explore operators and operands, distinguishing between unary and binary operators and grasping their function in manipulating data and variables. Arithmetic operators allowed you to efficiently perform numerical calculations, while compound assignment operators showed you how to generate concise and readable code. Relational operators facilitated the comparison of values, and the assignment operator enabled efficient variable assignment. Understanding the length unary operator helped determine the size of strings and tables, while the string concatenation operator provided seamless string manipulation. In conditionals, you mastered the art of decision-making by employing if, else, and elseif constructs. Logical operators empower you to express complex conditions succinctly. Additionally, you explored operator precedence and using parentheses to control the order of evaluation in expressions, optimizing your code for clarity and efficiency. Through practical insights and hands-on examples, this chapter has provided you with the crucial skills needed to navigate the intricacies of Roblox Lua and harness its potential to create engaging and dynamic virtual experiences.

CHAPTER 4

Loops

A loop is a fundamental control structure that allows you to repeatedly execute a block (chunk) of code. It's a way to automate the repetition of a particular task or set of instructions without having to write the same code again and again. Loops are handy when you must perform an action multiple times or want to iterate through a collection of items (like an array, dictionary, or list). In Lua, you can access three major loop structures: the while, repeat…until, and for loops. In this chapter, you will dive deep into all possible looping structures within Roblox Lua.

While Loops

The while loop allows you to repeatedly execute a block (chunk) of code if the loop's specified boolean condition is true. The loop is terminated when the loop boolean condition evaluates to false. A while loop starts with the while keyword, followed by a boolean condition and a do/end block (chunk). Listing 4-1 shows the while loop in action.

Listing 4-1. An example of a while loop

```
-- Example: Print even numbers less than 10 using a while loop
local num = 2          -- 1
while num < 10 do      -- 2 boolean condition (num < 10)
    print(num)         -- 3
    num += 2           -- 4
end
print("Loop Condition Evaluated to False-Loop Terminated )-- 5
```

© Christopher Coutinho 2023
C. Coutinho, *Roblox Lua Scripting Essentials*, https://doi.org/10.1007/979-8-8688-0026-9_4

1) local num = 2: This line declares a local variable named num and initializes it with the value 2. This variable will keep track of the current number being processed in the loop.

2) while num < 10 do: This line starts a while loop with the boolean condition num < 10. The loop will continue executing the block (chunk) of code inside it if this condition (num is less than 10) keeps evaluating to true.

3) print(num): Inside the loop, this line prints the value of the variable num. Since the loop will print even numbers less than 10, it will print 2, 4, 6, and 8.

4) num += 2: This line increments the value of num by 2 in each iteration of the loop. This is done to ensure that only even numbers are printed. After each iteration, the value of num becomes 2, then 4, then 6, then 8, and 10.

5) end: This line marks the end of the loop block (chunk). Once this end of the loop is reached, the program will loop back to the condition (num < 10) to check if it's still true. If the condition is true, the loop will execute again; otherwise, it will terminate.

6) print("Loop Condition Evaluated to False – Loop Terminated"): This line is placed outside the loop and will be executed only after the loop terminates. It prints a message indicating that the loop's condition has been evaluated as false and terminated.

Infinite Loops

An inherent risk of loops is encountering an infinite loop, where the loop's termination condition never evaluates as false. This situation leads to an endless repetition of the loop's instructions since the condition remains perpetually true. As a result, the program becomes stuck in an eternal loop, causing it to hang or crash.

Listing 4-2. An example of an infinite loop

```
-- Example: Creating an Infinite Loop
local counter = 1
while counter > 0 do
    print("This loop will run forever!")
-- The condition counter > 0 will never become false
end
```

The while loop is initialized in Listing 4-2 with a counter variable set to 1. The loop's condition, counter > 0, is true (as one is greater than zero) and will never evaluate as false since the counter remains positive. Consequently, the loop will endlessly print the message "This loop will run forever!" without ever terminating.

It's crucial to avoid unintentional infinite loops in your code by ensuring that the loop's termination condition eventually becomes false based on the changing state of your program or variables. Otherwise, your program's execution will be trapped in an infinite loop, causing it to become unresponsive and potentially crash the system.

Repeat...Until Loop

The repeat...until loop operates similarly to a while loop, with the vital distinction lying when the loop's condition is assessed. In the case of the repeat...until loop, the condition is evaluated after the loop's body (also known as a block/chunk) has been executed, ensuring the block/chunk is executed at least once during the loop's course. Contrasting this with the while loop, where the initial boolean condition is evaluated first, the repeat...until loop follows a reversed sequence. It initiates by executing the block/chunk of code and then evaluates the boolean condition. This sequential order guarantees the execution of the repeat...until the loop's block/chunk of code at least once.

To implement a repeat...until loop, the loop begins with the "repeat" keyword, followed by the code block/chunk that constitutes the loop's body. The block/chunk is concluded with the "until" keyword, which is succeeded by a logical boolean expression (condition). This expression dictates whether the loop should continue its execution or terminate.

The code snippet in Listing 4-3 is an example of a repeat...until loop that executes once but doesn't repeat.

Listing 4-3. A repeat...until loop executing just once

```
-- Example: Demonstrating a repeat-until loop executing once
local condition = true                      -- 1
repeat                                       -- 2
    print("This chunk will execute once.")  --3
until condition                              -- 4
```

1) local condition = true: This line declares a local variable named condition and initializes it to the boolean value true. The variable will be used as the condition for the repeat...until loop.

2) repeat: This keyword marks the beginning of a repeat...until loop. It indicates that the following code block/chunk should be executed at least once, regardless of the loop condition.

3) print("This chunk will execute once."): This line of code displays the specified message to the output window within the loop. Since the loop's condition is not evaluated at the beginning of the loop, this print statement will run once.

4) until condition: This line concludes the loop and specifies the loop's termination condition. The loop will continue to execute the block/chunk of code (print() function) so long as the loop condition (in this case, condition) keeps evaluating to false. The loop will be terminated only once the condition evaluates to true. However, since the condition is initialized as true, the loop's body will execute only once, and the loop will terminate immediately afterward. If the loop condition never becomes true, you will have an infinite loop.

Numeric For Loop

In Lua, the for loop comes in two variations: the numeric for loop and the generic for loop. The generic for loop is employed for iterating over collections such as arrays, dictionaries, lists, etc. In this section, we will go over the numeric for loop.

A numeric for loop in Lua follows a specific structure, comprising the "for" keyword, three expressions, and a "do/end" block (chunk). These expressions include the initial, final, and step expressions, separated by commas. The overall format of the loop is depicted in Figure 4-1.

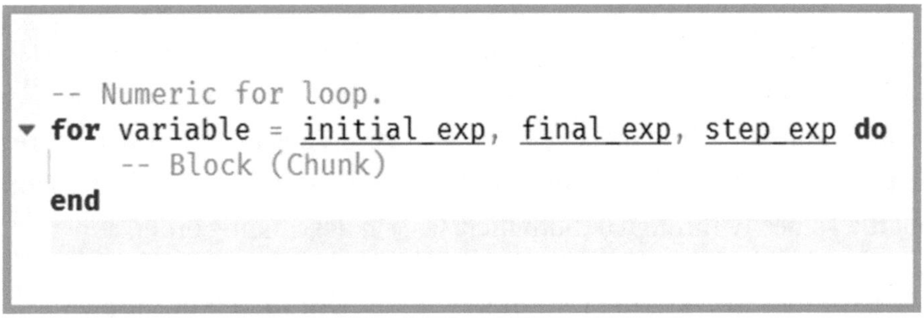

```
-- Numeric for loop.
for variable = initial_exp, final_exp, step_exp do
    -- Block (Chunk)
end
```

Figure 4-1. *Numeric for loop*

The initial expression should be a numeric value assigned to a local variable within the loop. The loop will continue to increment or decrement this variable as long as it hasn't reached the value of the final expression. The increment or decrement is determined by the value specified in the step expression.

The code snippet in Listing 4-4 iterates from 0 to 10, incrementing the variable i by one on each iteration of the loop and printing its value. This for loop prints out the values 0 through 10 (both inclusive) in ascending order.

Listing 4-4. A for loop that increments by a value of 1 during each iteration

```
for i = 0, 10, 1 do
    print(i)
end
```

However, the step expression need not be limited to incrementing by one. It can be any desired value. Setting the step expression to two will result in an increment of 2 during each iteration. Listing 4-5 iterates from 0 to 10, incrementing the variable i by two on each iteration of the loop and printing its value. This for loop will now print out the values 0, 2,4,6,8, and 10.

Listing 4-5. A for loop that increments by a value of 2 during each iteration

```lua
for i = 0, 10, 2 do
    print(i)
end
```

Additionally, numeric for loops are not restricted to counting upward only; they can also count downward. To achieve this, set the initial expression to a value that is larger than the final expression, and make the step expression negative. The step expression can still be any numerical value. Listing 4-6 demonstrates this, where the for loop now prints out the values 10 through 0 (both inclusive) in descending order.

Listing 4-6. A for loop that decrements by a value of 1 each iteration

```lua
for i = 10, 0, -1 do
    print(i)
end
```

Lua offers a shorthand within the for loop to cater to the common scenario of counting up by one. When you provide only the initial and final expressions, Lua assumes a count-up-by-one pattern with a default step expression of one. Listing 4-7 demonstrates this. This for loop prints out the values 0 through 10 (both inclusive) in ascending order.

Listing 4-7. A for loop that defaults to incrementing by 1

```lua
for i = 0, 10 do
    print(i)
end
```

Generic For Loops

In Lua, you can iterate through all elements of an array or table using the generic for loop. While similar to the numeric for loop, the generic for loop features slight differences in its syntax. This generic for loop is a versatile construct for iterating through table or array elements. It provides flexibility for iterating through the elements of a collection, whether it's an array, a table, or any other iterable data structure.

A generic for loop in Lua follows a specific structure, comprising the "for" keyword, two variables, and the "in" keyword, followed by an expression list that consists of a single iterator function and a "do/end" block (chunk). The format of the generic for loop used with an array is depicted in Figure 4-2. The index variable is the control variable which ensures that the loop keeps iterating until this control variable becomes nil. It holds the index of the array element being iterated over. The variable value has the actual value of the element. The iterator function used here for iterating through an array of elements is the ipairs() function, which iterates over each element within the month's array. The "do/end" block (chunk) displays the array index and the element value at that index. These values are displayed in ascending order.

Thus, with the first iteration of this generic for loop, the variable index will be one, and the variable value holds the value of the first element, "Jan." The loop continues iterating until all elements within the month's array have been displayed.

```
-- Generic for loop used with arrays
local months ={"Jan", "Feb", "Mar", "Apr", "May", "Jun"}

for index, value in ipairs(months)do
    print("Index: " .. index .. " Value: " .. value)
end
```

Figure 4-2. *Generic for loop used with arrays*

Lua provides a different iterator function to iterate over a table: pairs(). This pairs() iterator function also returns two variables which we call key and value. The key variable (optional) holds the table's current key (index). The variable value has the current value associated with the key. Figure 4-3 depicts this generic for loop used with tables.

```
-- Generic for loop used with tables
local fruitTable = {
    apple = "red",
    banana = "yellow",
    orange = "orange",
    grape = "purple"
}

for key, value in pairs(fruitTable) do
    print("Key: " .. key, " Value:" .. value)
end
```

Figure 4-3. *Generic for loop used with tables*

Utilizing the ipairs() iterator, we will iterate through a folder containing point lights, toggling their state between on and off. Additionally, we'll generate 7-point lights with randomized positions, organizing them within a "Lights" folder in the Explorer using code. Listing 4-8 illustrates this. Create a new script within the "ServerScriptService" available within the "Explorer" window, and then type in the code provided in Listing 4-8.

Listing 4-8. Generic for loop using the ipairs() iterator with an array

```
-- Create 7 point lights parenting them to parts & set properties
-- Create a Lights folder to hold the point lights
local lightsFolder = Instance.new("Folder") -- 1
lightsFolder.Name = "Lights"                 -- 2
lightsFolder.Parent = workspace              -- 3
for i = 1, 7 do                              -- 4
local part = Instance.new("Part")            -- 5
part.Name = "Light_" .. i
part.Size = Vector3.new(1, 1, 1)
part.Position = Vector3.new(                  -- 6
math.random(-20, 20),   -- Random X position between -20 and 20
math.random(10, 20),    -- Random Y position between 10 and 20
math.random(-20, 20)    -- Random Z position between -20 and 20
)
part.Anchored = true -- The part won't fall when the game starts
-- Parent the part to workspace so it appears in the game world
part.Parent = workspace
-- Create a new point light and set its properties
local randNum = math.random(0, 1) -- 7 Generate a random number
                                  -- (either 0 or 1)
local randBool = (randNum == 1)   -- 8 Set a boolean variable
                                  -- based on the random number
local light = Instance.new("PointLight")           -- 9
light.Brightness = 10
light.Range = 15
light.Color = Color3.new(1, 1, 0) -- Yellow light
light.Enabled = randBool -- 10 Light is either on or off
```

```
light.Parent = part -- Parent the pointlight to the part
part.Parent = lightsFolder -- Parent Light part to Lights folder
end
wait(3)
-- Assign all lights within Lights folder to an array variable
local lights = lightsFolder:GetChildren()            -- 11
-- Loop through all lights in lights array. If a light is on
-- turn it off & vice versa
for _, light in ipairs(lights) do                    -- 12
local pointLight = light:FindFirstChildWhichIsA("PointLight")
                                                     -- 13
pointLight.Enabled = not pointLight.Enabled          -- 14
end
print("Lights tested successfully")
```

1) local lightsFolder = Instance.new("Folder"): This line creates a new instance of a "Folder" object and stores it in the local variable lightsFolder.

2) lightsFolder.Name = "Lights": This line sets the name of the created folder to "Lights."

3) lightsFolder.Parent = workspace: This line sets the parent of the lightsFolder to the "workspace" object. This will place the folder in the game's workspace.

4) for i = 1, 7 do: This line starts a loop that will iterate seven times, creating 7-point lights and parent each to a new part.

5) local part = Instance.new("Part"): This line creates a new instance of a "Part" object and stores it in the local variable part. Each part will hold a child object which is a "PointLight."

6) part.Position = Vector3.new(...): This line sets the position of the part in 3D space using Vector3. The X, Y, and Z values are set randomly within specific ranges.

7) local randNum = math.random(0, 1): Generates a random number of 1 or 0.

8) local randBool = (randNum == 1): This line creates a boolean variable randBool based on the value of the random number randNum. If the value of the variable randNum == 1, then randBool is set to true; otherwise, if randNum == 0, then randBool is false.

9) local light = Instance.new("PointLight"): This line creates a new instance of a "PointLight" object and stores it in the local variable light.

10) light.Enabled = randBool: This line sets the "Enabled" property of the light to either true or false based on the value of randBool. This ensures that the light can be either on or off.

11) local lights = lightsFolder:GetChildren(): This line retrieves a list of all the children (point lights and parts) within the lightsFolder and stores them in the local array variable lights.

12) for _, light in ipairs(lights) do: This line starts a loop that iterates through each element in the lights array.

13) local pointLight = light:FindFirstChildWhichIsA("PointLight"): This line searches for the first child of the current light element, which is a "PointLight" object, and stores it in the local variable pointLight. Note that each light element comprises a child object which is the "PointLight." Here you get the "PointLight" from each Light part within the lightsFolder.

14) pointLight.Enabled = not pointLight.Enabled: This line toggles the "Enabled" property of the pointLight, turning it on if it's off and off if it's on.

In Roblox Lua (Luau), the generic for loop allows looping through arrays and dictionaries without needing iterators like ipairs and pairs. This provides a more concise and straightforward way of looping through a table structure such as an array or dictionary. Here you use the name of the table structure without an iterator. Note that just like when using the pairs() iterator with a dictionary structure, the items will not be in order when looping through a dictionary. Listing 4-9 demonstrates this.

Listing 4-9. An easier way to iterate through a table structure is using a generic for loop

```
-- Numeric array example
local numbers = {10, 20, 30, 40, 50}
for i,v in numbers do
    print(Index: " .. i .. value: " .. v)
end
-- Dictionary example
local inventory = {
    Sword = 1,
    Shield = 1,
    Potion = 5,
    Arrow = 20
}
for items, quantity in inventory do
    print("Item: " .. item .. ", quantity: " .. quantity)
end
```

Nested Loops

Like control structures, loops in Lua operate on a block of code and can be nested. Different loops can be nested within each other, adhering to the exact scope rules of other programming constructs introduced thus far. Nested loops involve placing an inner loop within an outer loop in your code. This technique enables you to construct intricate and comprehensive repetition patterns and control flows within your program. In practice, when utilizing nested loops, the entire execution cycle of the inner loop takes place for each iteration of the outer loop. This means that for each outer loop iteration, the inner loop must complete its own set of iterations first.

The primary purpose of employing nested loops in Lua is to address scenarios where you require iteration across multiple dimensions of data or the repetition of specific tasks within distinct contexts. This is particularly beneficial when dealing with intricate data structures like multidimensional arrays, matrices, grids, etc.

It's worth noting that while nested loops offer powerful capabilities, they can also introduce complexity and potentially lead to performance issues. Therefore, careful consideration and optimization are essential when working with nested loops to ensure efficient and effective code execution.

Listing 4-10 demonstrates a nested loop using Lua's for loop structure. This nested loop structure executes the outer loop (i loop) thrice, and for each iteration of the outer (i) loop, an inner loop (j loop) executes five times. Inside the inner loop, the current values of i and j are printed, resulting in a series of output that shows the combinations of iterations of the two loops.

Listing 4-10. Nested loops

```
for i = 1, 3 do            -- 1 Outer loop
    for j = 1, 5 do        -- 2 Inner loop
        print(i, j)        -- 3 Print the current values of i and j
    end                    -- 4
end                        -- 5
```

1) for i = 1, 3 do: This line starts an outer loop (i loop) that initializes the variable i with the value 1. The loop will continue iterating as long as i is less than or equal to 3. This outer loop iterates thrice.

2) for j = 1, 5 do: Within the outer (i)loop, this line starts an inner loop (j loop) that initializes the variable j with the value 1. This inner loop will continue iterating as long as j is less than or equal to 5. This inner loop iterates five times for each iteration of the outer loop.

3) print(i, j): Within the inner loop (j loop), this line prints the current values of i and j. The values of i and j represent the current iteration numbers of the outer and inner loops, respectively. This line outputs pairs of numbers indicating the combinations of iterations of the two loops.

4) end: This line marks the end of the inner loop's block (j loop). Once the end of the block is reached, the program loops back to the beginning of the inner loop and checks the condition (j <= 5) to determine whether the loop should continue or terminate.

5)   end: This line marks the end of the outer loop's block (i loop).
     Like the inner loop, once the end of the block is reached, the
     program returns to the beginning of the outer loop and checks
     the condition (i <= 3) to determine whether the outer loop should
     continue or terminate.

Breaking Out of a Loop

During the execution of a loop, there could be scenarios where it becomes necessary to
prematurely terminate the loop before the loop's condition naturally evaluates as false.
Such situations might arise due to error conditions or specific branches of logic within
the loop. The loop can be abruptly halted using the "break" keyword in these cases.
The code in Listing 4-11 illustrates the immediate cessation of loop execution using the
"break" keyword.

Listing 4-11.   Breaking out of a loop using «break»

```
-- Simulating a game loop with the possibility of encountering
-- an obstacle
local playerPosition = {x = 0, y = 0}              -- 1
local maze = {                                     -- 2 maze 2D array(table)
with 3 rows where
                -- each row comprises 3 columns.
    {0, 0, 0},
    {0, 1, 0},    -- The value 1 indicates an obstacle
    {0, 0, 0}
}
for i = 1, #maze do                                -- 3
    for j = 1, #maze[i] do                         -- 4
        if maze[i][j] == 1 then                    -- 5
            print("Player encountered an obstacle!")
            break  -- Exit the loop immediately    -- 6
        else                                       -- 7
            playerPosition.x = j
            playerPosition.y = i
```

```
            print("Player collected a coin at (" .. playerPosition.x .. ",
            " .. playerPosition.y .. ")")
        end                                             -- 8
    end                                                 -- 9
end                                                     -- 10
```

1) local playerPosition = {x = 0, y = 0}: This line declares a local
   variable named playerPosition and initializes it as a table with
   two fields, x, and y, both set to 0. This table represents the player's
   position in a 2D space in a game world. While the x and y fields
   might seem analogous to object properties, in Lua, they are just
   fields of a table, and you can access them using the same syntax as
   you would for object properties.

2) ```
   local maze = {
       {0, 0, 0},
       {0, 1, 0},
       {0, 0, 0}
   }:
   ```

   This line declares a local variable named maze and initializes it
   as a 2D array (table) representing the game maze. The values in
   this 2D array represent different elements of the maze, where 0
   represents an open path, and 1 represents an obstacle.

3) for i = 1, #maze do: This line starts a "for" loop that iterates over
   the rows of the maze table. (Note that, from point 2 above, there
   are three rows in the maze table (2D array). The loop runs from
   index 1 to the length of the maze table, which is three, as the table
   (2D array) has three rows.

4) for j = 1, #maze[i] do: This nested for loop iterates over the
   elements (columns) within "each row" of the maze table (2D
   array). It runs from index 1 to the length of the current row of
   the maze table, which is 3. (There are three columns (elements)
   within each row of the table).
   ```

5) if maze[i][j] == 1 then: This line starts an if statement that checks if the current cell in the maze table (2D array) (indicated by maze[i][j]) is equal to 1, which signifies an obstacle. Here maze[i][j] refers to the ith row and jth column in the maze table (2D array). Through the first iteration of both for loops, variables i and j would both hold the value one, and hence the first cell at maze[1][1] (i.e., the first rows, first column) would be accessed and would return the value stored there which is zero.

6) print("Player encountered an obstacle!") break: If the condition above is true (i.e., the ith row and jth column maze[i][j] in the maze table (2D array) holds the value 1), the message indicating that the player encountered an obstacle is displayed, and the break statement that follows ensures that the innermost loop (the j loop) is exited.

7) else: In the event the if statement's condition is false (no obstacle encountered), the code within the else block runs. This updates the player's x and y positions in the playerPosition table using the current values of j and i, representing their position within the maze. A message stating that the player collected a coin at the current x, y position is also displayed.

8) end: The end statement closes out the if...else code block.

9) end: This end statement closes the nested for loop (the j loop).

10) end: This last end statement closes the outer for loop (the i loop).

Continue Statement of a Loop

In Roblox Lua, the continue statement is used within loops to skip the current iteration of the loop and move to the next iteration. Listing 4-12 is an example of how you might use the continue statement with a generic loop that iterates through a collection (array) of enemies and skips enemies already defeated.

Listing 4-12. Skipping loop iteration, using «continue»

```
local enemies = {"Goblin," "Orc," "Dragon," "Skeleton"} -- 1
print("=== Defeat Enemies ===")
for _, enemy in ipairs(enemies) do                        -- 2
-- Simulate whether the enemy is defeated (true) or not (false)
--[[ Create a random boolean value using random numbers to
     Simulate random defeat status (true or false)]]
local isDefeated = math.random(0, 1) == 1                 -- 3
    if isDefeated then                                    --4
        print("You have defeated the: " .. enemy .. " !")
        -- Skip to the next iteration of the loop
        continue                                          --5
    end
print("You are facing a: " .. enemy .. " ! Prepare for battle...")
end
```

1) local enemies = {"Goblin," "Orc," "Dragon," "Skeleton"}: This line
   creates a local variable enemies and assigns it an array (table)
   containing four enemy names: "Goblin," "Orc," "Dragon," and
   "Skeleton."

2) for _, enemy in ipairs(enemies) do: This line starts a loop using
   the for statement. It iterates over each element (enemy name) in
   the enemies (array) table using the ipairs iterator function. The
   underscore _ is used to ignore the index.

3) local isDefeated = math.random(0, 1) == 1: This line generates
   a random boolean value, representing whether the enemy is
   defeated (true) or not (false). It uses math.random() function to
   generate a random number of either 0 or 1, and then compares it
   to 1 to create a boolean value that evaluates to either true or false
   and assigns it to the boolean variable isDefeated.

4) if isDefeated then: This line starts an if statement that checks
   whether the isDefeated variable is true. If it is, the print() function
   inside the if block will be executed, displaying the name of the
   enemy that has been defeated.

5)   continue: This "continue" statement skips the current iteration of the "for" loop and moves to the next iteration. In the event the "if...then...end" condition is evaluated to true, then the "continue" statement will not be executed, and the loop will complete its iteration displaying the message stating that you are facing one of the enemies and need to prepare for battle.

Summary

In this chapter, you explored a comprehensive range of essential topics crucial to understanding and harnessing the power of the Roblox Lua language. You began by looking at the basic data types provided by Lua and explored the table data structure, learning to create tables, arrays, and dictionaries. You examined variables and literals as well as delved deep into variable scope. You then went on to explore operators and operands, distinguishing between unary and binary operators and grasping their function in manipulating data and variables. Arithmetic operators allowed you to efficiently perform numerical calculations, while compound assignment operators showed you how to generate concise and readable code. Relational operators facilitated the comparison of values, and the assignment operator enabled efficient variable assignment. Understanding the length unary operator helped determine the length of strings and tables, while the string concatenation operator provided seamless string manipulation. In conditionals, you mastered the art of decision-making by employing if, else, and elseif constructs. Logical operators empower you to express complex conditions succinctly. Additionally, you explored operator precedence and using parentheses to control the order of evaluation in expressions, optimizing your code for clarity and efficiency. Armed with these powerful tools, you are better equipped to craft captivating experiences and build intricate games within the Roblox platform.

Objects, Data Types, and Properties

Understanding Roblox Objects (parts), additional Luau data types, and properties are essential for anyone looking to dive into the exciting world of game development on the Roblox platform. This chapter delves into these building blocks of Roblox creations, exploring the properties of Parts/Objects and understanding Roblox Luau's additional data types. You will uncover the concepts of the other data types made available via Roblox's Lua (Luau) implementation and learn how to use them like a pro. By the end of this chapter, you will have unraveled some essential concepts that bring virtual worlds to life, delving into the core constructs that enable you to create, manipulate, and imbue objects with functionality.

Roblox Parts and Objects

Over the last few chapters, you would have noted that "Parts" are the fundamental building blocks used to create 3D objects and environments within the Roblox platform. In Roblox, a "Part" is an object that represents a 3D shape in the game world. It can be a cube, sphere, cylinder, wedge, or any custom shape created by combining these primitives. They can build structures, characters, items, and various interactive elements within a game or experience. Each "Part" has properties such as size, position, rotation, color, and material, which can be adjusted to customize the appearance and behavior of the object it represents. Parts can be combined and manipulated through scripting to create dynamic and interactive gameplay elements.

Objects, in general programming, are self-contained units that encapsulate data (attributes) and behavior (methods or functions), representing a real-world or abstract entity in code via an object-oriented programming language that supports essential concepts of OOP (Object-Oriented Programming): Encapsulation, Inheritance, and

101

© Christopher Coutinho 2023
C. Coutinho, *Roblox Lua Scripting Essentials*, https://doi.org/10.1007/979-8-8688-0026-9_5

Polymorphism. Objects are instantiated from classes, which act as blueprints or templates for creating objects. A class defines the structure and behavior that its objects will have.

In Roblox, parts and objects are related in the sense that each Roblox "Part" represents an Object in the world created by a developer. These parts are the building blocks for creating the various objects that populate a Roblox game or experience. For instance, a part might represent a player's character, an enemy NPC, a weapon, or a collectible item.

In the context of Roblox's game development environment, the concept of objects aligns with the principles of object-oriented programming. Each "Part" (object) can have its unique properties and behaviors, and developers can use scripts embedded into a "Part" to define how these objects interact and behave within the game world.

Object Hierarchy Navigation

The Object Hierarchy within the "Explorer" window refers to the organization of game objects within one another, forming a parent-child relationship. Understanding this hierarchy is crucial for manipulating and interacting with objects using Lua code.

In the Object Hierarchy, game objects are organized in a tree-like structure. Each object can have zero or more children, and a parent can have multiple children. For example, in the hierarchy "Game > Workspace > Baseplate," the Baseplate is a child of Workspace, and Workspace is a child of the game object, even though the game object is not visible in the "Explorer" window. This nesting forms a chain of parent-child relationships.

To manipulate objects with code, specify their location within the hierarchy. You can navigate the hierarchy using the dot operator in Lua. The dot operator allows you to access a child object within a parent object. For example, game.Workspace.Baseplate is a Lua expression that refers to the Baseplate object, a child of Workspace, and a child of the game object.

Understanding the Object Hierarchy and navigating it using Lua code is fundamental for scripting in Roblox, as it allows you to interact with and manipulate game objects effectively.

Let's change the position of the Baseplate in the hierarchy by moving it up on the "Y" axis. Listing 5-1 shows one of several ways this could be achieved. You will continue to use the "Cuboid_Script" even though; ideally, you would use a new script attached directly to the Baseplate object. Either comment or delete all the existing code within the "Cuboid_Script" and then type in the code as provided within Listing 5-1.

Listing 5-1. Raising the Baseplate

```
-- Accessing the Baseplate object using the dot operator
local baseplate = game.Workspace.Baseplate
-- Changing the position of the Baseplate
baseplate.Position = Vector3.new(0, 10, 0)
```

In Listing 4-1, we first declare a local variable called Baseplate and assign it the value game.Workspace.Baseplate to access the Baseplate child object within the Workspace object, which is a child of the Game object. Then, by using the baseplate variable in conjunction with the dot operator, we access the Baseplate object "Position" property, assigning it a new Vector3 value which results in having the Baseplate moved to the newly specified "Y" coordinate of 10.

In the previous section, you learned about the Vector3 data type and can see it being used here. You create a new Vector3 value using the "Vector3.new()" constructor, a function that takes three arguments representing the vector's "X," "Y," and "Z" components, respectively. In Listing 4-1, you only change the "Y" component of the Vector.

To reduce the need for typing game.Workspace repeatedly, Roblox Lua provides the lowercase keyword "workspace." You could rewrite the first line of code in Listing 4-1 to read as:

```
local baseplate = workspace.Baseplate
```

Roblox (Luau) Additional Data Types

The native Lua language has just a few basic data types, as discussed in Chapter 3. However, Roblox (Luau), which is Roblox's implementation of Lua, extends the native language with several additional data types essential for game development. This section will explore some of these commonly used data types you will use most often.

Some of the essential additional data types provided as Part of Roblox's (Luau) implementation:

1) Vector3: The Vector3 data type in Roblox is a built-in data structure for representing three-dimensional vectors in 3D space, serving as points or directions. It finds widespread usage in Roblox game development to manage object positions, direction, and scale. Comprising three components (X, Y, and Z), a Vector3 denotes the position or direction within a three-dimensional Cartesian coordinate system. In 3D space, a Vector can be visually depicted as an arrow or line segment with a specific magnitude (length) and direction (Figure 5-1). Roblox provides various built-in properties and methods for its Vector3 data structure, such as the "Magnitude" property to calculate the length of the Vector, the "Unit" property to obtain a normalized vector with direction only, and "lerp" method to perform linear interpolation between two vectors. In a forthcoming chapter, you will learn to use vectors in conjunction with "Cframes."

2) CFrame: The CFrame data type (short for Coordinate Frame) is a fundamental and powerful representation of a 3D transformation. It describes an object's position, rotation, and scale in the game world. It comprises two Vector3 values, one representing position and the other representing rotation. A CFrame consists of a 3x3 rotation matrix and a 3D position vector. The rotation matrix represents the orientation (rotation) of the object in 3D space, and the position vector represents its position in the world. Together, they define the complete transformation of an object. It also holds the Look Vector, Up Vector, and the Right Vector of the CFrame (Figure 5-1).

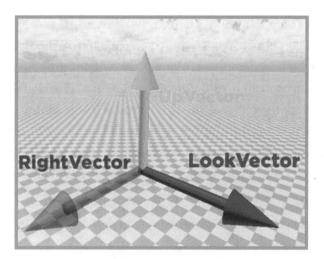

Figure 5-1. *Vector3 - vectors in 3D space*

3) Color3: The Color3 data type represents colors in a three-component format, specifically, RGB (red, green, blue) values. It is a built-in data type that allows developers to define and manipulate colors in their Roblox games and experiences. This combination of RGB can make up approximately 16.8 million different colors. Color3 values are commonly used for various purposes in Roblox, such as setting the color of parts, text, and GUI elements, defining ambient lighting, changing the appearance of characters, and implementing visual effects. Color3 values provide a versatile way to work with colors in Roblox.

4) Instance: The Instance data type is a fundamental building block in Roblox, used to represent objects in the game world. It can be used to create a new part, GUI, particle emitter, model, etc. Instances are the fundamental entities that make up a Roblox game. Each instance represents a unique object with specific properties and behaviors. Instances can be arranged in a hierarchical parent-child relationship to create complex structures and systems in the game world.

5) Enum: The Enum data type represents a set of predefined symbolic names, also known as enumerations. Enums are a way to organize related constants or values under a common type. They provide a more readable and structured approach to represent

options or choices in code. An example of an Enum is the "Shape" property available on a part, where you can change the shape of a part which by default is a block. This "Shape" property enumeration is used to re-define the shape of a "Base Part" via its "Shape" property allowing you to customize its appearance and physical behavior. (Base Part objects are the building blocks for 3D objects in Roblox). You can use Enums to declare the different types of weapons in your game (rifle, revolver, sword, axe, etc).

6) Random: In Roblox, the Random data type is not a distinct data type. Instead, it refers to the concept of generating pseudo-random numbers and directions.

Manipulating Parts: Vector3 Data Type

In Roblox Lua, manipulating parts using Vector3 is a compelling technique for transforming objects in 3D space. By creating Vector3 instances with desired coordinates, you can change the position, orientation, and size of parts within the game. The Vector3 data type allows you to perform arithmetic operations like addition, subtraction, scaling, and lerping to transition parts to new positions smoothly. Additionally, you can use dot and cross products to perform more complex transformations. Whether building dynamic environments or implementing gameplay mechanics, utilizing Vector3 enables precise and efficient manipulation of parts in Roblox Lua.

Changing the Position of a Part

Let's change the position of the "Cuboid" Part that currently exists in the world. Select the Cuboid Part in the "Explorer" window, and expand it to make its "Cuboid_Script" visible. Double-click the "Cuboid_Script" to open it in Roblox's script editor, and either comment or delete all the existing code it contains. Type in the code as provided in Listing 5-2.

Listing 5-2. Changing the position of a part

```
local cuboidPart = script.Parent --1
-- Creating a new Vector3 position
local newPosition = Vector3.new(-10, 0, 5) --2
-- Changing the position of the Part
cuboidPart.Position = newPosition --3
```

1) local cuboidPart = script.Parent: Declares a local variable "cuboidPart" and assigns it the value of the current script's parent object ("Cuboid" part).

2) local newPosition = Vector3.new(-10, 0, 5): Creates a new Vector3 variable named "newPosition" with X = -10, Y = 0, and Z = 5.

3) cuboidPart.Position = newPosition: Sets the position of the "cuboidPart" object to the coordinates specified in "newPosition," effectively moving the "Cuboid" Part to the new position.

Note   The syntax for creating a new Vector3 value is

local vector = Vector3.new(X, Y, Z)

Replace "X," "Y," and "Z" with the numerical values you want for each Vector component. For example, to create a Vector3 with X = 1, Y = 2, and Z = 3:

local position = Vector3.new(1, 2, 3)

Scaling a Part Using Multiplication

Let's make the "Cuboid" Part twice as large. This can be achieved by multiplying its "Size" property by a scalar value, as shown in Listing 5-3. Continue typing the code provided as Part of Listing 5-3 below the existing code provided as Part of Listing 5-2.

Listing 5-3. Scaling a part

```
local scaleFactor = 2                                    --1
-- Scaling the Part by multiplying its Size vector by 2
cuboidPart.Size = cuboidPart.Size * scaleFactor          --2
```

1) local scaleFactor = 2: Declares a local variable "scaleFactor," assigning it the value 2.

2) cuboidPart.Size = cuboidPart.Size * scaleFactor: Scales the "Cuboid" object by multiplying its "Size" vector by the value of "scaleFactor" (2 in this case). This effectively increases the size of the "Cuboid" Part. Note that the value of the expression on the right-hand side of the "=" operator results in a Vector3 being assigned to the cuboidPart.Size property, which is also a Vector3 data type.

You can view the concerned property values for the "Cuboid" Part within the "Properties" window to ensure they have changed from their original values.

Moving a Part Using Lerp

Let's use the Vector3 Lerp method to have the "Cuboid" Part move a certain distance from a starting point (Part) toward an endpoint (Part). Either comment or delete existing code within the "Cuboid_Script," and type in the code provided as Part of Listing 5-4. To see the Lerp method working with the Vector3 data type, you must first create two new parts within your world. Figure 5-2 displays the two new parts I have placed in the world: a green cylindrical part and a blue wedge part, and I have named them "Cylinder" and "Wedge," respectively, within the "Explorer" window. I have placed them on either side of the "SpawnLocation" part, trying to keep them somewhat equidistant from the center of the "SpawnLocation." The "Cuboid" Part has its "BrickColor" property set to red and has been positioned in front of the spawn location. Ensure that these parts are set up in your world to match what you see in Figure 5-2 closely. It doesn't have to be a replica.

Figure 5-2. *Moving a part using Vector3 Lerp*

Listing 5-4. Lerp using Vector3

```
local cuboidPart = script.Parent                    --1
local cylinderPart = workspace.Cylinder             --2
local wedgePart = workspace.Wedge                    --3
local startPosn = cylinderPart.Position             --4
local endPosn = wedgePart.Position                  --5
local dist = 0.75                                    --6
-- Moving the Cuboid from start to end position using Lerp
cuboidPart.Position = startPosn:Lerp(endPosn, dist)  --7
```

1) local cuboidPart = script.Parent: Declares a local variable "cuboidPart" and assigns it the object of which the script is a child.

2) local cylinderPart = workspace.Cylinder: Declares a local variable "cylinderPart" and assigns it the "Cylinder" object from the "workspace."

3) local wedgePart = workspace.Wedge: Declares a local variable "wedgePart" and assigns it the "Wedge" object from the "workspace."

4) local startPosn = cylinderPart.Position: Declares a local variable "startPosn" and assigns it the position of the "cylinderPart" object.

5) local endPosn = wedgePart.Position: Declares a local variable "endPosn" and assigns it the position of the "wedgePart" object.

6) local dist = 0.75: Declares a local variable "dist" (distance) and assigns it the value 0.75.

7) cuboidPart.Position = startPosn:Lerp(endPosn, dist): Sets the position of "cuboidPart" smoothly by linearly interpolating between "startPosn" and "endPosn" based on the "dist" value (0.75 in this case). This smoothly moves the "cuboidPart" 75% of the way from the "cylinderPart" position to the "wedgePart" position. If you set "dist" to the value 0.5, the "cuboidPart" would be moved 50% of the way (approximately to a center point) toward the "wedgePart." If "dist" were set to 0.25, the "cuboidPart" would be moved 25% of the way from the "cylinderPart" toward the "wedgePart." If "dist" were set to 0, the "cuboidPart" would be positioned in line with the "cylinderPart"; if "dist" were set to 1, the "cuboidPart" would be placed in line with the "wedgePart." Try out these different values in the code.

Computing Distance Between Parts

Let's explore how to use the Vector3 data type to compute the distance between two parts. Figure 5-2 shows that the distance between the cuboid and cylinder must be smaller than between the cuboid and wedge. Listing 5-5 shows you how to achieve this. Either comment or delete existing code within the "Cuboid_Script," and type in the code provided as Part of Listing 5-5.

Listing 5-5. Computing the Distance between Parts

```
local cuboidPart = script.Parent
local cylinderPart = workspace.Cylinder
local wedgePart = workspace.Wedge
-- Get the direction Vector from cuboidPart to cylinderPart
local dirToCylinder = cylinderPart.Position-cuboidPart.Position
                                                          -- 1
```

```
-- Get the direction Vector from cuboidPart to wedgePart
local dirToWedge = wedgePart.Position - cuboidPart.Position          --2
-- Calculate the distance between the cuboid and cylinder parts
local distToCylinder = dirToCylinder.magnitude                      --3
-- Calculate the distance between the cuboid and wedge parts
local distToWedge = dirToWedge.magnitude                            --4
-- 'distToCylinder' holds the distance between cuboid &
-- cylinder parts
print("Distance between Cuboid & Cylinder Part: " .. distToCylinder)
-- 'distToWedge' holds the distance between cuboid & wedge parts
print("Distance between Cuboid & Wedge Part: " .. distToWedge)
local normalizedCylinderDir =  dirToCylinder.Unit                  --5
local normalizedWedgeDir = dirToWedge.Unit                         --6
```

1) local dirToCylinder = cylinderPart.Position - cuboidPart.
    Position: Calculates the direction Vector from "cuboidPart" to
    "cylinderPart" (i.e., the length of the Vector (arrow) pointing
    from the cuboid to the cylinder) by subtracting the "cuboidPart"
    position from 'cylinderPart" position and stores it in the variable
    "dirToCylinder."

2) local dirToWedge = wedgePart.Position - cuboidPart.Position:
    Calculates the direction Vector from "cuboidPart" to "wedgePart"
    (i.e., the length of the Vector (arrow) pointing from the cuboid
    to the wedge) by subtracting "cuboidPart" position from
    "wedgePart" position and stores it in the variable "dirToWedge."

3) local distToCylinder = dirToCylinder.magnitude: Computes the
    distance between "cuboidPart" and "cylinderPart" using the
    magnitude property of "dirToCylinder" (the direction Vector
    calculated earlier) and stores it in the variable "distToCylinder."

4) local distToWedge = dirToWedge.magnitude: Computes the
    distance between "cuboidPart" and "wedgePart" using the
    magnitude property of "dirToWedge" (the direction Vector
    calculated earlier) and stores it in the variable "distToWedge."

5) local normalizedCylinderDir = dirToCylinder.Unit: The
    "normalizedCylinderDir" is a Unit vector that solely represents
    the direction from the cuboid to the cylinder and contains a
    magnitude of 1, referred to as a normalized vector.

6) local normalizedWedgeDir = dirToWedge.Unit: The
    "normalizedWedgeDir" is also a Unit vector that solely represents
    the direction from the cuboid to the wedge having a magnitude of 1,
    referred to as a normalized vector.

The "magnitude" property value represents the length of the Vector that points
from the "cuboidPart" to either the cylinder or wedge Part if the Vector has not been
normalized.

Manipulating Parts: Cframe Data Type

A Roblox Lua CFrame (Coordinate Frame) is a powerful data type used to represent
transformations in 3D space. Unlike a Vector3, which only represents a position,
a CFrame combines position and orientation information. It describes an object's
location and rotation, making it ideal for manipulating parts in a 3D environment.
With a CFrame, you can efficiently perform rotations, translations, and complex
transformations on parts, providing more control over their movements and
orientations. Overall, CFrame offers more flexibility and control over object positioning,
orientation, and animations, making them a preferred choice for manipulating parts and
creating dynamic 3D experiences in Roblox Lua.

A CFrame in Roblox Lua can do several things that a Vector3 cannot:

1) Position and orientation: A CFrame combines both position and
    orientation information, allowing you to represent not only the
    location of an object but also its rotation in 3D space. This enables
    more complex transformations that involve both translation and
    rotation.

2) Smooth animation: CFrames are ideal for creating smooth
    animations as you can interpolate between two CFrames using
    the lerp function, resulting in seamless and natural movements.

3) Complex transformations: CFrames support more complex transformations, such as scaling and shearing, which are impossible with just Vector3.

4) Efficient movement: CFrames are more efficient for handling movements, especially for objects that undergo multiple changes in position and rotation, as they are optimized for this purpose.

5) Parent-child relationship: CFrames are crucial for working with objects in a parent-child relationship. When you position a child object relative to its parent using a CFrame, it automatically inherits the parent's position and orientation.

6) Smoother rotations: When rotating objects with CFrames, you avoid the gimbal lock issue, which can occur when using Euler angles (XYZ rotations) with Vector3.

Offsetting a Part

Frequently, precise placement of objects isn't required, and instead, you may want to position them slightly above or offset to the side. By combining CFrame and Vector3 values, you can achieve such relative positioning, allowing for more flexible and versatile arrangements of objects in your game experience. Let's write a few lines of code to offset the cuboid Part to be positioned directly above the wedge part by five studs, using a combination of CFrame and Vector3 operations. We'll calculate the desired position above the wedge part and then set the CFrame of the cuboid Part accordingly. Either comment or delete existing code within the "Cuboid_Script," and type in the code provided as Part of Listing 5-6. Here's the code.

Listing 5-6. Offsetting the cuboid Part to be positioned above the wedge part

```
local cuboidPart = script.Parent                        -- 1
local wedgePart = workspace.Wedge                        -- 2
cuboidPart.Anchored = true
-- Define the offset in studs (5 studs above the wedgePart)
local offset = Vector3.new(0, 5, 0)                     -- 3
-- Calculate the desired position for the cuboidPart
local desiredPosition = wedgePart.Position + offset     -- 4
```

```
-- Create a new CFrame to position the cuboidPart above the
-- wedgePart
local newCFrame = CFrame.new(desiredPosition)            -- 5
-- Apply the new CFrame to the cuboidPart
cuboidPart.CFrame = newCFrame                            -- 6
```

1) local cuboidPart = script.Parent: This line declares a local variable cuboidPart and assigns it the value of the parent object of the script. Here, the "Cuboid_Script" is a child of the cuboid Part so that the variable cuboidPart will reference this object.

2) local wedgePart = workspace.Wedge: This line declares a local variable wedgePart and assigns it the value of the Wedge object in the workspace.

3) local offset = Vector3.new(0, 5, 0): This line defines a local variable offset and assigns a Vector3 value with X, Y, and Z components set to 0, 5, and 0, respectively. It represents an offset of 5 studs in the positive Y direction (above the wedgePart).

4) local desiredPosition = wedgePart.Position + offset: This line calculates a local variable desiredPosition by adding the offset to the Position of the wedgePart. It represents the position where the cuboidPart should be placed, that is, five studs above the wedgePart.

5) local newCFrame = CFrame.new(desiredPosition): This line creates a new local variable newCFrame and assigns it a CFrame value generated from the desiredPosition. It represents a CFrame that positions the cuboidPart above the wedgePart by five studs.

6) cuboidPart.CFrame = newCFrame: This line sets the CFrame property of the cuboidPart to the value of the newCFrame, effectively moving the cuboidPart to the desired position above the wedgePart.

Rotating a Part

To rotate a part using a CFrame, you must assign a new CFrame containing the desired rotation angle directly to the Part's CFrame property. The new CFrame can be created using the methods CFrame.Angles(). Once you have the new CFrame, you can apply it to the Part by assigning it to the parts CFrame property, effectively rotating the Part around its local axes. Listing 5-7 is a simple example of how you can rotate the Cuboid Part 45 degrees around its local "Y" axis. Ensure that the local orientation of your Cuboid Part has been set to zero for all axes to avoid encountering weird rotation. Either comment or delete existing code within the "Cuboid_Script," and type in the code provided as Part of Listing 5-7.

Listing 5-7. Rotating the Cuboid Part 45 degrees around its local "Y" axis

```
local cuboid = script.Parent
-- Define the rotation angle in radians
local rotationAngle = math.rad(45) --1 convert 45 degrees to
                                    --  radians
-- Get the current CFrame of the Cuboid Part
local currentCFrame = cuboid.CFrame               --2
--3 Create a new CFrame with the desired rotation where
-- ''rotationAngle'' must be in radians.
local rotatedCFrame = CFrame.Angles(0, rotationAngle, 0)
-- Apply the desired rotation to the Cuboids CFrame
cuboid.CFrame = currentCFrame * rotatedCFrame     --4
```

1) local rotationAngle = math.rad(45): Converts 45 degrees to radians and stores the result in the variable "rotationAngle."

2) local currentCFrame = cuboid.CFrame: Retrieves the current CFrame of the "cuboid" Part and stores it in the variable "currentCFrame."

3) local rotatedCFrame = CFrame.Angles(0, rotationAngle, 0): Creates a new CFrame with the desired rotation of "rotationAngle" radians around the Y-axis (vertical axis) and stores it in the variable "rotatedCFrame."

4) cuboid.CFrame = currentCFrame * rotatedCFrame: Applies the desired rotation to the "cuboid" Part by combining the current CFrame with the "rotatedCFrame" using the * (Multiplication) operator and assigns it back to the "cuboid" Part's CFrame property. This rotates the "cuboid" Part by 45 degrees around the Y-axis.

Moving a Part in a Specific Direction

Using a CFrame along with a Vector3, you can move a part in any direction you want. You could have it strafe either left or right along the "X" axis, move up or down along the "Y" axis, or move forward or back along the "Z" axis. Listing 5-8 shows how to achieve this. Ensure you either comment or delete existing code within the "Cuboid_Script," and type in the code provided as Part of Listing 5-8. You will be moving the cuboid Part along different axes.

Listing 5-8. Moving the cuboid Part along different axes

```
local cuboidPart = script.Parent
cuboidPart.Anchored = true
local moveSpeed = 5
local moveDirection = Vector3.xAxis -- 1 Move the cuboid in
                                    -- the X direction
cuboidPart .CFrame = cuboidPart .CFrame * CFrame.new(moveDirection *
moveSpeed)                 -- 2
wait(3)                    -- 3
moveDirection = Vector3.yAxis -- 4 Move the cuboid in the Y
                             --direction
cuboidPart .CFrame = cuboidPart .CFrame * CFrame.new(moveDirection *
moveSpeed)                 -- 5
wait(3)
moveDirection = Vector3.zAxis -- 6 Move the cuboid in the Z
                             --direction
cuboidPart .CFrame = cuboidPart .CFrame * CFrame.new(moveDirection *
moveSpeed)                 -- 7
```

1) local moveDirection = Vector3.xAxis: This line sets the moveDirection variable to a unit vector in the X direction (1, 0, 0), indicating that the cuboid will move in the positive X direction.

2) cuboidPart.CFrame = cuboidPart.CFrame * CFrame. new(moveDirection * moveSpeed): This line updates the CFrame of the cuboidPart by translating it in the X direction by an amount determined by moveSpeed.

3) wait(3): This line pauses the script for three seconds, causing a delay before the next movement.

4) moveDirection = Vector3.yAxis: This line sets the moveDirection variable to a unit vector in the Y direction (0, 1, 0), indicating that the cuboid will move in the positive Y direction.

5) cuboidPart.CFrame = cuboidPart.CFrame * CFrame. new(moveDirection * moveSpeed): This line updates the CFrame of the cuboidPart by translating it in the Y direction by an amount determined by moveSpeed.

6) moveDirection = Vector3.zAxis: This line sets the moveDirection variable to a unit vector in the Z direction (0, 0, 1), indicating that the cuboid will move in the positive Z direction.

7) cuboidPart.CFrame = cuboidPart.CFrame * CFrame. new(moveDirection * moveSpeed): This line updates the CFrame of the cuboidPart by translating it in the Z direction by an amount determined by moveSpeed.

Part Rotation to Face Another Part – (1)

Let's write another script to make the "cuboidPart" rotate to face the "cylinderPart" and then move 80% of the way toward it using CFrame, Lerp, and then rotate to face the "wedgePart" and move 75% of the way toward it. You would ideally need something like this to create an EnemyNPC that can turn to face the player and move toward it. Listing 4-9 shows you how to achieve this. Either comment or delete existing code within the "Cuboid_Script," and type in the code provided as Part of Listing 5-9.

Listing 5-9. Rotate to face another part and move a certain distance toward it

```
local cuboidPart = script.Parent
local cylinderPart = workspace.Cylinder
local wedgePart = workspace.Wedge
-- Get the normalized direction Unit Vector from cuboidPart to
-- cylinderPart
local dirToCylinder = (cylinderPart.Position - cuboidPart.Position).
Unit                                    -- 1
-- Get the normalized direction Unit Vector from cuboidPart to -- WedgePart
local dirToWedge = (wedgePart.Position - cuboidPart.Position).
Unit                                    -- 2
-- Rotate the cuboidPart to face the cylinderPart
cuboidPart.CFrame = CFrame.new(cuboidPart.Position, cylinderPart.
Position)                                -- 3
-- Calculate the position 80% of the way towards the cylinderPart
local distanceToMoveCylinder = 0.8 * (cylinderPart.Position - cuboidPart.
Position).magnitude                       -- 4
local newPositionCylinder = cuboidPart.Position + dirToCylinder *
distanceToMoveCylinder                   -- 5
-- Move the cuboidPart to the new position using CFrame:Lerp
-- Adjust this value to control the time it takes to move
local timeToMoveCylinder = 1                          -- 6
for t = 0, 1, 0.01 do                                 -- 7
    cuboidPart.Position = cuboidPart.Position:Lerp(newPositionCylind
er, t) -- 8
    wait(timeToMoveCylinder / 100)                    -- 9
end
-- Rotate the cuboidPart to face the wedgePart
cuboidPart.CFrame = CFrame.new(cuboidPart.Position, wedgePart.Position)
-- Calculate the position 75% of the way towards the wedgePart
local distanceToMoveWedge = 0.75 * (wedgePart.Position - cuboidPart.
Position).magnitude
local newPositionWedge = cuboidPart.Position + dirToWedge *
distanceToMoveWedge
-- Move the cuboidPart to the new position using CFrame:Lerp
```

```
-- Adjust this value to control the time it takes to move
local timeToMoveWedge = 1
for t = 0, 1, 0.01 do
    cuboidPart.Position = cuboidPart.Position:Lerp(newPositionWedge, t)
    wait(timeToMoveWedge / 100)
end
```

1) local dirToCylinder = (cylinderPart.Position - cuboidPart.Position).Unit: Calculates the normalized direction unit vector from "cuboidPart" to "cylinderPart." Here you are subtracting the Cuboid part position from the Cylinder part position to obtain a direction vector and then obtaining its normalized unit vector, which has a magnitude of 1.

2) local dirToWedge = (wedgePart.Position - cuboidPart.Position).Unit: Calculates the normalized direction unit vector from "cuboidPart" to "wedgePart." Here you are subtracting the Cuboid part position from the Wedge part position to obtain a direction vector and then obtaining its normalized unit vector, which has a magnitude of 1.

3) cuboidPart.CFrame=CFrame.new(cuboidPart.Position, cylinderPart.Position): Rotates the "cuboidPart" to face the "cylinderPart" using a new CFrame.

4) local distanceToMoveCylinder = 0.8 * (cylinderPart.Position - cuboidPart.Position).magnitude: Here, you first compute the total distance from the cuboid Part to the cylinder part using (cylinderPart.Position - cuboidPart.Position).magnitude. The "magnitude" property here provides the distance between the cuboid and the cylinder. Once you have this value and need to move only 80% of this distance, multiply this "magnitude" value by 0.8.

5) local newPositionCylinder = cuboidPart.Position + dirToCylinder * distanceToMoveCylinder: Calculates the new position for the "cuboidPart," 80% of the way toward the "cylinderPart."

6) local timeToMoveCylinder = 1: Sets the time it takes for the "cuboidPart" to move toward the "cylinderPart," where it will move to the new position over a period of 1 second.

7)
```
for t = 0, 1, 0.01 do
    cuboidPart.Position = cuboidPart.Position:
    Lerp(newPositionCylinder, t)
    wait(timeToMoveCylinder / 100):
end:
```

The for loop above iterates a specific number of times, executing the code within it repeatedly during each iteration. The above loop continuously moves the cuboid Part toward the cylinder part over the duration of one second. The loop iterates 100 times (t = 0 to t = 1 with an increment of 0.01). Through each iteration, it moves the cuboid Part in the direction it faces (forward direction) by an increment of 0.01 and waits for timeToMoveCylinder / 100 (i.e., 0.01) seconds before the next iteration.

8) cuboidPart.Position = cuboidPart.Position:Lerp(newPosition Cylinder, t): Smoothly interpolates the position of the "cuboidPart" toward "newPositionCylinder" as "t" varies from 0 to 1.

9) wait(timeToMoveCylinder / 100): Pauses the loop for a short duration to control the rate of movement toward "newPositionCylinder." In this example, the loop executes 100 times, and the total wait time is 0.01 seconds for each iteration.

Rotating the cuboid Part to face the wedge part follows the same steps, and the explanation of each line of code is essentially the same as rotating the cuboid Part to have it face the cylinder part.

The CFrame.new() function creates a new CFrame (Coordinate Frame) object representing a transformation in 3D space. This function takes two parameters: "cuboidPart.Position," which represents the position (Vector3) of the starting point or origin of the CFrame, and "cylinderPart.Position" that represents the position (Vector3) of the target point or destination of the CFrame.

The CFrame created by CFrame.new(cuboidPart.Position, cylinderPart.Position) represents a transformation that aligns the starting point (origin) to "cuboidPart. Position" and rotates it to face the target point (destination) at "cylinderPart.Position." It creates a CFrame that positions and orients "cuboidPart" to face the position of "cylinderPart."

Using this CFrame assignment, the "cuboidPart" will directly face the "cylinderPart," with its position remaining the same. This is useful for scenarios where you want to make one Part (cuboidPart) face another part (cylinderPart) while keeping their relative position unchanged.

Part Rotation to Face Another Part – (2)

Let's write a more straightforward script to have a part rotate and look at a specific position or another part using the CFrame.lookAt() function. The code listing here will only deal with rotating the Part and not lerping it. However, as discussed in Listing 5-9, you could use the Lerp method to have the part move to the new desired location. Either comment or delete existing code within the "Cuboid_Script," and type in the code provided as Part of Listing 5-10.

Listing 5-10. A simpler way to rotate a part to face another part

```
local cuboidPart =  script.Parent
local cylinderPart = workspace.Cylinder
cuboidPart.Anchored = true
cylinderPart.Anchored = true
-- 1 Set the position to look at
local targetPosition = Vector3.new(20, 10, 15)
cylinderPart.Position = targetPosition
wait(3)
-- 2 Calculate the direction to look at
local lookVector = (targetPosition - cuboidPart.Position).unit
-- 3 Have the cuboid turn and rotate to face the target position
cuboidPart.CFrame = CFrame.lookAt(cuboidPart.Position, targetPosition,
Vector3.new(0, 1, 0))
```

1) local targetPosition = Vector3.new(20, 10, 15): This line creates a new Vector3 named targetPosition with coordinates (20, 10, 15). This Vector represents the position the cuboid Part will finally rotate toward and look at.

2) cylinderPart.Position = targetPosition: This line of code sets the position of the cylinder Part to targetPosition, effectively moving the cylinder part to that position in the 3D World.

3) local lookVector = (targetPosition - cuboidPart.Position).unit: This line calculates the direction in which the cuboidPart needs to look to face the targetPosition. It does this by subtracting the position of cuboidPart from targetPosition to get the direction vector pointing from the cuboid to the target. The ".unit" property normalizes this Vector, turning it into a unit vector (a vector with a magnitude of 1), representing just the direction with a length of 1.

4) cuboidPart.CFrame = CFrame.lookAt(cuboidPart.Position, targetPosition, Vector3.new(0, 1, 0)): This line of code creates a new CFrame that, when executed, rotates and positions the cuboidPart to face the targetPosition. The CFrame.lookAt function takes three arguments: the starting position of the object (cuboidPart.Position), the position to look at (targetPosition), and the "Up" Vector, which defines the orientation of the object when facing the target. In this case, we use Vector3.new(0, 1, 0) as the "Up" Vector, which represents the positive Y-axis direction (what is considered the upward direction of the world). The resulting CFrame is then assigned to the cuboid Part's CFrame property, which reorients the cuboid accordingly.

Upon testing this code, you will note that when reoriented to face the cylinder at targetPosition, the cuboid Part performs a pitch rotation against itself (i.e., it's also rotated around its X-axis). You may need to focus on the Cuboid part and look at it from the left or right to notice this pitch rotation. If this object were an NPC enemy character, it would turn to face the player anytime it was within its viewing distance. It would be rotated a certain amount about the "X" axis, especially when the player was on higher ground than the NPC. Ideally, you would want to avoid both a pitch and roll rotation in this context. Listing 5-11 shows how you can achieve this. Ensure you either comment or delete existing code within the "Cuboid_Script," and type in the code provided as Part of Listing 5-11.

Listing 5-11. Yaw rotation only - excluding pitch and roll rotations

```
local cuboidPart =  script.Parent
local cylinderPart = workspace.Cylinder
cuboidPart.Anchored = true
cylinderPart.Anchored = true
-- Set the position to look at
local targetPosition = Vector3.new(20, 10, 15)
cylinderPart.Position = targetPosition
wait(3)
-- Calculate the direction to look at
local dirVector = (targetPosition - cuboidPart.Position).unit
-- 1 Get just the new Y-axis rotation from the dirVector which
-- points from the cuboid to the target position
local newRotationY = math.atan2(-dirVector.X, -dirVector.Z)
-- 2 Get just the current Y-axis rotation from the cuboid's
-- CFrame
local currentRotationY = math.atan2(cuboidPart.CFrame.LookVector.X,
cuboidPart.CFrame.LookVector.Z)
-- 3 Calculate the rotation difference about the Y axis
local rotationDiffY = newRotationY - currentRotationY
-- 4 Apply the rotation only around the Y-axis while setting the
-- X and Z rotations to zero
local rotatedCFrame = CFrame.Angles(0, rotationDiffY, 0)
local newCFrame = CFrame.new(cuboidPart.Position) *
rotatedCFrame                                    -- 5
-- 6 Set the Part's CFrame to the new rotated CFrame
cuboidPart.CFrame = newCFrame
```

1) local newRotationY = math.atan2(-lookVector.X, -lookVector.Z): Returns the angle in radians that the cuboid Part needs to rotate around its Y-axis (vertical axis) to face the targetPosition (cylinder part) while keeping its existing rotation around the X and Z axes unchanged. The math.atan2() function calculates this angle based on the lookVector, representing the direction the cuboid Part needs to face. Without a detailed explanation of the inverse tangent function in Trigonometry, it would suffice to think of this trigonometric function as extracting only the "Y" rotation from the directional Vector (i.e., lookVector).

2) local currentRotationY = math.atan2(cuboidPart.CFrame. LookVector.X, cuboidPart.CFrame.LookVector.Z): This line computes the current angle in radians (currentRotationY) that the cuboid Part is currently rotated around the Y-axis by. It extracts this information from the CFrame.LookVector, which represents the forward Vector (direction) of the Part.

3) local rotationDiffY = newRotationY - currentRotationY: This line calculates the difference (rotationDiffY) between the new desired Y-axis rotation (newRotationY) and the current Y-axis rotation (currentRotationY). This difference represents the amount the cuboidPart needs to rotate around the Y-axis to face the targetPosition (cylinder part).

4) local rotatedCFrame = CFrame.Angles(0, rotationDiffY, 0): This line of code constructs a new CFrame (rotatedCFrame) that rotates only around the Y-axis by an angle of rotationDiffY (calculated in the previous step).

5) local newCFrame = CFrame.new(cuboidPart.Position) * rotatedCFrame: The expression "CFrame.new(cuboidPart. Position)" creates a new CFrame at the current position of the cuboidPart. It uses the position of the cuboidPart as the origin of the new CFrame, meaning it sets the translation (position) of the new CFrame to be the same as the current position of the cuboidPart. The "* rotatedCFrame" expression applies the rotation represented by the rotatedCFrame to the newly created CFrame.

The * operator is used to combine transformations, and in this case, it combines the translation (position of the cuboidPart) with the rotation specified by rotatedCFrame. The result is assigned to newCFrame, a new CFrame that has the same position as the cuboidPart, but also includes the desired Y-axis rotation specified by rotatedCFrame

6) cuboidPart.CFrame = newCFrame: Finally, setting the CFrame property of the cuboid Part to newCFrame, the cuboid Part will be moved to the desired position and rotated only around the Y-axis while setting existing X and Z rotations to zero.

Parenting a Part to Another Part

Parenting a part to another part in Roblox refers to establishing a hierarchical relationship between two objects, where one object becomes the parent of the other. In this parent-child relationship, the child part is attached to the parent part and inherits its position and orientation. When the parent part moves or rotates, the child part moves and rotates with it, maintaining its relative position and orientation. When creating certain gameplay mechanics, you may want to parent certain interactive objects like weapons or collectibles to a character's hand or body to ensure they stay attached while the character moves around. Listing 5-12 shows how to implement this parenting. Ensure you either comment or delete existing code within the "Cuboid_Script," and type in the code provided as Part of Listing 5-12.

Listing 5-12. Parenting a part to another part

```
local parentPart = script.Parent -- make the cuboid the parent
                                  -- Part
parentPart.Anchored = true
local childPart = workspace.Wedge -- make the wedge the child
                                  -- Part
childPart.Anchored = true
-- 1 Offset the child part 5 studs relative (above) the parent
childPart.CFrame = parentPart.CFrame * CFrame.new(0, 5, 0)
-- 2 Set the parent of the child wedge to be the cuboid
childPart.Parent = parentPart
```

Having reviewed several examples, the above code should be self-explanatory and easy to follow.

Color3 Data Type

Color3 is a built-in data type used to represent colors. It is a simple data structure that holds information about a color using three components, each ranging from 0 to 1. A Color3 value is defined by three properties, red, green, and blue, representing the intensity of the respective color components. The Color3 data type is commonly used in Roblox to set the colors of GUI elements, parts, lights, and other graphical objects. It allows developers to specify colors precisely using RGB (red, green, blue) values, where 0 means no intensity (no color), and 1 represents full intensity (full color). Creating a Color3 value can be done using the constructor Color3.new(), passing in the RGB components as arguments. Listing 5-13 shows how the cuboid Part's color can be changed programmatically.

Listing 5-13. Changing the color of the cuboid part

```
local cuboidPart = script.Parent
cuboidPart.Color = Color3.new(0.7,0.2,0.9) -- purple color
                                           -- cuboid
```

When run, the code in Listing 5-13 results in the cuboid Part turning purple.

There are also some predefined Color3 constant values in Roblox, which, when used in conjunction with the Color3's fromRGB() function, make it easy to use some common standard colors. Listing 5-14 shows you how to use this function.

Listing 5-14. Using the Color3.fromRGB() function

```
local cuboidPart = script.Parent
-- Red - Equivalent to Color3.new(1, 0, 0)
cuboidPart.Color = Color3.fromRGB(255, 0, 0) -- Red
wait(2)
-- Blue - Equivalent to Color3.new(0, 0, 1)
cuboidPart.Color = Color3.fromRGB(0, 0, 255) – Blue
wait(2)
-- Green - Equivalent to Color3.new(0, 1, 0)
```

```
cuboidPart.Color = Color3.fromRGB(0, 255, 0) - Green
wait(2)
-- White - Equivalent to Color3.new(1, 1, 1)
cuboidPart.Color = Color3.fromRGB(255, 255, 255)—White
wait(2)
-- Black - Equivalent to Color3.new(0, 0, 0)
cuboidPart.Color = Color3.fromRGB(0, 0, 0)-- Black
```

Instance Data Type

In Roblox Lua, the Instance data type is a fundamental class representing objects in the game world. Instances are the building blocks of all objects in a Roblox game, such as parts, models, GUI elements, lights, and more. Each object in Roblox is an instance of a specific class. For example, the "Part" object is an instance of the "Part" class. Instances have properties and methods that allow developers to manipulate and interact with the objects they represent. Instances are created using the instance.new() method, where you specify the class name of the object you want to create as the argument to the new( ) method. For example, you use instance.new("Part") to create a new part in the game world. Listing 5-15 shows you how to create and manipulate object instances programmatically.

Listing 5-15. Creating objects using the Instance data type

```
-- Create a new part and set its properties
local part = Instance.new("Part")
part.Size = Vector3.new(4, 2, 1)
part.Position = Vector3.new(10, 12, 0)
part.BrickColor = BrickColor.new("Bright red")
part.Anchored = true -- The Part won't fall when the game starts
-- Parent the Part to workspace so it appears in the game world
part.Parent = workspace
-- Create a new point light and set its properties
local light = Instance.new("PointLight")
light.Brightness = 10
light.Range = 20
```

```
light.Color = Color3.new(1, 1, 0) -- Yellow light
light.Parent = part -- Parent the light to the previously
                    -- created Part
```

In Listing 5-15, we create a Part and a Point Light, each with different properties and parented to various instances in the game world. This demonstrates how you can programmatically create, configure, and arrange instances in a Roblox game experience to create a simple scene with a part and a light source. Developers can build complex and interactive game environments using instances and their properties in Roblox.

Enum Data Type

In Roblox Lua, the Enum data type representing enumerations is a special class representing a set of predefined symbolic values. Enums organize related constants into groups, making the code readable and maintainable. Enums are commonly used in Roblox to represent categories, states, or options where a limited and fixed set of values are expected. Enums are usually defined as a separate data type and consist of a collection of named members, each representing a specific constant value. Each member of an enum has a unique name and an associated integer value. The integer value starts at 0 for the first member and increases by 1 for subsequent members. However, if needed, you can manually assign specific integer values to enum members. Enums are handy when dealing with properties or settings with only specific, limited options (e.g., Shape property). They provide better clarity in code and reduce the risk of errors due to incorrect values. One common use case for an enum in Roblox is to represent different NPC states, such as "Idle," "Chase," and "Dead." Using an enum for such states allows you to avoid using arbitrary integer values and improves code readability, making it easier to understand and maintain the game's logic. Listing 5-16 uses the enum "PartType" available within Roblox to manipulate a part's "Shape" property. The enum "PartType" represents a part's different shapes and can be used to set the shape of a part instance.

Listing 5-16. Using the enum "PartType" to change the shape of a part at runtime

```
-- Create a new part
local part = Instance.new("Part")
part.Size = Vector3.new(5, 2, 5)
part.Position = Vector3.new(5, 12, 0)
```

```
part.Anchored = true
part.CanCollide = true -- Enable collision for the Part
-- Set the shape of the Part using the Enum.PartType Enum
local shapeEnum = Enum.PartType.Ball -- Set the shape to a sphere
part.Shape = shapeEnum
-- Parent part to the workspace so it appears in the game world
part.Parent = workspace
wait(3)
-- Change the shape of the Part to a Block using Enum.PartType
shapeEnum = Enum.PartType.Block
part.Shape = shapeEnum
wait(3)
-- Change the shape of the Part to a Cylinder using Enum.PartType
shapeEnum = Enum.PartType.Cylinder
part.Shape = shapeEnum
wait(3)
-- Remove the Part from the game
part:Destroy() -- Destroys the part
```

In Listing 5-16, we create a new Part instance, set its initial shape to a sphere (using Enum.PartType.Ball), and then change its shape to a block (using the Enum.PartType. Block) after three seconds. Later, we change the shape again, this time to a cylinder (using the Enum.PartType.Cylinder). Finally, we remove the Part from the game using the ":Destroy()" method of Part.

Let's now create a user-defined Enum with named members to represent the different states an NPC could be in, namely, "Idle," "Chase," and "Dead." Listing 5-17 shows you how to create and utilize this Enum.

Listing 5-17. Creating a user-defined Enum and utilizing it

```
-- Define an Enum 'NPCState' with named members
local NPCState = {
    Idle = 0,
    Chase = 1,
    Dead = 2,
}
```

```
-- Set NPC currentState state to 'Chase'
local currentState = NPCState.Chase
if currentState == NPCState.Idle then
    print("NPC is in the Idle state.")
elseif currentState == NPCState.Chase then
    print("NPC is Chasing the Player.")
elseif currentState == NPCState.Dead then
    print("NPC is Dead")
else
    print("NPC state not valid.")
end
```

1) local NPCState = { Idle = 0, Chase = 1, Dead = 2 }: This line defines a user-defined enum called NPCState with three named members: "Idle" with a value of 0, "Chase" with a value of 1, and "Dead" with a value of 2.

2) local currentState = NPCState.Chase: This line sets the variable currentState to the value "Chase" from the NPCState enum, meaning the NPC is currently in the chasing state.

3) if currentState == NPCState.Idle then: This line starts a conditional statement to check if currentState equals NPCState.Idle, which represents the "Idle" state.

4) print("NPC is in the Idle state."): If the condition above is true, this line prints the message "NPC is in the Idle state."

5) elseif currentState == NPCState.Chase then: This line checks if currentState is equal to NPCState.Chase, representing the "Chase" state.

6) print("NPC is Chasing the Player."): If the condition above is true, this line prints the message "NPC is Chasing the Player."

7) elseif currentState == NPCState.Dead then: This line checks if currentState is equal to NPCState.Dead, representing the "Dead" state.

8) print("NPC is Dead"): If the condition above is true, this line prints the message "NPC is Dead."

9) else: If none of the conditions above are true, this line represents the default case.

10) print("NPC state not valid."): If the currentState does not match any of the enum members, this line prints the message "NPC state not valid."

Random Data Type

In Roblox Lua, the "Random" data type allows generating random numbers and making random selections, which are crucial for creating dynamic behavior in games and simulations. Lua has a "math" library with several functions for working with random numbers. However, in this section, let's focus on the "Random" class and its object-oriented approach to generating random numbers rather than the "math" library. Listing 5-18 describes several methods in the "Random" class to generate pseudo-random numbers.

Listing 5-18. Generating random numbers

```
local random = Random.new()                           -- 1
local min = 1
local max = 100
local randomNumber = random:NextInteger(min, max)     -- 2
print("Random Integer using Random.new(): " .. randomNumber)
-- Generate and print a random floating-point number between
-- 0 (inclusive) and 1 (exclusive)
local randomFloat = random:NextNumber()               -- 3
print("Random float:" .. randomFloat)
```

1) local random = Random.new(): Creates a new instance (object) of the Random class and stores it within the variable random.

2) local randomNumber = random:NextInteger(min, max): This method generates a random integer between the specified min (inclusive) and max (inclusive) using the random object.

131

3) local randomFloat = random:NextNumber(): Using
    random:NextNumber(), you can call the NextNumber method on
    a random object. This method returns a random floating-point
    number between 0 (inclusive) and 1 (exclusive).

Listing 5-19. Generating random colors for a part

```
-- Create a new part
local part = Instance.new("Part")
part.Size = Vector3.new(5, 2, 5)
part.Position = Vector3.new(5, 12, 0)
part.Anchored = true
part.CanCollide = true -- Enable collision for the Part
-- Parent part to the workspace so it appears in the game world
part.Parent = workspace
local rnd = Random.new()
for i = 1, 5 do
part.Color =   Color3.fromRGB(rnd:NextInteger(0,255),rnd:NextInteg
er(0,255),
rnd:NextInteger(0,255))
wait(2)
end
```

In Listing 5-19, the given for loop generates random RGB color values for a part and changes its color every two seconds. Here's a breakdown of what the code does:

1) for i = 1, 5 do … end: This sets up a for loop that will execute the
    code within it five times. The loop variable "i" starts from 1 and
    increments by one each iteration until it reaches 5.

2) part.Color = Color3.fromRGB(rnd:NextInteger(0,255),
    rnd:NextInteger(0,255), rnd:NextInteger(0,255)): This line
    generates a new RGB color using random integer values for red,
    green, and blue components of the "fromRGB()" function.

3) rnd:NextInteger(0, 255) generates a random integer for each color
    component between 0 and 255 (inclusive). It uses the Random
    object "rnd" to obtain the random values.

4) Color3.fromRGB() is a function that takes three arguments (red, green, blue) representing the color components and returns a new Color3 value with the specified RGB color.

5) part.Color = ...: The generated RGB color is assigned to the Color property of the part object, which will change its appearance to the new color.

6) wait(2): This line pauses the script for two seconds before continuing to the next iteration of the loop. This creates a time delay of two seconds between each color change.

Properties of Parts (Objects)

Chapter 2 covered various Roblox properties and their manipulation using the Roblox Editor, including Shape, Transform, CanCollide, Anchored, CollisionGroup, etc. This section will look at some essential additional properties available to a "Part" (object). These properties can be manipulated through scripts or the Roblox Studio interface to create dynamic and interactive gameplay experiences. Let's explore some additional properties of Roblox Parts (objects):

1) BrickColor and Material: "BrickColor" defines the color of the "Part," while "Material" determines its surface texture and appearance. There are various BrickColors and Materials to choose from, giving you a wide range of visual options. Try changing these properties on one of your existing parts.

2) Transparency: This property controls how transparent the Part is. Setting a high transparency value will make the Part almost invisible, while a low value will make it fully opaque.

3) CanTouch: This property determines whether the "Part" can be interacted with by players, allowing them to click or touch the Part to trigger specific events.

4) Locked: This is a Boolean property that determines whether a part can be edited or manipulated using the parts tools. If set to true, you won't be able to move, rotate, or scale the Part. After setting the "Locked" property to true, you deselect it in "Scene View."

Then any attempt to select it will fail as the Part is now locked. However, you can still access the Part by selecting it within the "Explorer" window and then unchecking its "Locked" property.

5) Pivot: This category determines a part's positional and rotational pivot offset point. On the "MODEL" tab, within the "Pivot" section, clicking the "Edit Pivot" button places a rotational cum move gizmo on your Part, allowing you to change its pivot point from its default center position. The "Pivot Offset" properties are updated within the "Properties" window for the Part whose pivot point you have changed. Now you can rotate the Part around its new pivot position. Clicking the "Reset" button will reset the pivot point to its default central position.

6) Custom Physical Properties: This category, when checked, provides you access to the concerned part's physical properties such as Density, Elasticity, ElasticityWeight, Friction, and FrictionWeight. These properties deal with essential physics attributes that can change the behavior of your Part, for example, increasing its elasticity to enhance restitution, or perhaps you would like programmatically to change the friction of a part based on the type of surface it is colliding with.

7) Massless: This Boolean property determines whether your Part should retain its "Mass" when welded to another part that has "Mass." If set to false (unchecked), the Part will add its "Mass" to the total collective "Mass" of all the other parts when welded to another part. If set to true (checked), the Part will not add any "Mass" to the other Part; it is welded to that has "Mass."

8) Assembly Linear Velocity: This property is a "Vector3" that determines the physics force to apply against one of the global axes of a part assembly or Part whose "Anchored" property is false. This property needs to be set via a script on the Part. Launch the Roblox Script Editor by opening the "Cuboid_Script." Type in the code provided in Listing 5-20. Ensure that you have the "Cuboid" part in focus in "Scene View" so that it's visible. Click the "Run" button, and you will note that your cuboid Part jumped upward along its global "Y" axis.

Listing 5-20. Applying Linear Velocity to a Part

```
local cuboid = script.Parent
cuboid.AssemblyLinearVelocity = Vector3.new(0,50,0)
```

In Listing 5-20, we have declared a variable named cuboid that will reference the cuboid Part in the Explorer (game world). The statement "script. Parent" assigns the current scripts (i.e., "Cuboid_Script") parent (which is the cuboid Part) to the cuboid variable. Now you can access the properties of the cuboid Part using this cuboid variable (Figure 5-3). Ensure you either comment or delete existing code within the Cuboid_Script, and type in the code provided as Part of Listing 5-20. Try moving the cuboid Part forward along the global "Z" axis by setting a value for the Vector3 "Z" property in the script using Vector3.new(0, 0,15).

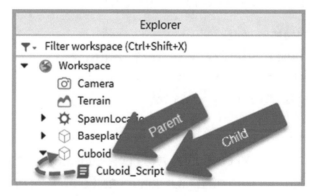

Figure 5-3. *Parent-child relationship*

Note   An Assembly is one or more parts connected by welds or animated joints.

The script keyword represents the current script object, irrespective of what the script object has been named. Using the dot operator, you can access the script's parent. It allows developers to access and manipulate the properties of the script itself. For instance, you could access the "Enabled" and "Disabled" properties to have the script deactivated and the script "Changed" event trigger whenever certain property values of an object the script is attached to change. This keyword is beneficial in the context of LocalScripts and ModuleScripts.

---

1) Assembly Angular Velocity: This property is a "Vector3" that determines the rotational /angular (torque) force to apply against one of the global axes of a part assembly or Part whose "Anchored" property is false. This property needs to be set via a script on the Part. Continuing from Listing 5-20, add the new lines of code to your script as shown in Listing 5-21, which should have your Part rotate around the global "Y" axis. Also, ensure to comment on the line of code that applies linear velocity to the Part by preceding it with two hyphens, as we want to see angular velocity working. Click the "Run" button, and you will note that your cuboid Part rotates 45 degrees around the global "Y" axis.

Listing 5-21. Applying Angular Velocity to a Part

```
local cuboid = script.Parent
--cuboid.AssemblyLinearVelocity = Vector3.new(0,50,0)
-- Rotate the block by 45 degrees about the global 'Y' axis
cuboid.AssemblyAngularVelocity = Vector3.new(0,45,0)
```

Note   In Lua, whenever you encounter two consecutive hyphens ("--" symbol), the remainder of that line is treated as a comment. Comments are solely meant to aid in code readability and comprehension; they do not get executed.

---

2) Attributes: Besides the standard properties, you can add custom properties to your Parts (objects), referred to as "Attributes." This handy but overlooked feature is extremely useful for storing additional data or metadata about your "Parts" (objects). Attributes are custom properties that can be named and provided with a value. For example, each "Part" could have a custom property (Attribute) named "Enabled" and provided with a value of either true or false that can be modified using Lua code to determine if the specific "Part" has been enabled or not. You can set up these custom properties (attributes) for your "Part" (object) by selecting the "Part" within "Scene View" or the "Explorer" window and then scrolling down to the very bottom

within the "Properties" window and expanding the "Attributes" category, followed by clicking the "Add Attribute" button, which should have the "Add Attribute" dialog pop up (Figure 5-4). Set the attribute name to "Enabled" (without the quotes). From the "Type" dropdown, select the value "Boolean," a basic Lua data type that can hold a true or false value. Finally, click "Save" to save your newly created custom property, which should now be visible within the "Properties" window within the "Attributes" category (Figure 5-5). Note that this "Enabled" custom property, a Boolean that can accept only a true or false value, has been represented as a check box that, when checked, is true and false when unchecked.

The properties available to a "Part" (object) may vary depending on the type of "Part" (e.g., BasePart, MeshPart, etc.) and whether it is a part of a specific Roblox class (e.g., Model, Script, etc.). Understanding and utilizing these properties effectively is crucial for creating engaging and interactive experiences within the Roblox platform.

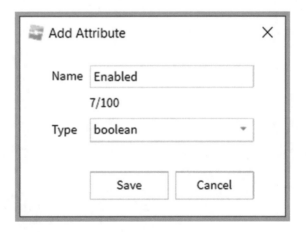

Figure 5-4. *Add Attribute dialog*

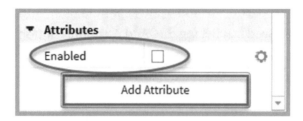

Figure 5-5. *Enabled Attribute*

Summary

Through this comprehensive chapter, you will have a solid grasp of fundamental Roblox concepts, namely, Objects, Data Types, and the intricate world of Object properties. Armed with a deeper understanding of Data Types, you have harnessed the ability to structure and manage information effectively, enabling seamless interactions with objects. With a robust toolkit of knowledge surrounding object Properties, you have now unlocked the art of customizing and fine-tuning behaviors, ultimately empowering you to craft immersive, dynamic, and captivating experiences.

Functions and Events

Functions and Events are the twin pillars within Roblox Lua scripting that empower you to breathe life into your game experiences, orchestrating a symphony of actions and reactions that captivate players. Functions are crucial in enabling developers to create specific actions that can be executed whenever needed. On the other hand, events facilitate communication and interaction between different elements in the game experience. By triggering responses based on user actions or system events, events contribute to the dynamic and ever-changing nature of Roblox experiences. In this chapter, we will deeply dive into Functions and Events using Roblox Lua.

Functions

A function in Roblox Lua serves as a designated code block bearing a distinct name. Unlike other code blocks, a function's contents remain inert upon the initial loading of the Lua file (its code doesn't execute). Instead, functions are merely defined during the file-loading phase. However, after a function is defined, it becomes accessible for execution through invocation. This characteristic bestows the ability to summon a function repeatedly. Functions adhere to the exact scope regulations that govern do/end blocks (chunks) that you have learned about in Chapter 3.

The terminology of a function abides by the same naming conventions applied to variables within Roblox Lua that you learned about in Chapter 3. Function declarations commence with the "function" keyword, followed by the function name. Following the name, a set of parameters may be specified, enclosed within parentheses (). Parameters constitute variable signatures that are pivotal to the function's internal operations. In cases where a function necessitates no parameters, an empty pair of parentheses suffices. Subsequently, the function's operative instructions are encapsulated within a code block (chunk), referred to as the function's body that is closed by the "end" keyword. Figure 6-1 describes the various components that comprise a function in Roblox Lua.

© Christopher Coutinho 2023
C. Coutinho, *Roblox Lua Scripting Essentials*, https://doi.org/10.1007/979-8-8688-0026-9_6

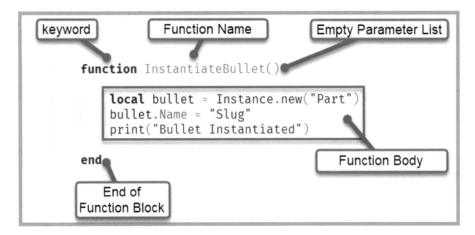

Figure 6-1. *Filter Properties Search box*

Invoking a Function

After defining a function, you can trigger its execution by typing its name followed by parentheses. This initiates the function call. For example, to call the "local" function depicted in Figure 6-1, all you need to do is invoke it as shown in Listing 6-1.

Listing 6-1. Define and Invoke a function

```
local function InstantiateBullet()
    local bullet = Instance.new("Part")
    bullet.Name = "Slug"
    print("Bullet Instantiated")
end
InstantiateBullet() -- invoke function defined above
```

Function Parameters

Parameters (also known as arguments) of a function are values or variables you provide when you call the function. They serve as inputs that the function can work with or manipulate to produce a desired result. When you define a function, you specify the parameters it expects to receive. When you call the function, you provide actual values or variables for those parameters. In Roblox Lua, parameter types are not explicitly declared within the function's signature as they might be in other programming languages. Lua is a dynamically typed language, meaning you don't explicitly specify data types for function parameters or variables. It's important to note that if you pass in values that don't match the implied parameter type within the function, your code will provide an error when run. Listing 6-2 illustrates the passing of parameters to a function and how to validate the arguments passed into a function and raise a customized error message.

Listing 6-2. Defining function parameters

```
local function calcRectangleArea(length, width)
if typeof(length) ~= "number" or typeof(width) ~= "number" then
    error("Both length and width must be numbers")
end
    return length * width
end
print("Rectangular Area is: " .. calcRectangleArea(4, 6))
```

When the function in Listing 6-2 is invoked, it will display the message "Rectangular Area is: 24." In the event the above function was called using non-numeric values, as follows: calcRectangleArea("a," "c"), the if condition within the function would evaluate to true, resulting in the error function terminating the function and displaying the message "Both length and width must be numbers."

Function Return Values

In Lua, not only can you pass values to a function, but you can also have a function return either a single value or multiple values as well as a nil value. When a function returns multiple values, they are typically separated by commas in the return statement. In the case of multiple returned values, when you call a function, you can assign each returned value to a separate variable using commas. The order of values returned by the function matters, and they are assigned to the variables in the order they appear in the return statement. It's important to note that Lua will automatically discard the extra values if you don't capture all the returned values. Listing 6-3 demonstrates this.

Listing 6-3. function return values

```lua
local function triangleAreaPerimeter(b,h,c)
      local perimeter = b + h + c
      local area = 0.5 * b * h
      return area, perimeter, c
end
local area, perimeter = triangleAreaPerimeter(3,4,5)
print("Triangle Area: " .. area .. " Perimeter: " .. perimeter)
```

When invoked, the function in Listing 6-3 is passed numeric arguments b, h, and c to compute the area and perimeter of a triangle. This function returns three values as part of its return statement, where only 2 of these returned values are captured into the variable's area and perimeter. As no third variable is specified to capture the return value of parameter c, its value is discarded when returned. The keyword "return" within the function's body returns values computed within the function. When a function encounters a return statement, it returns whatever data follows the "return" keyword and stops executing. If you have any code after the return statement, that code will never execute.

An Arbitrary Number of Parameters

In Lua, providing an identical number of arguments as stated in a function's declaration(signature) is unnecessary. For instance, including more arguments than declared will result in the surplus arguments being discarded. Conversely, if fewer arguments are added than indicated in the functions declaration(signature), the missing parameters will be assigned a nil value. Listing 6-4 illustrates this.

Listing 6-4. An arbitrary number of parameters are passed to a function

```lua
local function listTriangleSides(base,height,hypotenuse)
print("Base: " .. tostring(base) .. " Height: " .. tostring(height).."
Hypotenuse: "..tostring(hypotenuse))   -- 1
end
listTriangleSides(5,7,8.602)     -- 2
listTriangleSides(5,7)           -- 3
listTriangleSides(5)             -- 4
```

1) print("Base: " .. tostring(base) .. " Height: " .. tostring(height).." Hypotenuse: "..tostring(hypotenuse)): In this line of code, arguments base, height, and hypotenuse are converted to strings using the built-in tostring() function, before being concatenated to the output string. This prevents errors caused by attempting to concatenate nil with a string when a few or no arguments are passed to the function.

2) listTriangleSides(5,7,8.602): In this line of code, all three arguments are passed to the function, displaying all three argument values.

3) listTriangleSides(5,7): In this line of code, only the first two arguments are passed to the function, resulting in the value nil displayed for the Hypotenuse. If the tostring() function wasn't used in the print statement when attempting to print the value of the hypotenuse parameter, you would have encountered an error as nil without first being converted to a string cannot be concatenated.

4) listTriangleSides(5): In this line of code, only the first argument is passed to the function, resulting in the value nil displayed for the Height and Hypotenuse.

Anonymous Functions

In Roblox Lua, an anonymous function (also known as a lambda function or a function literal) is a function that doesn't have a predefined name. It's a way to define a function on the fly (at the same place it is invoked) without assigning it a specific name. Anonymous functions are often used when you need a short, simple function for a particular task or when you want to pass a function as an argument to another function. You will find such anonymous functions used often as Event handlers when Roblox Events are triggered. Listing 6-5 is an example of an anonymous function being passed as a parameter (argument) to another function.

Listing 6-5. Anonymous function passed as a parameter to another function

```
local function performOperation(operation, x, y)
     return operation(x, y)                         -- (1)
end
local result = performOperation(function(a, b)       --(2)
     return a * b
end, 5, 3)
print("Product is: ", result) -- Output: Result: 15
```

Here, an anonymous function, defined using the "function" keyword, is passed as an argument to the performOperation function (2). The performOperation function takes an operation (a function) and two numbers and calls the operation (1) with the given numbers. In this case, the anonymous function performs multiplication, resulting in the value 15 being displayed.

While some programmers discourage anonymous functions due to potential readability and maintainability issues, they can offer faster coding and prove beneficial as event handlers. However, they might be more challenging to update and reuse since they lack a distinct name for calling. Anonymous functions are ideally best suited for situations as event handlers where return values aren't necessary.

Events

In Roblox, Events are a way to respond to specific actions or changes in the game environment. Events provide a way for your scripts to be notified when something specific happens, enabling you to create interactivity, animations, gameplay mechanics, and more. They allow you to execute custom code when certain conditions are met, such as when a player interacts with an object, when a property changes, or when user input is detected.

In Roblox Lua scripting, there are instances where you want to execute a function not at a predetermined point in your code but rather when a specific event occurs during gameplay. These events can include actions like a player clicking on a loot chest to collect loot, automatically assigning players to teams upon joining a game, destroying a part when the player touches it, etc. The idea here is that you're anticipating and waiting for these events to occur, and once they do, you want a specific set of code to execute in response.

Roblox's event-driven architecture is designed to handle these scenarios. When the expected event occurs, a signal is dispatched as a notification to instruct specific code to run. To ensure your function is called whenever such an event is fired, you can employ the Connect() method. This method requires you to specify the function you want to run in response to the triggered event. Using Roblox's event system and Connect() method, you can dynamically trigger functions to execute based on player interactions and other game events, creating engaging and interactive gameplay experiences.

Note   In Lua, functions that are built-in or associated with existing objects, like print(), wait(), destroy(), and Connect(), are technically referred to as methods in other languages. We will continue to refer to such built-in functions as methods whenever encountered.

Here's how Roblox Lua's built-in events work:

1) Event Creation: Many Roblox objects, like parts, GUI elements, characters, and services, have built-in events associated with them.

2) Connecting to Events: To respond to an event, you connect a function (also called a callback or event handler) to the event using the :Connect() method. The connected function will be executed whenever the event is triggered.

3) Event Triggering: An event is triggered when a specific action or condition occurs. For example, a "Touched" event is triggered when a part encounters another part, or a "MouseButton1Click" event is triggered when a player clicks a GUI button.

4) Execution of Event Handlers: When an event is triggered, all the functions connected to it are executed in the order they were connected. Each function is called with arguments passed by the triggered event into the function.

5) Disconnecting Events: You can disconnect event handlers using the:Disconnect() method. This prevents the handler from being executed when the event is triggered.

Touched Event

Listing 6-6. Events and Event Handlers – Touched event

```
-- Move a bullet to collide with a target and trigger the
-- bullet's Touched event
-- 1. Create a Target Object
local target = Instance.new("Part")
-- 2. Set properties for the target
target.Name = "Target"
target.Anchored = true
target.Color =  Color3.fromRGB(255, 136, 0)
target.Parent = workspace
target.Position = Vector3.new(
math.random(-20, 20),   -- Random X position between -20 and 20
math.random(10, 20),    -- Random Y position between 10 and 20
math.random(-20, 20)    -- Random Z position between -20 and 20
)
-- 3. Create a sphere bullet object
local bullet = Instance.new("Part")
-- 4. Set properties for the bullet
bullet.Name = "Bullet"
bullet.Shape = Enum.PartType.Ball
bullet.Size = Vector3.new(0.15, 0.15, 0.15)
bullet.Parent = workspace
bullet.Anchored = true
bullet.BrickColor = BrickColor.new("Really black")
bullet.Position = Vector3.new(
math.random(-10, 10),   -- Random X position between -10 and 10
math.random(10, 10),    -- Random Y position between 10 and 10
math.random(-30, 20)    -- Random Z position between -30 and 20
)
-- 5. Store initial positions of bullet and target
local curBulletPosn = bullet.Position
local targetPosn = target.Position
local TIME_TO_TARGET = 3
```

```lua
local startTime = tick()
-- 6. Function to move the bullet toward the Target
local function moveBullet()
    local elapsedTime = tick() - startTime
    -- Calculate the interpolation factor 't' based on the
    -- elapsed time and the total duration.
    local t = elapsedTime / TIME_TO_TARGET
    local newPosn = curBulletPosn:Lerp(targetPosn,t)
    bullet.Position = newPosn
    curBulletPosn = newPosn
end
-- 7. Function to handle bullet collision when bullet's
--    Touched event is triggered
local function onBulletCollision(hitPart)
    print("Bullet collided with: ", hitPart.Name)
    bullet:Destroy()
end
-- 8. Connect collision handler to the bullet's Touched event
bullet.Touched:Connect(onBulletCollision)
-- 9. Loop that moves bullet towards target within approx 3
-- seconds
while tick() - startTime < TIME_TO_TARGET  do
    moveBullet()
    wait(0.01) -- Small delay to control the loop rate
end
-- 10. Set bullet position to target position when it reaches
-- the target
bullet.Position = targetPosn
-- 11. Wait for 5 seconds
wait(5)
-- 12. Set bullet 'Anchored' property to false to allow the
-- Physics Simulation needed for the 'bullet.Touched' event to
-- be triggered
bullet.Anchored = false
```

1) A Part object named target is created using the Instance.new function.

2) The target object's properties are set, including name, anchored state, color, parent, and position. When set to true, the "Anchored" property ensures that the part is not under any physics simulation such as gravity. This ensures that the target part doesn't fall. Parenting target to workspace ensures that it is part of the game world.

3) A Part object named bullet is created using the Instance.new function.

4) The properties of the bullet object are set, including name, shape (ball), size, parent, anchored state, brick color, and position. The bullet object is assigned a spherical shape. Its "Anchored" property has been set to true so that physics simulations do not initially affect it.

5) Variables are initialized to store the initial positions, duration, and starting times. "TIME_TO_TARGET" indicates how many seconds the bullet will take to reach the target. The tick() function returns a numerical value representing the current time in seconds. It starts counting when the game begins or the script executes.

6) A function named moveBullet is defined to interpolate the bullet's position using linear interpolation (Lerp).

7) A function named onBulletCollision, the Event Handler for the bullet's Touched event, is defined to handle the collision event when the bullet touches another object (i.e., the target in this case).

8) The onBulletCollision function is connected to the Touched event of the bullet object, ensuring that the moment the bullet's Touched event is triggered, this onBulletCollisioin event handler function will execute.

9) A loop continuously calls the moveBullet function and updates the bullet's position over time.

10) The bullet's position is set to the target position once it reaches the target.

11) The script waits five seconds before continuing, allowing you time to focus on the bullet within "Scene View," should you want to.

12) The "Anchored" property of the bullet is set to false, enabling physics simulation for the bullet object, which in turn allows the Touched event to be triggered when the bullet collides with another object. When an object's "Anchored" property is set to true, physics simulations on the object do not occur. The Touched event of an object will not be triggered by simply changing its position using the Position property along with Lerp. The Touched event is typically triggered by the Roblox physics engine when the object's bounding box physically contacts another object's bounding box. To achieve this, you ideally need to have Roblox's physics engine handle the movement using a "BodyVelocity" component or other body mover classes or constraints. However, an easier way to achieve this is to have the bullet's movement controlled by Lerp, and once the bullet reaches the target position, set its "Anchored" property to false, allowing the physics engine to take over and handle collisions and trigger the Touched event. The Lerp function is just a method to interpolate the bullet's position over a duration, making the movement appear smooth.

Changed Event

The Changed event in Roblox Lua is a general-purpose event triggered when an object's property changes. It can be used to monitor changes made to various properties of an object. Listing 6-7 provides a few examples of the Changed event.

Listing 6-7. Events and Event Handlers – Changed event – Size property

```
local part = Instance.new("Part")
part.Anchored = true
part.Parent = workspace
part.Position = Vector3.new(-1,20,-10)
```

```
-- Connect the part Changed event to monitor Size changes using
-- an Anonymous function as the Event Handler.
part.Changed:Connect(function(property)          -- 1
    if property == "Size" then                   -- 2
        local newSize = part.Size
        print("Part's new size: ", newSize)
    end
end)
wait(3)
-- Change the size of the part to trigger the Changed event
part.Size = Vector3.new(5, 10, 5)                -- 3
```

1) part.Changed:Connect(function(property)...end): This line sets
up an event handler for the Changed event of the part object. The
:Connect() function is used to attach a function (in this case, an
anonymous function) to be executed when the Changed event
is triggered. The anonymous function is defined immediately
after the function(and before the closing end). It accepts a single
parameter from the Changed event, which is the name of the
property that was changed.

2) if property == "Size" then: This line checks if the value of the
property parameter passed to the anonymous function event
handler (which represents the property that changed) is equal to
the string "Size." This conditional statement aims to determine
if the change that occurred is related to the "Size" property of
the part. If so, it retrieves the new size of the part and displays a
message indicating the new size.

3) part.Size = Vector3.new(5, 10, 5): This line of code triggers the
Changed event by changing the physical size of the part.

This code demonstrates how to use an anonymous function as an event handler
to respond to changes to a specific property "Size" of an object and execute custom
behavior when that property changes.

Listing 6-8. Events and Event Handlers – Changed event – Color property

```
local part = Instance.new("Part")
part.Anchored = true
part.Parent = workspace
part.Position = Vector3.new(-1,20,-10)
-- Connect the part Changed event to monitor Color change using
-- an Anonymous function as the Event Handler.
part.Changed:Connect(function(property)
    if property == "Color" then
        local newColor = part.Color
        print("Part's new Color: ", newColor)
    end
end)
wait(3)
-- Change the color of the part to trigger the Changed event
part.Color = Color3.new(0.345098, 1, 0.858824)
```

Listing 6-9. Events and Event Handlers – Changed event – Transparency property

```
local part = Instance.new("Part")
part.Anchored = true
part.Parent = workspace
part.Position = Vector3.new(-1,20,-10)
-- The part Changed event monitoring Transparency change using
-- an Anonymous function as the Event Handler.
part.Changed:Connect(function(property)
    if property == " Transparency " then
        local newTransparency = part.Transparency
        print("Part's new Color: ", newTransparency)
    end
end)
wait(3)
-- Change part transparency to trigger the Changed event
part.Transparency = 0.15
```

Listing 6-10. Events and Event Handlers – Changed event – Anchored property

```
local part = Instance.new("Part")
part.Anchored = true
part.Parent = workspace
part.Position = Vector3.new(-1,20,-10)
-- The part Changed event monitoring Anchored property setting -- using an
Anonymous function as the Event Handler.
part.Changed:Connect(function(property)
    if property == " Anchored " then
        local newAnchored = part.Anchored
        print("Part's new Anchored status: ", newAnchored)
    end
end)
wait(3)
-- Change Anchored property value to trigger the Changed event
part.Anchored = false            -- causes part to fall
```

Listing 6-11. Events and Event Handlers – Changed event – Position property

```
local part = Instance.new("Part")
part.Anchored = true
part.Parent = workspace
part.Position = Vector3.new(-1,20,-10)
-- Connect the part Changed event to monitor Position changes
-- using an anonymous function as the Event Handler.
part.Changed:Connect(function(property)
    if property == "Position" then
        local newPosn = part.Position
        print("Part's new Position : ", newPosn)
    end
end)
wait(3)
-- Change the part's Position to trigger the Changed event
part.Position = Vector3.new(5, 5, 0)
```

ClickDetector.MouseClick Event

This event is fired when a player clicks on a part with a "ClickDetector" component. Let's first create a part with a "ClickDetector" component attached to it. Begin by inserting a block part in the game world using the Roblox Studio Editor. In the "Explorer" window, with the newly added part selected, rename it to "ClickablePart." Hover over the name of this part in the "Explorer" window, and click the plus icon beside it. From the list that shows up, select the item "ClickDetector" to add it as a child of the "ClickablePart." You might want to resize the "ClickablePart" game object by increasing its height and depth using the "Properties" window and adjusting its Transform – Size property.

Let's create a script attached to the "ClickablePart" object to handle the interaction between the player's click and the "ClickDetector." Hover over the "ClickablePart" in the "Explorer" window, click the plus icon beside it, and select the item script from the list to add a new script to this "ClickablePart" object. Delete the default print() function in the newly created Script, and type in the code provided in Listing 6-12.

Listing 6-12. Events and Event Handlers – ClickDetector.MouseClick event

```
local part = script.Parent  -- Assuming this script is a child of the part
local clickDetector = part:FindFirstChild("ClickDetector")
if clickDetector then
    clickDetector.MouseClick:Connect(function(player)
    print(player.Name .. " clicked on the part!")
    end)
end
```

This script checks if the "ClickablePart" object contains a ClickDetector component (as a child). If so, it connects the MouseClick event to an anonymous function. When a player clicks on the "ClickablePart" object, the anonymous function will be called and display the player's name that clicked the object.

To test the experience, you must play the game within Roblox Studio. Instead of selecting "Run" as you have been doing so far, you now need to select either "Play" or the "Play Here" button from the toolbar ribbon made available upon selecting the "HOME" tab. The "Play Here" button is a convenient feature that allows you to load the game with the player spawned into the area you have focused on. For example, you could focus on your "ClickablePart" object and then click the "Play Here" button to have your player spawn close to the "ClickablePart" object. Once your player is near the "ClickablePart" object, hover your mouse pointer over this "ClickablePart" object. You will note that your mouse pointer morphs into a hand icon. Now click on the "ClickablePart" object to display the players' name within the "Output" window.

This is a fundamental example. You can customize the interaction by adding more functionality within the MouseClick event handler, such as opening a door, triggering an action, or awarding points. Additionally, you can use the "Player" parameter of the event handler to identify the player who clicked the part and perform specific actions for that player.

MouseButton1Click Event

This event is triggered when a player clicks a GUI button using the primary (Left) mouse button. Like the "MouseButton1Click" event, Roblox provides a "MouseButton2Click" event triggered by the secondary (Right) mouse button. Both events work identically. Listing 6-13 shows you how to set up the "MouseButton1Click" event that displays a message when its GUI button is clicked.

Listing 6-13. Events and Event Handlers – MouseButton1Click event

```
local button = script.Parent
button.MouseButton1Click:Connect(function()
    print("Hurray ! You Clicked Me")
end)
```

Listed as follows are the steps to create a "ScreenGui" with a single button positioned at the top-middle of the screen using the Roblox Studio Editor:

1) From the "Explorer" window, select the item "StarterGui," and click the plus icon beside it. From the list that shows up, use the "Search Object" box at the top to search for the component "ScreenGui" and select it, adding it as a child of "StarterGui." Rename the newly created "ScreenGui" object if desired. You will note that within the Roblox Editor, you now have a new "UI" tab made available to you to design your very own highly customizable UI interface. We will use it to add just a single button, as shown in Figure 6-2.

2) With "ScreenGui" selected in the "Explorer" window, ensure that you have the "UI" tab selected. Click the "Text Button" icon on the "UI" toolbar ribbon to add a Text button object as a child of the "ScreeGui." You will note that a button object is added to the Roblox Studio Editor. Select this button in the editor and drag it to the right to center it at the top-middle within the editor (Figure 6-2). The editor provides helpful guides to position your button precisely where you want.

3) With the "TextButton" selected in the editor, within the "Properties" window, locate its "Text" property and change it to "Click Me !."

4) You may further customize the button's appearance using properties such as the "BackgroundColor3" (sets the background color of the button), "TextColor3" (sets the text color of the button), "FontFace" (sets the font for the button's text), "TextSize" (sets the size of the button text), etc.

5) Finally, you create a new script as a child of the "TextButton" by hovering over it in the "Explorer" window and selecting "Script" from the list. Delete the default print() function from the newly added script, and type in the code provided in Listing 6-13.

6) The code in Listing 6-13 ensures that when a player clicks the "TextButton" in the game experience, the "MouseButton1Click" event is triggered, and the code inside the anonymous function executes, resulting in the message "Hurray! You Clicked Me" displayed in the "Output" window.

7) To test the "ScreenGui" and button, you need to play the game within Roblox Studio by selecting "Play" or "Play Here." Once your player spawns into the game world, the "Click Me !" button will appear at the screen's top-middle. Clicking on this button using your mouse pointer displays the message "Hurray! You Clicked Me" to the "Output" window.

Once you're satisfied with your "ScreenGui" and button setup, you can continue adding more elements and interactions to create a complete and engaging user interface for your game. The "UI" toolbar ribbon allows you to add various GUI elements to your "ScreenGui."

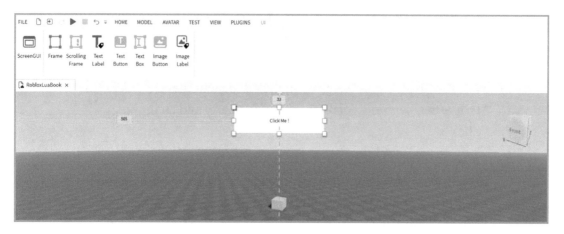

Figure 6-2. *UI Editor Window*

PlayerAdded Event

The "PlayerAdded" event in Roblox Lua is triggered whenever a new player joins the game. It allows you to execute code when a player enters the game world. This event is often used to set up player-specific functionality, initialize player data, and manage interactions unique to each player. In this example, we'll create an experience where players earn points by clicking on clickable parts, and their scores will be displayed using a leaderboard. You will use the leaderboard that's built into Roblox.

You already have a "ClickablePart" object within your game world that you created earlier in this chapter in the section titled "ClickDetector.MouseClick Event." Select this "ClickablePart" object within the "Explorer" window, expand it, and double-click "Script" to open the script attached to this "ClickablePart" object in Roblox's editor. Replace the contents of this script with the code provided in Listing 6-14.

Listing 6-14. Events and Event Handlers – clickDetector.MouseClick event

```
local part = script.Parent   -- this script must be a child of
                             -- the 'ClickablePart' object
local clickDetector = part:FindFirstChild("ClickDetector")
if clickDetector then
    clickDetector.MouseClick:Connect(function(player)
    player.leaderstats.Score.Value += 1
    part:Destroy()

    end)
end
```

With this "ClickablePart" object still selected within the "Explorer" window, duplicate it thrice so you have four "ClickablePart" objects within your game world. Using the move tool, move them around so they don't overlap. You will have your player visit each "ClickablePart" object within the game world and click on it to have the score updated on the leaderboard.

Whenever a player enters the game experience, they should be added to the leaderboard. This can be achieved by creating a new leaderboard script within the "ServerScriptService" that can be accessed from the "Explorer" window. Hover over this "ServerScriptService," click the plus icon beside it, and select "Script" from the available list. Rename this "Script" to "leaderboard," and ensure it has been opened in Roblox's editor. Delete the default print() function, and type in the code provided in Listing 6-15 into the leaderboard script.

Listing 6-15. The leaderboard script

```
game.Players.PlayerAdded:Connect(function(player)    -- 1
    local leaderStats = Instance.new("Folder")       -- 2
    leaderStats.Name = "leaderstats"                 -- 3
    leaderStats.Parent = player                      -- 4
    local score = Instance.new("IntValue")           -- 5
    score.Name = "Score"                             -- 6
    score.Value = 0                                  -- 7
    score.Parent = leaderStats                       -- 8
end)
```

The code in Listing 6-15 is all about setting up the leaderboard and the score item:

1) game.Players.PlayerAdded:Connect(function(player): This line of code connects an anonymous function to the PlayerAdded event, which is fired whenever a new player joins the game. The anonymous function will be called each time a player joins and will receive the player object as a parameter.

2) local leaderStats = Instance.new("Folder"): This line of code creates a new instance of a Folder object that will hold player-specific leaderstats data.

3) leaderStats.Name = "leaderstats": This line of code sets the name of the newly created folder to "leaderstats." This is a convention often used to store player-specific stats. You must ensure the name is "leaderstats" (all lowercase), as Roblox won't add the player to the leaderboard if any other name variation is used.

4) leaderStats.Parent = player: This line of code sets the leaderStats folder as a child of the player object. This effectively associates the folder with the specific player.

5) local score = Instance.new("IntValue"): This line of code creates a new instance of an IntValue object named score. This IntValue will only accept integers and will store the player's score.

6) score.Name = "Score": This line of code sets the name of the IntValue to "Score." This will be the key to accessing the leaderstats folder's score value.

7) score.Value = 0: This line of code initializes the value of the score to 0 when the player joins the game.

8) score.Parent = leaderStats: This line of code sets the score IntValue object to be a child of the leaderStats folder. This organizes the score value within the player's leaderstats.

Figure 6-3 displays the leaderboard after clicking on two of the "ClickablePart" objects. Upon clicking these objects, they disappear from the game world, and the player's score is incremented by 1.

Figure 6-3. *Roblox built-in leaderboard in the game*

The code in Listing 6-14 is all about setting up the clickDetector.MouseClick event, which, when triggered, executes an anonymous function that gets passed in the player object as its parameter, which is then used to access the score, which is a child of leaderstats, which in turn is a child of the player. Here, the score value is incremented each time a "ClickablePart" object is clicked.

ChildAdded and DescendantAdded Events

In Roblox Lua, the "ChildAdded" and "DescendantAdded" events are essential for handling changes to the hierarchy of objects within a game. They track when new objects are added to a parent object, such as a part added to an object or a UI element added to a screen GUI. Both "ChildAdded" and "DescendantAdded" events help monitor changes to object hierarchies, such as managing in-game items, dynamic UIs, and more. They provide a way to respond to changes in real time and take appropriate actions based on those changes.

The "ChildAdded" event is triggered whenever a new child object is parented to an object whose event you are listening for. This event is explicitly used to listen for a non-nested child getting added to a parent object. On the other hand, the "DescendantAdded" event is a more general event triggered whenever a new descendant object is added to the parent, no matter how deeply nested the descendant object is within the parent hierarchy. Listing 6-16 demonstrates both these events using a simple block part.

Begin by inserting a new block part into the game world using Roblox Studio. Select this newly added block part in the "Explorer" window, and rename it to "Parent_Brick." Click the plus icon beside this item, and add a Script object as a child to the newly created "Parent_Brick" part. Open this script and delete its contents. Now, type the code provided in Listing 6-16 into the script.

Listing 6-16. The ChildAdded and DescendantAdded events

```
local brick = script.Parent
brick.Anchored = true
brick.ChildAdded:Connect(function(child)
     print("A child has been added to the Parent Brick: ", child.Name)
end)
brick.DescendantAdded:Connect(function(descendant)
     print("A descendant has been added to the Parent Brick: ",
     descendant.Name)
end)
for i=1, 2 do
     local brickChild = Instance.new("Part")
     brickChild.Name = "ChildBrick_" .. i
     -- brickChild.Parent = brick      -- (1)
     brickChild.Parent = brick:FindFirstChildWhichIsA("BasePart") or
     brick      -- (2)
end
```

For both events in Listing 6-16, the "ChildAdded" and "DescendantAdded" events would fire twice. This is because the "ChildAdded" event would see both parts being added when the for loop executes as there are no nested children, and each "ChildBrick" would be directly parented to the brick object. On the other hand, the "DescendantAdded" event is looking for every descendant. As a "ChildBrick" is considered a direct descendant, it will also be notified when a "ChildBrick" is added. Ideally, you would want the "ChildAdded" event to fire only once upon a "ChildBrick" being parented to the brick. You would also like the "DescendantAdded" event to fire twice, first when "ChildBrick_1" is parented to the brick and then again upon a new "ChildBrick_2" being parented to the existing "ChildBrick_1." To achieve this, you must ensure that when the for loop instantiates "ChildBrick_2," it is parented to "ChildBrick_1" and not to the brick object. This is possible by commenting statement (1) and using statement (2) instead. In statement (2), "brick:FindFirstChildWhichIsA("BasePart")" is being used to locate a child of the brick object that is of the Class type "BasePart." As we are using only "Part" objects in this code, every "Part" being instantiated will be of type "BasePart." Through the first iteration of the for loop, "ChildBrick_1" is created, and its parent is set to be the brick object as the statement "brick:FindFirstChildWhichIsA("Ba sePart")" will return nil, which evaluates to false and, instead, the second expression of the "or" is evaluated which results in assigning the brick as the parent of "ChildBrick_1." However, through the second iteration of the for loop, "ChildBrick_2" is created, and its parent is set to be "ChildBrick_1" on account of the statement "brick:FindFirstCh ildWhichIsA("BasePart")" evaluating to true. Thus, you now have a nested child (i.e., "ChildBrick_2") as part of the "Parent_Brick" object, as shown in Figure 6-4.

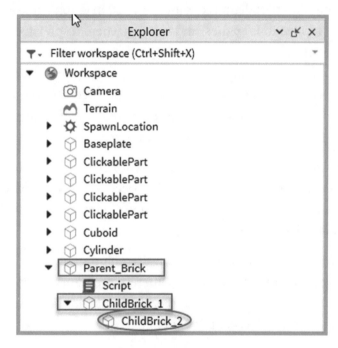

Figure 6-4. *Parenting objects – ChildAdded and DescendantAdded events*

Other Miscellaneous Event

Roblox provides several other events attached to its Services feature, such as UserInputService.InputBegan, UserInputService.InputEnded, RunService.Heartbeat, ProximityPromptService.PromptTriggered, etc., some of which will be discussed in upcoming chapters.

Event-Driven Programming

Event-driven programming is a programming paradigm that revolves around responding to events or occurrences rather than executing code in a linear and predetermined manner. In event-driven programming, the flow of the program is driven by external events, such as user actions, sensor inputs, system notifications, or messages from other parts of the program. This paradigm is commonly used in graphical user interfaces (GUIs), interactive applications, games, and systems where responsiveness and real-time interactions are essential.

In Roblox Lua, event-driven programming involves designing your game's logic and interactions around events. Events are actions or occurrences during gameplay, and event-driven code responds to these events by executing specific functions or actions.

Some of the benefits of Event-Driven Programming:

1) Responsiveness: Event-driven programs are highly responsive because they can react to events as they occur. This is essential for user interfaces and interactive applications (games) where real-time feedback is crucial.

2) Modularity and encapsulation: Event-driven programming encourages modular code design. Different program components can be encapsulated as event handlers, making the codebase more organized and easier to maintain.

3) Loose coupling: Components in an event-driven system are loosely coupled, meaning they interact through events without having direct dependencies on each other. This makes it easier to modify or extend functionality without affecting other code.

4) Scalability: Event-driven systems can be easily expanded by adding new event types and corresponding event handlers. This makes it simpler to introduce new features without rewriting existing code.

5) Debugging: Event-driven programs are often easier to debug since you can focus on specific events and their handlers. This makes it simpler to isolate and troubleshoot issues.

6) Flexibility: Event-driven programming allows you to change the behavior of your program without changing its overall structure. You can modify event handlers or add new ones to introduce new behaviors.

7) Real-time systems: Event-driven programming is crucial for real-time systems where timely responses to external stimuli are essential, such as simulations and games.

In summary, event-driven programming is a powerful paradigm that offers responsiveness, modularity, loose coupling, and scalability. It is particularly effective for applications that require user interaction, real-time updates, and a dynamic and flexible structure.

Some of the key concepts of Event-Driven Programming using Roblox Lua:

1) Events: In Roblox Lua, events are actions or occurrences that can trigger code execution. Events can be user interactions (e.g., button clicks, key presses), game updates (e.g., frame updates), or custom events triggered by scripts. Roblox provides various event classes, such as "UserInputService," "RunService," "RemoteEvent," "RemoteFunction," "BindableEvent," "BindableFunction," etc. that you can use to invoke, listen, and respond to events.

2) Event handlers: Event handlers in Roblox Lua are functions that you define to respond to specific events. These handlers contain the code to execute when a particular event occurs. For example, when a player clicks a button in the game, you might have an event handler that triggers an action, updates the game state, or prints a message.

3) Connecting event handlers: In Roblox Lua, you attach event handlers to events using the :Connect() method.

4) Custom events: Besides built-in events, you can create custom events using "RemoteEvent" and "BindableEvent" classes. These custom events allow communication between different parts of your game, such as between clients and the server. This is especially important for multiplayer games, where events need to be synchronized between players.

So far, within this chapter, you have already explored several of Roblox Lua's built-in events and how to use the :Connect() method. In this section, you will focus on the "BindableEvent," and the "RemoteEvent" will be discussed in the next chapter.

Script vs. LocalScript

Before proceeding, it's essential to understand the difference between a Script and a LocalScript object. Roblox's security model and execution context rules dictate where a LocalScript can run and what services it can access. Placing a LocalScript as a child of a Part may cause unexpected behavior or restrictions, such as the inability to access Roblox's UserInputService. On the other hand, placing LocalScripts in StarterPlayerScripts aligns with the intended design of Roblox, ensuring they have proper access to handle user input.

Note   The UserInputService in Roblox is a service that provides a way to detect and process user input, including keyboard, mouse, touch, and gamepad input. It's essential to creating interactivity within Roblox games, allowing developers to respond to player actions. This UserInputService is only accessible via a LocalScript created within StarterPlayerScripts. The UserInputService is not accessible within a regular Script that is a child of a part or located elsewhere in the server-side context. The UserInputService is specifically designed for use within a LocalScript, as it deals with input on the client's device (such as key presses, mouse movements, touch input, etc.).

A Script object that is a child of a Part is a server-side script, even though it's not explicitly placed within the "ServerScriptService." Scripts like this run on the server and cannot access individual player's input devices. They can't directly receive or respond to player input like key presses or mouse clicks. Suppose you need to handle user input within a part of the game that involves server-side logic. In that case, you will typically need to use a LocalScript to capture the input using UserInputService and then communicate with a server-side Script using mechanisms like "RemoteEvent" or "RemoteFunction." This way, the client-side LocalScript can handle just the user input. This separation of client-side and server-side logic is essential to networked game development in Roblox, allowing for responsive player interactions while maintaining authoritative control over the game's state and behavior. A LocalScript should never be created as a child of a part or within the ServerScriptService as it will result in unpredictable behavior. A LocalScript should be used within StarterPlayerScripts.

Understanding script placement in engines like Roblox is crucial for hobbyist game developers. It helps avoid issues, streamline code design, and achieve desired game mechanics. Always refer to the official Roblox documentation and best practices for accurate and current information.

BindableEvent

A BindableEvent in Roblox is an object that facilitates the creation of custom events, enabling communication between different scripts. It organizes code by allowing functions to remain separate while still interacting with each other. A bindable event can be advantageous in complex games where different systems must communicate. You could use a bindable event to notify the achievement system when a player completes a particular task. A bindable event could fire whenever certain game data changes, triggering a UI update. A bindable event provides a robust and flexible way to handle custom events in Roblox Lua, allowing clear communication between different parts of your code. A bindable event supports clean, modular design, particularly in more complex projects, by enabling functions to be connected and disconnected from events and triggering events at will.

The key components of a BindableEvent are its Event property and the Fire() method. The Event property can be used with the :Connect() method to link a specific function, known as an event handler, to the custom BindableEvent. When the event is triggered using the Fire() method, the connected event handler function will be executed.

Listing 6-17 lists code for a simple BindableEvent that is listened for and called upon from within the same script. A bindable event, once created, needs to be parented, and you could parent the bindable event object under any parent object, like the workspace or a part. However, parenting a bindable event under ReplicatedStorage is a common practice in Roblox game development, especially in complex projects where synchronization and communication between different parts of the game (such as client-side UI and server-side game logic) are required. It provides a standardized way to handle custom events and ensures they are accessible where needed. You will ensure that all bindable events reside within ReplicatedStorage.

Within the "Explorer" window in the Roblox editor, an item exists in
ReplicatedStorage. All your remote events need to be children of this ReplicatedStorage.
Objects such as BindableEvent, RemoteEvent, RemoteFunction, and BindableFunction,
etc., don't need to be created programmatically only. They can be created via the editor,
too. Within the "Explorer" window, hover over the ReplicatedStorage item and click the
plus icon beside it. From the list that shows up, you can search for BindableEvent using
the search object text box, followed by clicking on the BindableEvent item to add it to
ReplicatedStorage. You can then rename this BindableEvent suitably based on the event
it represents.

Note   ReplicatedStorage is a unique service in Roblox that stores objects that
should be visible and accessible from both the server and all clients. It's a shared
container, making it useful for storing assets and data that need to be accessed or
manipulated by multiple parts of a game, whether they're running on the server or
client side.

Begin by creating a new Part within the game world. You could name it "Weapon."
With the "Weapon" part selected in the "Explorer" window, click the plus icon beside
it, add a new Script, and open it within the Roblox editor. Replace the code within this
script with the code provided in Listing 6-17.

Listing 6-17. "BindableEvent" listened for and Invoked within the same script

```
local replStorage = game:GetService("ReplicatedStorage")    -- 1
local shootEvent = Instance.new("BindableEvent")            -- 2
shootEvent.Name = "Shoot"                                   -- 3
shootEvent.Parent = replStorage                             -- 4
-- Event Handler function onShootEvent()
local function onShootEvent(message)                        -- 5
print("'shootEvent' triggered with message : " .. message)
end
shootEvent.Event:Connect(onShootEvent)                      -- 6
-- Invoke the shootEvent
shootEvent:Fire("Hello 'Event' World")                      -- 7
```

1) local replStorage = game:GetService("ReplicatedStorage"): This line of code obtains a reference to the "ReplicatedStorage" service and stores it in a variable named replStorage. "ReplicatedStorage" stores objects that should be visible and accessible by both server and client, facilitating shared data.

2) local shootEvent = Instance.new("BindableEvent"): This line of code creates a new instance of a "BindableEvent," creating a custom "shootEvent" that other scripts can connect to.

3) shootEvent.Name = "Shoot": This line of code sets the name of the custom "BindableEvent" to "Shoot." This helps identify and reference the event in other parts of your code.

4) shootEvent.Parent = replStorage: This line of code parents the "BindableEvent" (shootEvent) under the previously retrieved "ReplicatedStorage," making it accessible to both the server and clients.

5) local function onShootEvent(message) ... end: This line of code defines a local function (event handler) named onShootEvent(), which takes a single parameter message. This event handler function is called once the "shootEvent" is triggered.

6) shootEvent.Event:Connect(onShootEvent): This line of code functions as a listener that listens for the "shootEvent" to be triggered. It connects the previously defined onShootEvent() (event handler) function to the "shootEvent" bindable event's "Event" property. It essentially sets up a connection so that the onShootEvent() function will be called whenever "shootEvent" is fired. This establishes a clear link between the event and the response, allowing for organized and responsive code behavior.

7) shootEvent:Fire("Hello 'Event' World"): This line of code fires the "shootEvent," which in turn triggers the connected onShootEvent() (event handler) function, passing it the string "Hello 'Event' World." This results in the message "shootEvent" triggered with the message: "Hello 'Event' World" to be displayed.

One of the limitations of a BindableEvent and a BindableFunction is that they cannot handle communication between client and server scripts in Roblox. They can be used for synchronous communication within the same context, such as between two LocalScripts on the client or between two regular Scripts on the server. If you need to communicate between the client and server in Roblox, you should use RemoteEvent or RemoteFunction.

RemoteEvent

Let's explore an example that illustrates a typical use of RemoteEvent in event-driven programming. In this scenario, the RemoteEvent is created and fired from one script (client-side), while a separate script(server-side) is set up to listen for this event. The listener script waits for the specific event to be triggered, and once it is, it responds by executing a connected event handler function. This example represents a standard approach to organizing code modularly, where different parts of the system can communicate and react to events without being directly linked.

A BindableEvent won't work for the above scenario as communication between client and server scripts is required. A RemoteEvent, on the other hand, is ideally suited to this situation. A RemoteEvent can be used for asynchronous communication, meaning you can send a message from the client to the server (or vice versa) without expecting an immediate response. A RemoteEvent object can be placed within ReplicatedStorage, which makes it accessible to both client and server scripts.

Listing 6-18. "RemoteEvent" ClientSide code within StarterPlayerScripts

```
--This 'Shoot' script is a LocalScript that is placed within
-- StarterPlayerScripts
local rplStorage = game:GetService("ReplicatedStorage")-- 1
local shootEvent = rplStorage.ShootEvent                 -- 2
-- Event Handler function onShootEvent()
local function onShootEvent(input, gameProcessedEvent) -- 3
if gameProcessedEvent then -- 4 Ignore clicks processed by
                                -- the game itself
    return
end
```

```
if input.UserInputType == Enum.UserInputType.MouseButton1
then                                                     -- 5
print("Weapon fired!") -- Debug message
shootEvent:FireServer("shot")-- 6 Fire the 'RemoteEvent'
                             -- passing in the argument "shot"
end
end
-- Connect the input handling function
game:GetService("UserInputService").InputBegan:Connect(onShootEvent)
                                                         -- 7
```

You should have a "Weapon" part in the game world, should you have tested out Listing 6-17. Delete the script attached to this "Weapon" part. Now, within the "StarterPlayerScripts" folder that is available within the "StarterPlayer" folder, create a new folder called "Weapon." The code in Listing 6-18 will reside in a "Shoot" script within this "Weapon" folder. Create a new "LocalScript" within the "Weapons" folder and rename it to "Shoot." Type in the code provided in Listing 6-18 into this script. Within the Roblox editor "Explorer" window, select the ReplicatedStorage item, and click on the plus icon beside it. Using the search box at the top of the list that shows up, search for RemoteEvent and add it as a child of ReplicatedStorage. Rename this RemoteEvent object to ShootEvent.

1) Retrieves the ReplicatedStorage service, a special storage container where objects can be seen and accessed from both server and client and stores it in the variable rplStorage.

2) Looks for an object named ShootEvent within the ReplicatedStorage and stores it in the variable shootEvent. This object is the RemoteEvent you created within the editor. It is used for communication between the client and server.

3) Defines a function named onShootEvent, which will be connected to the user's input later. It takes two parameters: input, which contains information about the input (like the key or mouse button that was pressed), and gameProcessedEvent, a boolean that indicates whether the game itself has processed the input.

4) Inside the function, this line checks whether the input was already processed by the game itself (e.g., the user pressed a key bound to a built-in game function). If it has been processed, the function returns early without doing anything.

5) Checks if the input was a left mouse button click (MouseButton1). If it was, the code continues executing the code block within this condition, displaying the message "Weapon Fired!."

6) Calls shootEvent:FireServer("shot"), which fires the RemoteEvent named shootEvent, with the string "shot" passed as an argument to the server.

7) Connects the onShootEvent function (event handler) to the InputBegan event of the UserInputService. This means that the onShootEvent function will be called whenever an input begins (e.g., a key is pressed, a mouse button is clicked), passing along information about the input.

Overall, this code sets up a system where a left mouse button click from the client triggers a "shot" event, sending a signal to the server via a RemoteEvent named ShootEvent. This pattern allows for modular and decoupled code design, where different parts of the game can respond to events without knowing where or why they were triggered. It provides a level of abstraction that can make the code clean, maintainable, and scalable.

Listing 6-19. Listener script ShotSound, listening for the "shootEvent" and plays a shot sound

```
-- This 'ShotSound' script is a server-side script that is a
-- child of the weapon object.
-- Find the 'RemoteEvent' that was named 'ShootEvent' that
-- resides in 'ReplicatedStorage.'
local rplStorage = game:GetService("ReplicatedStorage")-- 1
local weapon = script.Parent                            -- 2
local shootEvent = rplStorage.ShootEvent                -- 3
-- Create a sound object to play the shot sound
local sound = Instance.new("Sound")                     -- 4
```

```
sound.SoundId = "rbxassetid://sound_id_here"            -- 5 Replace with
                                                -- your sound asset ID
sound.Parent = weapon --Parent the sound to the weapon
-- Define the function to execute when shootEvent is triggered
local function onShotEvent(player,action)               -- 6
    if action == "shot" then                            -- 7
        print("Playing shot sound")
        sound:Play()                                    -- 8
    end
end
-- Connect the 'RemoteEvent' (shootEvent) to the function
shootEvent.OnServerEvent:Connect(onShotEvent)          -- 9
```

Hover over the Weapon object in the Workspace, click the plus icon beside it, and select Script. Rename this script to "ShotSound." Type in the code provided in Listing 6-19 into this "ShotSound" script. The code in this script only ensures that the weapon emits a shot sound upon the player clicking the left mouse button.

1) Retrieves the ReplicatedStorage service, a shared container that stores objects visible to both the server and clients and stores it in the variable rplStorage.

2) Retrieves the parent object of the script, which is the weapon object in this case, and stores it in the variable weapon.

3) Looks for an object named ShootEvent within the ReplicatedStorage and stores it in the variable shootEvent. This is a RemoteEvent, used to handle communication between the server and clients.

4) Creates a new Sound object, which is used to play audio within the game, and stores it in the variable sound.

5) Sets the SoundId property of the sound object, identifying the specific audio asset to be played. It also sets the Parent property of the sound object to the weapon, making the sound a child of the weapon object and associating the sound with the weapon.

6) Defines a function named onShotEvent, which will be executed when the shootEvent is fired from the client. It takes two parameters: player, which refers to the player that triggered the event, and action, a string describing the action that was triggered.

7) Inside the function, this line checks if the action passed is "shot." If it is, the code block within this condition is executed, displaying a message "Playing shot sound."

8) Plays the sound object created earlier.

9) Connects the onShotEvent function to the OnServerEvent of the shootEvent. This means that the onShotEvent function will be called whenever the RemoteEvent named shootEvent is fired from a client, with the arguments that the client passed.

Overall, this server-side code sets up the logic to play a shot sound whenever the "shot" event is received from a client through the RemoteEvent named "ShootEvent." It also sets up the sound object and connects the event to the corresponding function that handles the logic.

The code in Listings 6-18 and 6-19 contribute to a Weapon system for managing shootable weapons. Along with the "ShotSound" script, you can add scripts to the Weapon object for independent actions like DisplayMuzzleFlash, TakeAmmo, ReloadWeapon, AnimateTrigger, and more.

RemoteFunction

In Roblox, a RemoteFunction is a unique object that acts as a bridge to allow various parts of your game (such as different scripts across the server and client) to communicate by calling a specific function. Unlike a RemoteEvent that allows for one-way communication only, letting you signal that something has happened without expecting a response, a RemoteFunction provides two-way communication, invoking a function and obtaining a return value. Unlike simple event signaling, which is achievable using a RemoteEvent, a RemoteFunction can pass arguments to the function it's invoking and receive a value back from that function. This makes it a two-way communication channel.

A RemoteFunction allows you to invoke functions across different contexts within your game, such as between the server and client. This can be useful if, for example, the client needs to ask the server for some information and wait for a response. For example, you may have a player's character in a game that can pick up items. The server has information about the number of items available. When a player tries to pick up an item, the client can use a RemoteFunction to ask the server if any items are left to pick up. The server checks and then returns a response, letting the client know whether this action is possible. You might want to use a RemoteFunction when an event occurs in your game, and you need to not only notify another part of the game but also receive information back. For example, when a player presses the "R" key to reload a weapon, you might call a RemoteFunction to check if sufficient ammo exists and whether a reload is possible.

Thus, a RemoteFunction acts as a kind of telephone line, allowing two distant parts of your game to converse, ask questions, and receive answers. It helps in creating a responsive and well-structured game.

Create a new LocalScript named ReloadWeapon within the Weapon folder available in StarterPlayerScripts. Type in the code provided as part of Listing 6-20 into this script.

Listing 6-20. "RemoteFunction" being invoked within LocalScript - ReloadWeapon

```
-- This script must be a 'LocalScript,' placed within
-- StarterPlayerScripts since the 'UserInputService' is only
-- accessible via a 'LocalScript' created within
-- StarterPlayerScripts
local uis = game:GetService("UserInputService")        -- 1
local rplStorage = game:GetService("ReplicatedStorage")  -- 2
local reloadFunction = rplStorage:WaitForChild("ReloadFuncti
on")                                                     -- 3
uis.InputBegan:Connect(function(input, isProcessed)      -- 4
if isProcessed then return end                           -- 5
if input.KeyCode == Enum.KeyCode.R then                  -- 6
local result = reloadFunction:InvokeServer() -- 7 Invoke the
                                        -- RemoteFunction
print(result) -- Handle the result if needed, such as updating
            -- the UI
end
end)
```

173

The overall purpose of the code provided in Listing 6-20 is to set up a client-side detection for the "R" key press and then invoke a server-side function when that key is pressed. This code is used to initiate a reload ammo action for a weapon.

1) local uis = game:GetService("UserInputService"): This line of code fetches the UserInputService from the Roblox game, storing it in a local variable uis. It allows you to work with user input, such as keyboard presses or mouse clicks.

2) local rplStorage = game:GetService("ReplicatedStorage"): Here, you're obtaining a reference to the ReplicatedStorage service and storing it in the variable rplStorage. ReplicatedStorage stores objects that should be visible and accessible to client and server scripts.

3) local reloadFunction = rplStorage:WaitForChild("ReloadF unction"): This line of code looks for a child object named "ReloadFunction" inside rplStorage, which is a RemoteFunction that allows the server script and client script to communicate directly. The reference to this function is stored in the variable reloadFunction.

4) uis.InputBegan:Connect(function(input, isProcessed): This line of code sets up an event listener for the InputBegan event available to the UserInputService. This event is fired whenever an input action starts, such as pressing a key. The code within this function will be executed when this event occurs.

5) if isProcessed then return end: This line of code checks if the input has already been processed by the system (e.g., for opening an in-game menu). If it has, the function returns early, and the rest of the code inside the function will not be executed.

6) if input.KeyCode == Enum.KeyCode.R then: This line of code checks if the input's key code equals "R." If the "R" key has been pressed, the code inside this if statement will be executed.

7) local result = reloadFunction:InvokeServer(): This line invokes the RemoteFunction stored in reloadFunction, calling a corresponding function on the server. The result of the server function (if there is any) is stored in the variable result.

Listing 6-21. "RemoteFunction" is being listened for within CanWeaponReload script

```
local rplStorage = game:GetService("ReplicatedStorage")
local weapon = workspace:WaitForChild("Weapon")        -- 1
local currentAmmo = weapon:FindFirstChild("CurrentAmmo")
local maxMagazineCapacity = weapon:FindFirstChild("MaxMagazineCapacity").
Value                                                  -- 2
local reloadFunction = Instance.new("RemoteFunction") -- 3
reloadFunction.Name = "ReloadFunction"
reloadFunction.Parent = rplStorage                     -- 4
function reloadFunction.OnServerInvoke()               -- 5
local ammo = currentAmmo.Value
if ammo < maxMagazineCapacity then
print("Reloading weapon...")
-- Code to handle reloading the weapon (e.g., playing
-- animation, resetting ammo count, etc.)
return "Reloading weapon..."
else
print("Cannot reload, magazine is full.")
return "Cannot reload, magazine is full."
end
end
```

Before being able to run the code provided as part of Listings 6-20 and 6-21, you need to set up the IntValue objects MaxMagazineCapacity and CurrentAmmo. You can manually create and configure the CurrentAmmo and MaxMagazineCapacity objects in Roblox Studio:

1) Select the Weapon object in the "Explorer" window. Click the plus icon beside it, use the search box to find IntValue, and add it as a child of the Weapon object.

2) Rename the new IntValue object to CurrentAmmo.

3) Set the Value property of CurrentAmmo using the "Properties" window to your desired initial ammunition count (e.g., 45).

Follow the same steps to create a MaxMagazineCapacity object of type IntValue. Once the CurrentAmmo and MaxMagazineCapacity objects have been set up and parented to the Weapon object, you can access them via server-side and client-side scripts, as shown in Listing 6-21.

1) This line obtains the Weapon object from the workspace using the WaitForChild() method. This method waits until the child Weapon object is available within the workspace.

2) The script locates a child object named MaxMagazineCapacity within the Weapon object and accesses its Value property. This represents the maximum ammunition capacity of the weapon's magazine.

3) This line of code creates a new RemoteFunction object. Remote functions facilitate communication between the server and client scripts, allowing function calls to be made across these boundaries.

4) The newly created RemoteFunction is set as a child of the ReplicatedStorage object. This makes it accessible to both the server and the client, allowing them to communicate via this remote function.

5) This line of code defines what will happen when the RemoteFunction is invoked from the client. This is the server-side part of the function (event handler code). When reload Function:InvokeServer() is triggered on the client side, it is listened for within this "CanWeaponReload" script via the event handler function defined using 'function reloadFunction. OnServerInvoke()... end.

BindableFunction vs. RemoteFunction

A BindableFunction is like a RemoteFunction, which functions like a bridge between two scripts, where one script invokes the function and the other responds. However, it differs from a RemoteFunction in that it can invoke a function within the same client or the same server. It cannot be used to communicate between the client and server. A

BindableFuction is used for invoking functions within the same context (either client-to-client or server-to-server) and is always synchronous. A RemoteFunction, on the other hand, is used for invoking functions across the client-server boundary. Calls from the client to the server are synchronous, while calls from the server to the client are asynchronous.

When a BindableFunction is invoked, the script will wait for the function to return a value. It is a blocking call, and the script will not continue until a response is received. When a client calls a RemoteFunction on the server using :InvokeServer(), it's a synchronous call, meaning the client will wait for a response. Conversely, when the server calls a RemoteFunction on the client using :InvokeClient(), it's an asynchronous call, meaning the server will not wait for a response. Thus, a RemoteFunction is Synchronous on the Client and Asynchronous on the Server.

In short, you would typically use a BindableFunction when you need to call a function within the same context and want to receive a return value. A RemoteFunction would be used when communicating across the client-server divide.

Summary

In this chapter, you delved into the world of functions and events in Roblox Lua. You learned how functions serve as modular blocks of code, encapsulating specific tasks or operations and improving code organization, readability, and reusability by allowing developers to define a set of instructions that can be executed upon invocation. You learned about function parameters, how to pass an arbitrary number of parameters to a function, and how to return values from a function. You learned how to invoke functions, what anonymous functions are, and how they can be used effectively to create event handlers.

You then went on to learn about Events in Roblox and how Roblox provides a comprehensive set of built-in events that developers can leverage to respond to specific occurrences within a game or experience. You learned how to use these events to enable interaction between players, objects, and the game environment to create dynamic and engaging gameplay. You learned how to use the Touched event, Changed events, MouseClick event, MouseButton1Click event, PlayerAdded event, ChildAdded event, and the DescendantAdded event. You also learned how to create a leaderboard for your game experience. Finally, you were introduced to event-driven programming in Roblox Lua, where you learned to use bindable events, remote events, and remote and bindable functions.

CHAPTER 7

Roblox Services

Roblox Services is pivotal in providing developers with essential functionalities and interfaces. These services are predefined objects offering various features, from user authentication to in-game physics management. Understanding these services is crucial for creating immersive and dynamic games, as they are the building blocks that enable communication between different parts of a game and grant access to core game functionalities. In this chapter, we will delve into an exploration of key Roblox Services, including the Workspace, ReplicatedStorage, Players, UserInputService, TweenService, ProximityPromptService, RunService, SoundService, Lighting service, ContextActionService, TeamsService, TeleportService, and PhysicsService. Each of these services serves a distinct purpose and offers unique capabilities, and together, they form the backbone of Roblox game development.

Roblox Services

In the context of the Roblox game engine, "Services" plays a pivotal role in enhancing the complexity and functionality of games by providing essential tools to handle diverse aspects of gameplay. These services act as libraries, offering a collection of predefined functions, events, and methods that empower developers to create more intricate and engaging experiences. While they are not mandatory components, services are invaluable sets of code that extend the capabilities of scripts. By utilizing the GetService() function to bind them to variables, developers gain access to various functionalities. In essence, services are like pre-built modules that encapsulate specialized features, enabling seamless interaction with multiple elements of a Roblox game. Whether managing player interactions, controlling animations, orchestrating in-game physics, or networking, services are the backbone of the Roblox game engine, offering a structured framework that empowers developers to shape and control every facet of their game experience.

© Christopher Coutinho 2023
C. Coutinho, *Roblox Lua Scripting Essentials*, https://doi.org/10.1007/979-8-8688-0026-9_7

Roblox provides developers with several "Services." Some of the more important ones that are used most frequently in developing game experiences and that will be discussed in this chapter have been listed as follows:

Workspace: This "Service" represents the game world where the game takes place. Developers can use it to create, manipulate, and manage objects like parts, models, and terrain in the game world.

ReplicatedStorage: This "Service" is used for sharing data and objects between the Client and the Server. It's often used to store assets, variables, and other information that needs to be synchronized between the Client and Server sides of the game.

Players: This "Service" allows developers to interact with players currently in the game. It provides methods to manage player-related operations such as retrieving player data, handling player connections and disconnections, and managing player inventories.

UserInputService: This "Service" provides access to player input, such as keyboard and mouse interactions. Developers can use it to capture and respond to player input actions, enabling interactivity in the game.

TweenService: This "Service" creates smooth animations and transitions in the game. It provides methods for creating and managing tweens (animated transitions) for various properties of objects.

ProximityPromptService: This "Service" allows developers to create and manage prompts that respond to a player's proximity to particular in-game objects. These prompts inform players about interactive elements within the game environment, such as objects they can interact with, actions they can take, or places they can visit. The ProximityPromptService simplifies the process of adding interactive prompts and handling player input in a user-friendly manner.

RunService: This "Service" allows you to execute code at specific points during the game's frame update cycle, essential for implementing game logic, animations, physics simulations, and other time-dependent behaviors in your Roblox games. It offers different "heartbeat" events that fire at specific intervals during each frame update. Using the RunService, you can attach functions (callbacks) to these heartbeat events. These functions will then be executed when the corresponding heartbeat event occurs.

SoundService: This "Service" provides functionality for playing and managing audio in your game. You can play background music, sound effects, and other audio assets.

Lighting: This "Service" controls the lighting and ambiance of the game world, allowing you to set the scene's lighting conditions and effects.

ContextActionService: This "Service" enables you to create custom user input actions and bind them to specific input events.

TeamsService: This "Service" allows you to add teams to your games and then assign players to a team. Once players are assigned to teams, you can design gameplay mechanics that implement team-specific scoring systems or restrict interactions between players on different teams. This "Service" can be used to balance teams by ensuring an equal distribution of players based on skill level or other criteria, allowing for fair and competitive gameplay experiences.

TeleportService: This "Service" enables developers to facilitate seamless player teleportation between different game instances or places within the Roblox platform. It provides a standardized and secure way to transition players from one game environment to another, maintaining their data and ensuring a smooth user experience.

PhysicsService: This "Service" allows developers to customize and control various aspects of the physics simulation within their games. It provides a way to modify how physics interactions behave, apply forces and constraints, and create unique gameplay mechanics that go beyond the default physics behavior provided by the engine.

To access a service in Roblox Lua, you use the game:GetService() method, followed by the name of the service you want to access. This method returns an instance of the requested service, allowing you to interact with its properties, methods, and events. Figure 7-1 displays a few examples of accessing different Roblox Services.

```
local workspaceService = game:GetService("Workspace")
local playersService = game:GetService("Players")
local lightingService = game:GetService("Lighting")
```

Figure 7-1. *Accessing different Roblox Services*

Workspace Service

The Workspace is considered a service in Roblox. It allows developers to create, manipulate, and manage objects such as parts, models, and terrain within the game world. You can access the Workspace service using the GetService() method of the all-encompassing "game" object. The "game" object is the root object of your game experience that provides access to various services and properties that pertain to the entire game instance. It is the entry point for interacting with the Roblox game environment, allowing developers to access game-wide information, manage services, and control game behavior. The game object acts as a bridge between your script and the broader game world. Listing 7-1 demonstrates different ways to access the Workspace Service.

Listing 7-1. Accessing the Workspace Service

```
local workspaceService = game:GetService("Workspace")
local wSpace = game.Workspace
workspace.Name = "MyWorkspace"
```

As the Workspace service is the most fundamental and essential component, Roblox has provided us a shortcut to accessing this service by simply using the "workspace" keyword, which you have been using so far. The Workspace service provides access to all objects within the Workspace and all properties, methods, events, and functions.

As a developer, you can manipulate properties of objects within the Workspace, such as their positions, sizes, colors, and more, to shape the gameplay experience. The Workspace service acts as the canvas on which you build your game environments, enabling you to create dynamic and interactive worlds for players to explore and enjoy.

ReplicatedStorage Service

The ReplicatedStorage service in Roblox acts as a shared container, making objects accessible to both the Server and all client devices in a multiplayer game. It is essential to synchronize data, such as models, sounds, events, etc., between different player computers and the Server. By ensuring that everyone has consistent information about the game's state, ReplicatedStorage facilitates a cohesive gaming experience.

Let's consider a simple example where we want to sync a message to all players in the game. This can be achieved using ReplicatedStorage with a RemoteEvent (remote events were discussed in Chapter 6).

Begin by creating a RemoteEvent object within ReplicatedStorage using the Roblox editor. Select the item ReplicatedStorage within the "Explorer" window, click the plus icon beside it, search for RemoteEvent, and add it to ReplicatedStorage. Rename this RemoteEvent to SyncMessage.

Create a LocalScript within StarterPlayerScripts for the client-side script, and rename it to MessageFromServer. Type in the code provided as part of Listing 7-2 into this script.

Listing 7-2. Client-side script that displays a message from the Server

```
local rplStorage = game:GetService("ReplicatedStorage") -- 1
local messageRemoteEvent = rplStorage.SyncMessage        -- 2
print("client-side Script")
local function onMessageReceived(message)
    print(message) -- Output will be: "Hello, players!"
end

                                                         -- 3
messageRemoteEvent.OnClientEvent:Connect(onMessageReceived)
```

1) This line of code retrieves the ReplicatedStorage service and stores it in a local variable named rplStorage. ReplicatedStorage is a special service in Roblox used for storing objects that need to be accessible from both the Server and clients.

2) This line of code gets a child of ReplicatedStorage named SyncMessage (a RemoteEvent) and stores it in the local variable messageRemoteEvent. SyncMessage is a RemoteEvent object used to facilitate communication between the Server and clients.

3) This line of code connects the function onMessageReceived to the RemoteEvent's OnClientEvent. When the RemoteEvent is fired from the Server, the connected function (onMessageReceived()) will be called, and the message passed by the Server will be displayed.

Create a new Part within the game world, and rename it to Server. Add a Script as a child of this Server part. Type in the code provided as part of Listing 7-3 into this script.

Listing 7-3. Server-side script that sends a message to the Client

```
local rplStorage = game:GetService("ReplicatedStorage")
local messageRemoteEvent = rplStorage.SyncMessage     -- 1
print("server-side Script")
local function sendMessageToClients(message)
```

```
    messageRemoteEvent:FireAllClients(message)          -- 2
end
wait(5)
sendMessageToClients("Hello, players!")                 -- 3
```

1) This line of code assigns the SyncMessage (RemoteEvent) reference within ReplicatedStorage to the local variable messageRemoteEvent.

2) Within the function sendMessageToClients(), this line of code invokes the :FireAllClients() method on the messageRemoteEvent object. This will trigger the associated RemoteEvent on all connected clients, sending the message argument to them. Any client-side scripts connected to this RemoteEvent will respond to it, receiving the message as an argument.

3) In this line of code, the previously defined function sendMessageToClients()is invoked, passing in the string "Hello, players!" as the argument. As a result, the messageRemoteEvent: FireAllClients(message) line inside the function will be executed, sending the "Hello, players!" message to all connected clients via the RemoteEvent.

These lines of code create a server-side script that waits for five seconds and then sends a message to all clients using a RemoteEvent. Any client-side scripts (Listing 7-2) listening to this event will be able to receive and handle the message.

Players Service

In Roblox, the Player's service is an essential component that provides access to various aspects of players within a game, such as their characters, user information, and other player-specific attributes. You can obtain information about players, such as their usernames and user IDs. It offers functions to monitor when players join or leave the game. You can also remove a player from the game, get a list of all players, teleport a player to another place within the same game, etc. Through Player's service, you can create personalized experiences, like welcoming a player by their username or adjusting game behavior according to their preferences. Listing 7-4 demonstrates how you can use the Players service in Roblox to create a welcome message displayed to the player when they join the game.

Listing 7-4. Welcome message displayed to the player on joining the game

```
local players = game:GetService("Players")
local function onPlayerJoin(player)
    print("Welcome, " .. player.Name .. "!")
wait(5)
player:Kick("You have been Red Carded in 5 seconds.")
end
players.PlayerAdded:Connect(onPlayerJoin)
```

Begin by creating a Script within the ServerScriptService. Rename it to PlayerWelcomeMessage. Type in the code provided in Listing 7-4 into this script. In Listing 7-4, we first obtain the Players service using game:GetService("Players"). Then, we define a function onPlayerJoin, which takes a player object as a parameter and displays a welcome message using the player's name. After five seconds of being in the game world, the player receives a red card and is kicked out. Finally, we connect this function to the PlayerAdded event using Players.PlayerAdded:Connect(onPlayerJoin).

UserInputService

In Roblox, the UserInputService is an essential service that handles user inputs such as keyboard presses, mouse clicks, touchscreen inputs, and gamepad button presses. This service is vital for designing intuitive controls and player interactions within Roblox games. It can be used to check for a particular key press, mouse movement, touch input, etc., and to associate specific actions with certain inputs, such as jumping when a key is pressed or reloading a weapon upon the "R" key on the keyboard being pressed. Using this service, you can design specialized controls for your games. This UserInputService should be used on the client side, typically within a LocalScript. This ensures that the input is detected and processed on the player's machine, allowing for real-time responsiveness and better control. Placing this code on the server side would introduce latency and may lead to inconsistent behavior across different clients.

This service provides you with several interesting methods, events, and properties as listed as follows:

1) IsMouseButtonPressed(mouseButton): This method checks if a specific mouse button is pressed.

2) IsGamepadButtonDown(gamepadNum, button): This method checks if a specific button on the chosen gamepad is currently down.

3) InputBegan: This event is triggered when an input begins (e.g., a key is pressed, mouse button is clicked). This is very useful for detecting the start of an input action. You have seen this in action by detecting a key press and a mouse button click in Chapter 6.

4) InputEnded: This event is triggered when an input ends (e.g., a key and mouse button are released) and is used to detect the conclusion of an input action.

5) InputChanged: This event is triggered when an input changes (e.g., mouse movement). Handy for tracking changes in input, like continuous mouse movement.

6) TouchTap: This event is fired when a tap is registered on a touch-enabled device, useful for mobile and tablet interactions. Roblox also provides other touch events, such as TouchPan, TouchEnded, TouchPinch, and TouchMoved.

7) MouseEnabled: A read-only boolean property that indicates whether the user's device has a mouse.

8) TouchEnabled: A read-only boolean property that indicates whether the user's device supports touch input.

9) GamepadEnabled: A read-only boolean property that indicates whether the user's device supports gamepad input.

10) KeyboardEnabled: A read-only boolean property that indicates whether the user's device supports keyboard input.

11) MouseBehavior: A property that sets the mouse behavior, such as locking the cursor to the center of the screen in a first-person shooter.

12) MouseDeltaSensitivity: A property that can be used to slow down the mouse.

Listing 7-5. Check to see if a game pad is connected

```
local UserInputService = game:GetService("UserInputService")
-- Function to check for connected gamepad and print its type
local function checkGamepad()
local gamepadTypes = UserInputService:GetConnectedGamepads()
    if #gamepadTypes > 0 then
        for _, gamepad in gamepadTypes do
            print("Gamepad connected:", gamepad)
            -- For more details, you can access the gamepad enum
            if gamepad == Enum.UserInputType.Gamepad1 then
                print("This is the first gamepad connected")
            end
        end
    else
        print("No gamepad connected")
    end
end
-- Call the function to check for the gamepad
checkGamepad()
```

In Listing 7-5, the UserInputService:GetConnectedGamepads() method is called to get a table of connected gamepads. The method returns a table with the gamepad enums for each connected gamepad. If the table is not empty, the code iterates through it and prints the type of each connected gamepad. This approach enables you to detect the presence of a gamepad and identify its type, thereby allowing you to tailor the controls and gameplay experience to suit the specific input device. As you work on your game development projects, this can help you create a more versatile and responsive user experience for players using various types of gamepads.

Listing 7-6. Check if Button A on an Xbox controller was pressed

```
local UserInputService = game:GetService("UserInputService")
local function onInputBegan(input, isProcessed)
if isProcessed then return end -- If input is already being
                               -- processed, then exit
-- Check if the input is from the gamepad and, specifically, the
-- "A" button
if input.UserInputType == Enum.UserInputType.Gamepad1 and input.KeyCode ==
Enum.KeyCode.ButtonA then
        print("A button on the Xbox gamepad was pressed")
    end
end
UserInputService.InputBegan:Connect(onInputBegan)
```

In Listing 7-6, the onInputBegan function is connected to the InputBegan event, which fires when an input starts (e.g., a button is pressed). The input is checked inside the onInputBegan() function to see if it is from Enum.UserInputType.Gamepad1, which refers to the first connected gamepad, specifically the "A" button. When the "A" button is pressed, a message is displayed. This code should be placed in a LocalScript within StarterPlayerScripts, as the UserInputService should be used on the client side. Utilizing this code can create specific controls for Xbox gamepad users, enhancing their gaming experience and providing optimized interaction that caters to their specific device.

Tween Service

The TweenService is a service used for smoothly transitioning properties of objects over time. It's commonly used to create animations, such as moving GUI elements or parts, changing their size, rotation, transparency, or other properties, allowing for a polished and fluid user experience. It enables a smooth transition between the current value of a property and the target value over a specified duration. You can specify different easing styles and directions to control how the animation behaves, making it easier to create complex animation effects. Since the TweenService is a built-in Roblox feature, it's generally more efficient than manually coding an animation loop.

Let's see the TweenService in action by smoothly rotating a door from a closed to an open position. Note, as this is a Roblox Lua scripting book, this example doesn't set up a true-to-life door using a door hinge and frame. Its sole purpose is to demonstrate the TweenService in action. Begin by setting up the door manually in Roblox Studio. You'll need to adjust its pivot offset to the left corner to have the door rotate around the left corner. Follow the following steps listed to setup a door in your game world:

1) Within the HOME tab, click on Part to insert a part into the Workspace. This part will serve as the door. Rename the part to Door. Should you want to, you can change its BrickColor property.

2) Select the Door object, and within the Properties window, adjust its Transform – Size property as follows: X = 2; Y = 5; Z = 0.2.

3) With the Door object still selected, locate its PivotOffset - Position property within the Properties window and set its Vector3 values as follows: X = 1; Y = 1; Z = 0. This setting ensures that the pivot point is set up at the left edge of the door at its center. By setting the door's pivot point in the editor to the left edge and defining the rotation in the tween goal, within a script, the door rotates around this left corner, simulating a typical door-opening effect.

Listing 7-7. Using the TweenService to rotate a door

```
local TweenService = game:GetService("TweenService")
local door = script.Parent
local goal = {} -- 1 the door properties to change
-- 2 rotating door 60 degrees on the Y axis
goal.Orientation = door.Orientation + Vector3.new(0, 60, 0)
local tweenInfo = TweenInfo.new(                          -- 3
    2,                     -- 4 duration of the tween (in seconds)
    Enum.EasingStyle.Linear,                       -- 5 easing style
    Enum.EasingDirection.Out                       -- 6 easing
direction
)
local tween = TweenService:Create(door, tweenInfo, goal)  -- 7
tween:Play()                                              -- 8
```

Typically, you would place the TweenService code in a LocalScript if it's handling client-side animations, such as GUI elements. For world objects like doors that all players must see, you must use a Script on the server side. Ensuring that the code is placed correctly is essential to achieve the desired effect and performance, as running client-side operations on the Server or vice versa can lead to issues. For the Door script here, you will create a new script that is a child of the Door object (server-side script). Type in the code provided as part of Listing 7-7 into the Door Script you created as a child of the door object.

1) This line of code initializes an empty table that will be used to store the properties of the door that you want to change. This table will later be populated with the desired target values for the tween to utilize.

2) This line of code sets the target orientation for the door. It takes the current orientation of the door and adds 60 degrees to the Y-axis, meaning the door will rotate 60 degrees around the vertical axis. This is the property that the TweenService will animate.

3) This line of code creates a new TweenInfo object, which describes the tween's behavior, such as its duration, easing style, and direction. The parameters within the parentheses define these characteristics.

4) This is the duration of the tween, specified in seconds. The tween will take two seconds to rotate the door by 60 degrees.

5) This defines the easing style of the tween as Linear. The property changes constantly in Linear easing, resulting in a smooth and uniform transition.

6) This sets the easing direction to Out, which means that the tween will start slowly and then accelerate toward the end. Since the easing style is Linear, the easing direction has no effect; the transition will be uniform regardless.

7) This line of code creates the tween using the TweenService. The method takes three arguments: the object being tweened (in this case, the door), the TweenInfo object (which describes how the tween should behave), and the goal table (which contains the target properties for the tween). This line of code doesn't start the animation but prepares it for playback.

8) Lastly, this line of code starts the tween, linearly causing the door to rotate 60 degrees around the Y-axis over two seconds, simulating a typical door-opening effect.

This script sets up and plays a tween that rotates the door 60 degrees around its vertical Y-axis, using a linear easing style, over two seconds.

ProximityPrompt Service

The ProximityPrompt service creates an interactive experience between players and in-game objects or NPCs (non-player characters). When a player approaches within a specific distance of an object or NPC with a ProximityPrompt attached, a prompt appears on the screen, telling the player what action they can take.

The ProximityPrompt service is a feature that simplifies the creation of prompts that appear to players when they approach an object within a specified range. It signals interactive objects, triggers events, or initiates conversations within a game. It aligns well with various game genres, whether it's a role-playing game where a ProximityPrompt can initiate conversations with NPCs or an action game that signals interactive objects like levers, doors, or items. It enhances the player's immersion by providing intuitive visual cues and effectively enriches the in-game experience.

The code related to a ProximityPrompt should typically be hosted in a server-side script. This ensures that the Server controls the interaction and can be appropriately validated, preventing issues such as cheating or inconsistencies between players. However, suppose the ProximityPrompt requires a response from the player where the UserInputService needs to be utilized. In that case, any code that needs to detect input (e.g., a key press) after the ProximityPrompt is triggered must be a client-side script located within StarterPlayerScripts.

Let's assume you are creating an adventure game where the player needs to collect various items to proceed to the next level. You could use a ProximityPrompt to highlight a chest containing a key as one of the items the player needs to collect. This PromximityPrompt would prompt you with a message stating that you must press the "O" key to open the chest and collect the key. To set this up, you first need to add a ProximityPrompt object as a child of the chest part within Roblox Studio (you could achieve this using code, too). You would then need to set various properties like ActionText (e.g., "Press 'O' to Open"), ObjectText (e.g., "Chest"), MaxActivationDistance (e.g., 5 for five studs away), and KeyboardKeyCode to utilize the "O" key. You extend the

script provided as part of Listing 7-8 to define what happens when the player engages
with the prompt, such as opening the chest and adding the key to the player's inventory.
This would be a server-side script. Let's implement this script. We will use a simple
Wedge part to represent our chest in the world. Begin by creating a new Wedge part
within Roblox studio, and attach a Script to it. This Script is a server-side script that
is a child of the Wedge part. Rename this Wedge part to Chest. Now, type in the code
provided as part of Listing 7-8 into this script.

Listing 7-8. Setting up a proximity prompt

```
local chest = script.Parent
local proximityPrompt = Instance.new("ProximityPrompt") -- 1
proximityPrompt.ActionText = "Open Key Chest"            -- 2
proximityPrompt.ObjectText = "Key Chest"                 -- 3
proximityPrompt.MaxActivationDistance = 7                -- 4
proximityPrompt.Parent = chest
proximityPrompt.KeyboardKeyCode = Enum.KeyCode.O         -- 5
proximityPrompt.Triggered:Connect(function(player)       -- 6
    print(player.Name .. " Opened the Chest!")
-- Code to open the chest and add the key to the player's
-- inventory here
end)
```

1) This line of code creates a new instance of the ProximityPrompt
   class. A ProximityPrompt is an object used in Roblox to prompt
   players to interact with a nearby object, and here, a new instance
   is being created and assigned to the proximityPrompt variable.

2) This line of code sets the ActionText property of the proximity
   prompt to "Open Key Chest." This text will be displayed as an
   instruction to the player, along with information on the key that
   must be pressed to interact with the prompt.

3) This line sets the ObjectText property of the proximity prompt
   to "Key Chest." This text serves as a description or name for the
   object the player can interact with (in our case, the key chest).

4) This line sets the MaxActivationDistance property of the proximity prompt to 7. This determines the maximum distance, in studs, that the player must be from the object for the prompt to be displayed.

5) This line sets the KeyboardKeyCode property of the proximity prompt to the "O" key. This means the player must press the "O" key on their keyboard to interact with the proximity prompt.

6) This line of code connects an anonymous function to the Triggered event of the proximity prompt. This event is fired when the player successfully interacts with the prompt (in this case, by pressing the "O" key when within the activation distance). The connected function will be executed, and the data on the player who triggered the event is passed as the parameter to this anonymous function. Inside the function, you can add code to handle what happens when the player interacts with the chest, such as opening the chest, adding a key to the player's inventory, etc.

RunService

In Roblox, the RunService is an instrumental service in creating game loops, managing rendering, and handling client-server interactions. The commonly used events are the Heartbeat event, which fires as quickly as the engine can render frames, and the RenderStepped event, which fires immediately before the frame renders. Both events are often used for game processes that must be updated as often as possible. You can use RunService to create main game loops that update essential aspects of your game, such as game physics, animations, or custom logic.

If you're dealing with player-specific actions, such as HUD updates or client-side physics, the RunService code should be placed in LocalScripts. On the other hand, if you're handling gameplay mechanics that need to be consistent across all players, like spawning enemies or handling game rounds, it should be placed in a server-side script.

For example, you have a player's health bar that needs to be constantly updated. Whenever players run into an obstacle part, their health should be decreased by ten, and the health bar displayed over their heads should be updated to reflect the change in health. This health bar needs to be made available to all players within the game; hence, it must be contained within a server-side script placed in ServerScriptService. Begin by creating a Script within ServerScriptService, and rename it to PlayerHealthBarGUI. Type in the code provided in Listing 7-9 into this script.

Listing 7-9. Using the RunService Heartbeat event within a server-side script

```
local runService = game:GetService("RunService")          -- 1
local humanoid
local head
local healthBar
local billboardGui
local function updateHealth()
    healthBar.Size = UDim2.new(humanoid.Health /
    humanoid.MaxHealth, 0, 1, 0)                           -- 2
end
local function createHealthBar(character)                  -- 3
humanoid = character:FindFirstChildWhichIsA("Humanoid")   -- 4
head = character:FindFirstChild("Head")                   -- 5
if humanoid and head then                                 -- 6
billboardGui = Instance.new("BillboardGui")               -- 7
billboardGui.Adornee = head                               -- 8
billboardGui.Size = UDim2.new(0, 100, 0, 25)              -- 9
billboardGui.StudsOffset = Vector3.new(0, 4, 0)           -- 10
healthBar = Instance.new("Frame")                         -- 11
healthBar.Size = UDim2.new(humanoid.Health / humanoid.MaxHealth, 0, 1, 0)
                                                          -- 12
healthBar.BackgroundColor3 = Color3.new(0, 1, 0)          -- 13
healthBar.Parent = billboardGui                           -- 14
billboardGui.Parent = character                           -- 15
-- Update the health bar with every frame rendered
runService.Heartbeat:Connect(updateHealth)                -- 16
end
end
game.Players.PlayerAdded:Connect(function(player)          -- 17
-- When a new player joins, we want to create the health bar
```

```
-- for their character if it's already present
    if player.Character then                          -- 18
        createHealthBar(player.Character)
    end
end)
game.Players.PlayerAdded:Connect(function(player)
-- We also want to create a health bar for any future
-- characters this player might have (e.g., after respawning)
player.CharacterAdded:Connect(createHealthBar)        -- 19
end)
```

1) This line of code gets a reference to Roblox's RunService, allowing the script to connect to rendering events, such as the Heartbeat event used later.

2) Inside the updateHealth() function, this line calculates the new size of the health bar based on the player's current health and updates the health bar accordingly.

3) Defines the createHealthBar() function that sets up the health bar for a given character.

4) Finds the Humanoid object within the character (passed into the createHealthBar() function), which contains information about the character's health.

5) Finds the Head part within the character, which will be used as the adornee for the billboardGui, making it follow the character's head.

6) Check if both the humanoid and the head were found. The function will exit without creating the health bar if either is missing.

7) Creates a new BillboardGui object, displaying the health bar above the character's head.

8) Sets the Adornee property of the billboardGui to the character's head, causing it to follow the head's position.

9) Sets the size of the billboardGui.

10) Adjusts the offset of the billboardGui in studs, moving it four studs above the character's head.

11) Creates a new Frame object, which will be used as the health bar itself.

12) Sets the initial size of the health bar based on the character's current health.

13) Sets the background color of the health bar to green.

14) Sets the parent of the health bar to the billboardGui, making it a child of the billboardGui, causing it to be displayed.

15) Sets the parent of the billboardGui to the character, adding it to the game.

16) Connects the updateHealth function to the Heartbeat event, causing it to be called every time a frame is rendered. This allows the health bar to update smoothly as the character's health changes. The frequency of the Heartbeat event (and thus the rendering of a frame) depends on the game's frame rate. In most cases, the target frame rate for Roblox games is 60 frames per second (FPS), which means the Heartbeat event would be fired 60 times per second. However, this can vary depending on the player's device's performance capabilities, the game's complexity, and other factors. If the game runs at the target frame rate of 60 FPS, the Heartbeat event would be called approximately every 1/60 seconds or roughly every 16.67 milliseconds. If the frame rate drops, the time between Heartbeat events would increase accordingly, and if the frame rate increases (on devices that support higher frame rates), the time between Heartbeat events would decrease.

17) Connects an anonymous function to the PlayerAdded event, which fires when a player joins the game. It is passed in the data of the player.

18) Check if the player's character is already present when they join the game, and if so, call the createHealthBar() function to create the health bar for the character.

19) Here, we connect the createHealthBar() function to the CharacterAdded event for each player, ensuring that the health bar will be created for any future characters the player might have (e.g., after respawning).

Now, we need to create an obstacle object with which the player can collide. Every player's collision with this obstacle object will result in the player losing some health, and the health bar that has been set up reflects this. Begin by creating a new part within the game world. Rename it to Obstacle. Create a script as its child, and type in the code provided in Listing 7-10 into this script.

Listing 7-10. Obstacle object that causes damage to the player

```
local part = script.Parent -- Part the script is attached to
local damageAmount = 10                          -- The amount of
health to decrement
local debounceTime = 3                           -- 1 The amount
of time (in seconds)
        -- that must pass before the part can be damaged again
local playersDebounced = {}                      -- 2 A table to
track which
               -- players are currently in a debounce period
local function onTouched(hit)                     -- 3
    local character = hit.Parent                  -- 4
local player = game.Players:GetPlayerFromCharacter(character)
                                                  -- 5
local humanoid = character:FindFirstChildWhichIsA("Humanoid")
                                                  -- 6
if not player or not humanoid then
    return                                        -- 7 Exit if no
player or humanoid
end
-- Check if the player is in the debounce table and has a
```

```
-- valid debounce time
if playersDebounced[player.UserId] and tick() - playersDebounced[player.
UserId] < debounceTime then                                    -- 8
    return
end
humanoid.Health = humanoid.Health - damageAmount              -- 9
playersDebounced[player.UserId] = tick()                      -- 10 Store the
                    -- current time in the debounce table
end
part.Touched:Connect(onTouched)                               -- 11
```

1) This line of code sets the time (in seconds) that must pass before
    the part can cause damage again. This is used to prevent rapid
    repeated damage if a player continues to touch the part.

2) This line of code initializes a table to track which players are
    currently in a debounce period. It will store the time when each
    player last touched the part "debounce" refers to a programming
    technique to ensure that an event doesn't fire too frequently
    within a short time. In this specific case, the debounce is used to
    prevent a player's health from being continuously reduced if the
    player is touching the damaging part.

3) This line of code defines a function called onTouched that will be
    called whenever something touches the part. The hit parameter
    will contain information about the object that touched the part.

4) This line of code retrieves the parent of the hit object, which is
    usually the character model if a player's avatar touches the part.

5) This line of code retrieves the player object corresponding to the
    character that touched the part.

6) This line of code attempts to find a Humanoid object within the
    character. The Humanoid object contains information about the
    avatar's health.

7) This line of code checks whether the touching object is a player
    character with a Humanoid object. If not, it exits the function.

8) The playersDebounced table keeps track of the last time each player touched the part. When a player touches the part, the code checks whether the player is in the playersDebounced table and whether the current time minus the stored time is less than the debounceTime (three seconds in this case). If the time that has passed since the last touch is less than the debounceTime, the function returns, and the player's health is not reduced. This ensures that the player must wait for at least debounceTime seconds before touching the part again to have their health reduced. If the time that has passed since the last touch is greater than or equal to the debounceTime, the player's health is reduced, and the current time is stored in the playersDebounced table for that player.

9) This line of code reduces the player's health by the damage amount.

10) This line of code stores the current time in the debounce table for the player who touched the part. This is used to track when the player last touched the part.

11) This line of code connects the onTouched function to the part's Touched event so that the function will be invoked whenever something touches the part.

SoundService

The SoundService in Roblox is a service that handles the overall control of sounds and music within a game. The SoundService controls sound properties and behavior across the entire game, allowing the developer to create immersive auditory experiences for players. This can include background music, sound effects, voice overs, and other audio cues. It will enable you to set properties like volume, pitch, and other global sound settings. Additionally, you can create 3D sound effects that change based on the player's location within the game environment. If the sound needs to be controlled across all players in a game, then the code should be hosted on the server side within a Script. Background music intended to be the same for all players in a game would typically be controlled by a server-side script in Roblox. Using a server-side script ensures that the background music is synchronized and consistent across all clients. If the sound is specific to a single player (e.g., adjusting the volume based on proximity to an object), it should be hosted on the client side within a LocalScript.

Listing 7-11 provides an example of how you might play background music using a server-side script.

Listing 7-11. Playing background music using a server-side script

```
local soundService = game:GetService("SoundService")
local backgroundMusic = Instance.new("Sound")
backgroundMusic.SoundId = "rbxassetid://your_music_id_here"
backgroundMusic.Looped = true
backgroundMusic.Volume = 0.5
backgroundMusic.Parent = soundService
backgroundMusic:Play()
```

Within ServerScriptService, create a new Script and rename it to BackgroundMusic. Type in the code provided in Listing 7-11 into this script. Placing this script in the ServerScriptService will run on the Server and control the background music for all players. The Looped property is set to true, so the music will continue to play in a loop so long as players are in the game. It's worth noting that even though the Server controls the music, individual players can still have client-side control over certain aspects like volume (e.g., if you want to allow players to adjust the music volume in their settings).

Using server-side scripts for background music ensures a consistent experience across all players, which can be particularly important in creating a cohesive atmosphere or mood within the game.

Let's look at another example in a game where a player needs to find hidden treasures. When the player gets closer to the treasure, you can use SoundService to increase the volume of a treasure humming sound gradually. This audible cue would help guide the player to the hidden treasure's location. As the sound here would depend on the individual player's position relative to the treasure, we use a LocalScript placed within StarterPlayerScripts. Listing 7-12 demonstrates this. Begin by creating a new LocalScript within StarterPlayerScripts and rename it to HummingTreasure. Type in the code provided in Listing 7-12 into this script.

Listing 7-12. Playing a sound using a client-side LocalScript

```
local SoundService = game:GetService("SoundService")
local player = game.Players.LocalPlayer
local treasure = workspace:WaitForChild("Treasure")
local sound = Instance.new("Sound")
sound.SoundId = "rbxassetid:// your_sound_id_here"
sound.Parent = player.PlayerGui
local function updateSound()
    local character = player.Character                      -- 2
-- 3 Ensure the character and its PrimaryPart are valid
if character and character.PrimaryPart then
local distance = (character.PrimaryPart.Position - treasure.Position).
Magnitude                                                   -- 4
-- 5 assuming the sound gets completely quiet when the player
-- is 100 studs away
local volume = math.clamp(1 - distance / 100, 0, 1)
        sound.Volume = volume                               -- 6
        sound:Play()                                        -- 7
end
end
game:GetService("RunService").Heartbeat:Connect(updateSound)  -- 1
```

1) This line of code connects the updateSound( ) function to the Heartbeat event of RunService. Heartbeat is an event that fires approximately 60 times per second, so the connected function will repeatedly run at this rate. This allows the code to continually update the sound based on the player's proximity to the treasure.

2) This line of code gets the Character object of the player, which contains all the parts associated with that player's avatar (such as head, arms, legs, etc.). This is used to determine the player's location within the game world.

3) This line of code ensures that the character and its PrimaryPart are valid before proceeding. The PrimaryPart is a specific part within the character model designated as the main part (often the HumanoidRootPart). This validation is essential to prevent errors if the character or the PrimaryPart is not yet loaded or accessible.

4) This line of code computes the distance between the player's PrimaryPart and the treasure using the Magnitude property. This provides the straight-line distance between these two points in 3D space and is used to modify the sound volume.

5) This code line computes the sound volume based on the distance calculated in the previous step. The math.clamp() function ensures the value stays within the specified range (0 to 1). In this case, the volume is set to 1 when the distance is 0, and it decreases linearly until the player is 100 studs away, at which point it becomes 0.

6) This line of code sets the Volume property of the sound object to the value calculated in the previous step. This controls how loud the sound will be when played.

7) This line of code triggers the sound to be played. If the sound is already playing, this command will have no effect, so it's safe to call it repeatedly.

Here, we have set up a sound object that continuously adjusts its volume based on the distance between the player's character and the treasure object. (Ensure you create a Part named Treasure in the game world). It connects a function to the Heartbeat event, which runs every frame to provide smooth, real-time adjustments to the sound. This pattern is typical for creating dynamic, responsive sound in a Roblox game.

Lighting Service

The Lighting service in Roblox is vital for creating an immersive game environment. It controls lighting, shadows, atmosphere, and visual effects, influencing the scene's mood and aesthetics. This service allows adjustments to ambient lighting, the direction and intensity of sunlight for realistic shadows and weather effects, the creation of fog for depth, and the addition of bloom or blur for aesthetic appeal. Additionally, it enables the customization of various light sources like spotlights and point lights to illuminate specific areas. The Lighting service in Roblox provides a versatile set of features that can enhance game visuals and immersion. By creatively experimenting with these settings, developers can align visual elements with game themes, resulting in a cohesive and engaging experience.

The code for Roblox's Lighting service can be hosted in a server-side Script or a LocalScript, depending on the desired effect required. For consistent lighting effects among all players, such as day-night cycles, the code must be placed within a Script controlled by the Server. If specific effects are to be unique to individual players, like a player-controlled flashlight, the code would be hosted within a LocalScript. Listing 7-13 sets up an orange ambient light using the Ambient property of the Lighting service. It controls the overall ambient color in the game environment. The code in Listing 7-13 needs to be set up on a server-side script.

Listing 7-13. Setting up the ambient lighting for a scene

```
local lightingService = game:GetService("Lighting")
lightingService.Ambient = Color3.new(1, 0.5, 0) -- Sets up an
                                   -- orange ambient light
```

The Roblox Lighting service offers extensive properties that enable developers to craft engaging and visually appealing environments. Here are some additional properties:

1) Brightness: Adjusts the brightness of the entire game world.

2) ColorShift_Bottom: Alters the color of the skybox at the horizon.

3) ColorShift_Top: Changes the color of the skybox away from the horizon.

4) OutdoorAmbient: Sets the outdoor ambient color, allowing for more specific control in outdoor settings.

5) FogColor: Defines the color of the fog in the environment.

6) FogEnd: Determines where the fog will completely obscure objects, while FogStart sets where the fog begins to appear.

7) ExposureCompensation: Helps control the scene's exposure, making it appear darker or lighter.

8) GeographicLatitude: This can simulate sunlight based on real-world geographic locations.

9) GlobalShadows: Enables or disables shadows from sunlight.

10) ShadowSoftness: Adjusts how soft or sharp the edges of the shadows appear.

11) TimeOfDay: Allows the setting of the specific time of day, which can affect the appearance of the sun and sky.

12) ClockTime: Like TimeOfDay but advances independently, allowing you to create custom day-night cycles.

13) Atmosphere: An object that controls various atmospheric properties like density, color, glow, and haze.

Listing 7-14. Setting up lighting service properties to create lighting at dawn

```lua
-- Access the Lighting service
local lighting = game:GetService("Lighting")
-- Set the time of day to dawn (6:00 AM)          -- 1
lighting.TimeOfDay = "06:00:00"
-- Set the fog color to a light grey
lighting.FogColor = Color3.fromRGB(200, 200, 200)
-- Set the fog start and end to create a dense fog that
-- obscures distant objects
lighting.FogStart = 10                            -- 2
lighting.FogEnd = 50                              -- 3
-- Create an Atmosphere object to enhance the scene
local atmosphere = Instance.new("Atmosphere")     -- 4
atmosphere.Density = 0.5
atmosphere.Color = Color3.fromRGB(150, 150, 200) -- Slightly bluish hue
atmosphere.Haze = 0.1
atmosphere.Glare = 0.2
atmosphere.Parent = lighting
```

Using the code provided in Listing 7-14, you can create a mystical forest scene at dawn, with a dense fog that gradually clears as the sun rises. By adjusting these properties further, you can create an engaging and visually striking scene that feels mysterious and otherworldly.

1) TimeOfDay: Setting it to "06:00:00" represents dawn, allowing you to craft a scene with the early morning light.

2) FogColor: A light gray fog color creates a soft, misty appearance.

3) FogStart and FogEnd: These values make the fog begin close to the camera and gradually fade away, adding a sense of depth and mystery.

4) Atmosphere: Here, you create an Atmosphere game object whose properties are then set to create a subtle bluish hue with some haze and glare, adding to the mystical and magical feel of the scene.

ContextActionService

The ContextActionService in Roblox is an essential part of the game development process, especially for those creating games that must be responsive across various devices. It is a service in Roblox that handles user input across different platforms, allowing developers to define specific actions triggered by various inputs like button presses on a controller, keyboard key presses, or touchscreen taps. Using the ContextActionService, developers can ensure that their games respond to player inputs consistently, regardless of the device, making it crucial for games to be accessible on mobile devices, VR Devices, consoles, and PCs. As a powerful tool in Roblox's Luau scripting language, ContextActionService enables uniform handling of diverse input methods, facilitating engaging and accessible games with a consistent player experience across different devices. It is an indispensable service for anyone aiming to make their games more versatile and user-friendly.

The code utilizing the ContextActionService in Roblox is generally placed within a LocalScript on the client-side. This approach is favored as it involves dealing with user input, a factor that can differ significantly among players. Handling this on the Client rather than the Server promotes efficiency, as it eradicates latency in input processing. Consequently, this leads to an enhanced gameplay experience that is both smoother and more responsive.

Listing 7-15. Binding the JumpAction to different input methods

```
local ContextActionService = game:GetService("ContextActionService")
                                                          -- 1
                                                          -- 2
local function handleJump(actionName, inputState, inputObject)
if inputState == Enum.UserInputState.Begin then        -- 3
local inputPosition = inputObject.Position             -- 4
local player = game.Players.LocalPlayer                 -- 5
local character = player.Character                      -- 6
                                                          -- 7
local humanoid = character:FindFirstChildOfClass("Humanoid")
local screenHalfHeight = workspace.CurrentCamera.ViewportSize.Y / 2
                                                          -- 8
if inputPosition.Y < screenHalfHeight then             -- 9
-- Code to make the character jump higher
humanoid.JumpPower = 200                                            -- 10 Sets the jump
power higher
humanoid.Jump = true                                               -- 11 Makes the
character jump
        print("Set Higher Jump Power")
else
-- Code to make the character jump normally
humanoid.JumpPower = 50                                             -- 12 Sets the jump
power to normal
humanoid.Jump = true                                               -- Makes the
character jump
        print("Set Normal Jump Power")
    end
end
end
```

```
ContextActionService:BindAction("JumpAction", handleJump, false, Enum.
KeyCode.Space, Enum.KeyCode.ButtonA, Enum.UserInputType.Touch)
```
-- 13

The code in Listing 7-15 invokes the handleJump() function when the player presses the space key, the A button on a game controller, or touches a touch-enabled device. When you play the experience, clicking anywhere within the upper top position of the screen, followed by executing a jump, will have the player perform its higher jump power, and clicking anywhere within the lower extremities of the screen will have the player perform the normal jump.

1) Retrieves the ContextActionService from the game, allowing you to bind specific user inputs to custom functions.

2) Here, a local function called handleJump is declared, taking three parameters: actionName, inputState, and inputObject. This function will be executed when the relevant input is detected.

3) Inside the function, this line checks if the current input state equals Begin. In other words, it's checking if the input has just started, such as a key press, a gamepad button press, or a screen touch occurs, in which case this if statement is executed.

4) Gets the position of the input, which can be the location of a mouse click or touch event.

5) Retrieves the LocalPlayer, representing the player on the Client where this code runs.

6) Gets the player's character object, which contains all the parts related to the player's avatar, such as the head, arms, legs, etc.

7) Retrieves the humanoid object from the character, which controls properties like health, animations, jump power, and more.

8) Computes half the viewport's height, allowing for a comparison with the Y coordinate of the input position. This line of code that calculates half the viewport's height is a key part of the logic to determine whether the player's input (mouse click or touch) occurred in the upper or lower half of the screen. By dividing the Y component (height) by 2, you obtain the value representing

the vertical midpoint of the screen. This essentially divides the screen into two halves. Once the half height is calculated, it can be compared with the Y coordinate of the player's input (mouse click or touch). If the Y coordinate of the input is less than this half-height, it means the input occurred in the upper half of the viewport. If it's greater or equal, it occurred in the lower half.

9) Checks if the Y coordinate of the input is less than half the screen height (upper extremity of the screen). If true, the code inside the block will execute, leading to a higher jump.

10) Changes the jump power of the humanoid to 200, which determines how high the character can jump. The higher the value, the higher the jump.

11) Sets the jump property to true, causing the character to perform the jump with the previously set higher jump power.

12) Changes the jump power of the humanoid to 50, reverting it to a normal jump. This line of code is executed if the condition evaluates to false.

13) Associates the handleJump() function with specific inputs: the space key, the ButtonA on a game controller, and any touch input. Whenever these inputs are activated, the handleJump function is called, executing the logic defined within it.

It is important to note that the "JumpAction" used in Listing 7-15 is a custom name for the specific action being defined and can be named anything you like. It doesn't refer to a predefined action in Roblox. You can create actions with unique names and determine what inputs will trigger those actions using the ContextActionService. Some common actions that you might define in a Roblox game, along with typical keys or gamepad inputs that could be used to capture these actions, would be the following:

1) Move forward: Often captured with the "W" key, up arrow key, or the left thumbstick on a game controller.

2) Move back: Typically associated with the "S" key, the down arrow key, or the left thumbstick on a game controller.

3) Turn left/right: Might be captured with the "A" and "D" keys, the left/right arrow keys, or the right thumbstick on a game controller.

4) Crouch: This could be tied to the "C" key or a specific button on a game controller like the "B" button.

5) Attack: Often mapped to the left mouse button or a trigger on a game controller.

6) Interact: Frequently linked to the "E" key or a button like "X" or "A" on a game controller.

7) Reload: It might be associated with the "R" key or a button like "Y" on a game controller.

8) Pause/menu: Often captured with the "Esc" key or the "Start" button on a game controller.

9) Sprint: This could be tied to the "Shift" key or a button like the "Left Trigger" on a game controller.

These are just examples, and the keys or buttons used can be completely customized to fit your game's particular controls and mechanics. The main idea is to use the ContextActionService to bind these actions to specific inputs so that your game responds appropriately regardless of whether the player uses a keyboard, mouse, touch screen, or game controller. By using the ContextActionService, you can create a flexible control scheme that offers a consistent and accessible experience for players across various platforms and input methods.

TeamsService

The TeamsService in Roblox is a dynamic feature used to manage teams within a game, allowing developers to create various team-based gameplay mechanics like capturing the flag or team deathmatch. By differentiating players into teams and applying specific attributes like team color or name, TeamsService enhances the multiplayer experience by offering rich, competitive gameplay opportunities. By creating a Team object within the TeamsService, developers can assign players to specific teams using the player.Team property, as well as set up events to listen for changes in a player's team membership. This reactive design allows the execution of specific code when a player switches teams, thus facilitating nuanced control over the game's mechanics. By effectively utilizing TeamsService, game developers can open up exciting gameplay possibilities, adding depth and strategic layers to their Roblox game development projects.

The code involving TeamsService should be hosted on the server side, typically in a ServerScript. This ensures that the game logic related to teams is handled centrally by the Server rather than individually by each Client, thereby maintaining the integrity of the game's rules.

Listing 7-16. Assigning players to teams

```
-- Create Team Red
local redTeam = Instance.new("Team")              -- 1
redTeam.Name = "RedTeam"
redTeam.TeamColor = BrickColor.Red()
redTeam.Parent = Teams                            -- 2
-- Create Team Blue
local blueTeam = Instance.new("Team")             -- 3
blueTeam.Name = "BlueTeam"
blueTeam.TeamColor = BrickColor.Blue()
blueTeam.Parent = Teams                           -- 4
-- Assign players to teams based on some criteria
game.Players.PlayerAdded:Connect(function(player) -- 5
    if player.UserId % 2 == 0 then                -- 6
        player.Team = redTeam
    else
        player.Team = blueTeam
    end
end)
```

The code provided as part of Listing 7-16 creates two teams, red and blue, and assigns players to these teams based on the even or odd nature of their UserId. If the UserId is even, the player is assigned to the red team; otherwise, the player is assigned to the blue team.

1) This line of code creates a new instance of a "Team" object and assigns it to the local variable redTeam.

2) This line of code sets the redTeam object's parent property to the Teams service in Roblox. By setting the parent to Teams, the redTeam object becomes a child of the Teams service, thus finalizing the creation of the red team within the game's hierarchy.

3) Similar to point 1, this line of code creates a new instance of a "Team" object and assigns it to the local variable blueTeam.

4) This line of code sets the blueTeam object's parent property to the Teams service in Roblox, making it a child of Teams. This finalizes the creation of the blue team within the game's hierarchy.

5) This line of code sets up an event connection that listens for the PlayerAdded event. Whenever a new player joins the game, the anonymous function defined within the parentheses will be called, receiving the newly joined player's object as an argument.

6) This line of code checks whether the player's UserId is even or odd by taking the modulo of the UserId with 2. If the result is 0 (i.e., the UserId is even), the subsequent line of code assigns the player to the red team using the player's Team property; otherwise, the player is assigned to the blue team.

TeleportService

In Roblox, the TeleportService is a multifaceted service that facilitates the movement of players between different places within a game or to entirely different games, and it can even refer to teleporting a player to a new location in a VR experience. A "place" in Roblox represents a specific level or area, each with a unique PlaceId, and games can have multiple such places. Teleporting between places means moving a player from one place to another, either within the same game or different ones. On the other hand, a game instance is a single running copy of a game, and when multiple instances are needed to accommodate various players, teleporting between game instances enables a player's movement from one instance to another. This capability can balance player loads or group friends together, creating a dynamic and interconnected gaming experience.

The code related to teleporting a player should be hosted on the server side, not the client side. This ensures that players can't manipulate the teleporting process, which might lead to potential cheating or game-breaking issues.

Listing 7-17. Teleporting a player to a new place (Level) of the game experience

```
local teleportService = game:GetService("TeleportService")-- 1
local targetPlaceId = 14445924217 -- 2 Replace with your target
                                      -- PlaceId

                                                       -- 3
local teleportPart = workspace:FindFirstChild("TeleportPart")
local function onTeleportPartTouch(hit)                -- 4
-- the Model containing the humanoid and other character parts
     local character = hit.Parent                      -- 5
     local player = game.Players:GetPlayerFromCharacter(character)
                                                       -- 6
     if player then   -- 7 Check if the touching object is
                       -- indeed, a player
     print("Player touched the teleport part, teleporting...")
     teleportService:Teleport(targetPlaceId, player)   -- 8
     end
end
teleportPart.Touched:Connect(onTeleportPartTouch)      -- 9
```

Begin by creating a new TeleportPlayer Script within the ServerScriptService, and type in the code listed 7-17 into this script. You must create a new part within the game world and rename it TeleportPart. Upon your player colliding with this TeleportPart, it will be teleported to the new place (level). You will need to create a new place and obtain its PlaceID. Creating a new place is straightforward. Create a new game by selecting File - New and then design your new place (Level). Save your new place(Level) and publish it to Roblox. Once you have created and published the new place, you can obtain its PlaceId by visiting the page of the newly created place (you can find it within your creations) on the Roblox website. The PlaceId is a part of the URL for that specific place. The URL will look something like this: `www.roblox.com/games/PLACE_ID_HERE/Name-of-Your-Place`. The PlaceId is the numeric part in the URL where "PLACE_ID_HERE" is. You can copy this number and use it in your script for teleportation.

1) This line of code retrieves the TeleportService from the game, which handles teleportation between places and game instances in Roblox.

2) This line of code assigns the PlaceId of the target location (place, i.e., Level) to which players will be teleported. The PlaceId is a unique identifier for a particular place (Level) within a Roblox game.

3) This line of code searches for a child object named "TeleportPart" within the workspace. The returned object is expected to be a part that, when touched, triggers the teleportation. It's stored in the variable teleportPart for later use.

4) This line of code defines a new function named onTeleportPartTouch. This function will be called whenever a player touches the teleport part. It takes one parameter, hit, representing the object that touched the teleport part.

5) Within the onTeleportPartTouch function, this line of code gets the parent of the touched object (the hit). In this context, it's a model representing a player character, containing parts like the humanoid, head, arms, etc.

6) This line of code calls the GetPlayerFromCharacter() method on the Players service to get the player object associated with the character. It stores the player object in the variable player.

7) This "if" block checks if the touching object is indeed associated with a player (i.e., player is not nil). If it is, it prints a message to the output.

8) Here, the Teleport method on teleportService is called to teleport the player to the target PlaceId specified earlier.

9) This line of code connects the onTeleportPartTouch() function to the Touched event of teleportPart. This means that when a player touches the teleportPart, the onTeleportPartTouch() function will be called, potentially resulting in a teleport to the new place (Level).

This entire code snippet sets up a teleportation mechanism where players are teleported to a specified place when they touch a specific part within the game world.

PhysicsService

The PhysicsService is a service in Roblox used to control various physics-related properties within the game world, allowing for managing different aspects of the physics engine. This includes collision groups, where you can define which objects will collide and which won't. This feature could help segregate objects so they do not collide with each other, such as preventing players from colliding with their own bullets. The Gravity property can also control the gravitational force in the game world, creating specialized environments like a lighter or heavier gravity zone, which is particularly useful in a space-themed game. Moreover, by utilizing the ThrottleAdjustTime property, developers can adjust the physics engine's performance by limiting the number of calculations made within a given time frame, optimizing the overall game experience.

As the code here deals with physics, which must be consistently calculated across all clients, this code would need to run on a server-side script.

Listing 7-18. PhysicsService – setting up Collision Groups

```
local physicsService = game:GetService("PhysicsService")           -- 1
physicsService: RegisterCollisionGroup ("Players")                 -- 2
physicsService: RegisterCollisionGroup ("Bullets")                 -- 3
physicsService:CollisionGroupSetCollidable("Players", "Bullets", false)  -- 4
```

The code in Listing 7-18 could be used to ensure that players don't collide with their own bullets.

This line of code gets the PhysicsService from the Roblox game engine and assigns it to a local variable named physicsService.

This line of code attempts to register a collision group named "Players" with the physics engine.

Similar to point 2, this line of code attempts to register a collision group named "Bullets" with the physics engine.

This line of code sets the collision behavior between the "Players" and "Bullets" groups to be non-collidable. That means any parts assigned to the "Players" group will not collide with parts assigned to the "Bullets" group. It allows you to have more specific control over how different groups of objects interact with each other physically.

The code provided in Listing 7-18 would function to create two collision groups and set them as non-collidable with each other, which would be a typical pattern in a shooting game to prevent players from colliding with their own bullets.

However, Listing 7-18 is only part of the solution. You also need to ensure that you assign a player's character or specific parts of a character (such as the HumanoidRootPart) to the "Players" collision group. You would ideally do this when a new player character is added to the game. Likewise, the bullets fired by the player would need to be assigned to the "Bullets" collision group. The assignment of player bullets to the collision group "Bullets" would depend on how you create and manage them in your game. If you instantiate a bullet part when a gun is fired, you can assign it to the "Bullets" collision group at that time. Listing 7-19 demonstrates how to assign a player HumanoidRootPart to the "Players" collision group, and Listing 7-20 demonstrates how to assign player bullets to the "Bullets" collision group upon being instantiated.

Listing 7-19. Assigning player HumanoidRootPart to "Players" collision group

```
game.Players.PlayerAdded:Connect(function(player)                    -- 1
    player.CharacterAdded:Connect(function(character)                -- 2
    local humanoidRootPart = character:FindFirstChild("HumanoidRootPart")  -- 3
    if humanoidRootPart then                                         -- 4
        humanoidRootPart.CollisionGroup = "Players"                  -- 5
    end
    end)
end)
```

1) This line of code connects an anonymous function to the PlayerAdded event within the Players service. The PlayerAdded event is triggered whenever a new player joins the game. The anonymous function takes a player argument, representing the player that has just joined. The code within this function (including the nested event) will be executed when this event is triggered.

2) Nested within the PlayerAdded event, this line of code connects another anonymous function to the CharacterAdded event of the specific player that just joined. The CharacterAdded event is triggered when the player's character is added to the game (i.e., when they spawn). The anonymous function takes a character argument, representing the newly spawned character of the player. Any code within this function will be executed when the player's character is added to the game.

3) Inside the nested CharacterAdded function, this line of code looks for the first child part within the character object named "HumanoidRootPart" and assigns it to the local variable humanoidRootPart. In the context of Roblox, the HumanoidRootPart is typically the central part of a player's character, and it's often used as a reference point for various interactions with the character.

4) This line of code checks if the humanoidRootPart variable is not nil. If the FindFirstChild() method did not find a part named HumanoidRootPart within the character object, it would return nil, and the code inside this 'if' conditional block would not be executed.

5) If humanoidRootPart is not nil, this line of code sets its CollisionGroup property to "Players." In Roblox, collision groups define how different objects interact with each other in terms of collisions.

The nesting of events here allows for sequential and dependent handling of specific game events:

- First, the code waits for a player to join the game (using PlayerAdded).

- Once that happens, the nested code waits for that specific player's character to be added to the game (using CharacterAdded).

- Finally, once the character is added, the code assigns the HumanoidRootPart of that character to the "Players" collision group.

This sequence ensures that the action (assigning the collision group) depends on a player joining the game and their character being loaded. If these events were not nested, there would be no way to guarantee that the CharacterAdded event was connected to the player that had just joined, making it more difficult to perform player-specific actions like the one demonstrated in this code. The nesting of events in this way creates a logical flow that represents the sequence of actions in the game. It can make the code more readable and maintainable, mirroring the natural hierarchy of dependencies between these events.

Listing 7-20. Assigning an instantiated player bullet part to the "Bullets" collision group

```
local bullet = Instance.new("Part")
bullet.Name = "playerBullet"
local startPosn = Vector3.new(0,0,0)
bullet.Size = Vector3.new(0.15, 0.15, 0.15)
bullet.Position = startPosn -- Set this where you want the
                            -- bullet to start
bullet.Parent = workspace
bullet.CollisionGroup = "Bullets"
```

The code provided in Listing 7-20 is responsible for creating a new part in Roblox, representing a bullet, and configuring its properties. It starts by creating an instance of a Part object, naming it playerBullet, and initializing its size to be 0.15 x 0.15 x 0.15 studs. The bullet's starting position is set to the origin point (0,0,0), although this would typically be customized to match the position of the player's weapon or a firing point (muzzle). The bullet is then added to the workspace, making it part of the game's scene, and its collision group is set to "Bullets." This places the bullet within a predefined collision group, which manages how it interacts with other objects in the game, such as defining that it should collide with enemies but not the player.

Let's look at the Region3 object provided by Roblox and understand what it is and how it can be used in your game experience. A Region3 object in Roblox represents a three-dimensional region in world space, defined by two Vector3 values representing opposite corners of an axis-aligned bounding box. In other words, it defines a cubic or rectangular space in the 3D World by specifying the minimum and maximum extents along the X, Y, and Z axes. This object is not a visible entity in the scene but a mathematical construct used for programming purposes, such as finding parts within a specific area or triggering actions when something enters or exits the region. Placing parts within a Region3 object is not done directly through Region3 itself. Instead, you would position parts within the 3D space corresponding to the region defined by the Region3 object. Although you won't see it represented visually in the Roblox Studio or during gameplay, Region3 provides a powerful tool for managing spatial relationships in a game, allowing for complex interactions and behaviors based on the relative positions of objects and players. Whether used for collision detection, AI pathfinding, procedural generation, weather effects, or various gameplay mechanics, Region3 serves as an essential building block in creating immersive and dynamic virtual environments. Some typical use cases of a Region3 object in game development:

1) Collision detection: Using the FindPartsInRegion3() method, you can detect all parts within a specific area. This is commonly used for triggering events when an object enters a region, such as activating traps, starting missions, or spawning enemies.

2) AI pathfinding: You can use Region3 to define zones where AI-controlled characters can or cannot go. By querying the parts within these regions, you can dynamically adapt the pathfinding algorithms to navigate around obstacles or through specific pathways.

3) Procedural generation: Region3 objects can be used in procedural content generation to define areas where specific structures, objects, or terrain features should be created or modified.

4) LOD (Level of Detail) management: By defining regions around the player, you can dynamically load or unload content based on the player's position. For instance, you might want to display highly detailed models when the player is close and simpler models or none when the player is far away.

5) Weather effects: If you want to create localized weather effects (like rain or a tornado in a specific area), you can use a Region3 object to determine where those effects should be applied.

6) Gameplay mechanics: You can create specific gameplay mechanics using Region3, such as stealth zones where the player must avoid detection, healing zones where players can regenerate health, or danger zones with increased enemy activity.

7) Building systems: In building or crafting systems, Region3 can be used to check if a certain space is clear before allowing a structure to be built, ensuring that buildings don't overlap or intersect with other objects.

8) Animation and visual effects: Region3 can trigger specific animations or visual effects when an object or player enters, remains in, or exits a particular region.

9) Event management: Define regions where certain in-game events are triggered or controlled. For example, starting a boss battle when the player enters a certain room or controlling where random events can occur within the game world.

In Listing 7-21, you will create a Region3 object in our game world and position specific parts within its defined boundaries. You will then use the FindPartsInRegion3() method to locate the parts within the boundaries of the Region3 object and use the physics BodyVelocity object to have only the parts within the Region3 boundaries levitate upward using a custom gravity value. The script you create using the code provided in Listing 7-21 needs to be a server-side script.

Listing 7-21. Implementing a Region3 object

```
local runService = game:GetService("RunService")
-- Define a Region3 with given bounds
local minBound = Vector3.new(5, 5, 5)                 -- 1
local maxBound = Vector3.new(15, 15, 15)              -- 2
local region = Region3.new(minBound, maxBound)        -- 3
-- Function to generate a random number within a range
local function randomInRange(min, max)
    return math.random() * (max - min) + min
end
local parts = {} -- Table to store the created parts   -- 4
local meshTypes = {"Brick", "Wedge", "Cylinder","CornerWedge"}
                                                       -- 5
-- Create four unique parts within the Region3 bounds
for i = 1, 4 do
    local part = Instance.new("Part")
```

```
    part.Size = Vector3.new(1, 1, 1)
    part.Anchored = false
    part.Position = Vector3.new(randomInRange(minBound.X, maxBound.X),
    randomInRange(minBound.Y, maxBound.Y),
    randomInRange(minBound.Z, maxBound.Z)
    )                                              -- 6

    part.Parent = workspace
    part.Name = "Region3_Part_" .. i
    parts[part] = true -- Add part to the table
    -- Creating a mesh for the part
    local mesh = Instance.new("SpecialMesh")        -- 7
    mesh.MeshType = meshTypes[i]                     -- 8
    mesh.Parent = part                              -- 9
    print("Created Part: " .. part.Name)
end
print("Created 4 parts within a Region3 object.")
-- Function to apply custom upward movement to parts
local function movePartsUp()                        -- 10
local partsInRegion = workspace:FindPartsInRegion3(region, nil)
                                                    -- 11 Finding parts
within the defined region
    for _, part in pairs(partsInRegion) do          -- 12
    if part:IsA("BasePart") and not part.Anchored then -- 13
    local bodyVelocity = Instance.new("BodyVelocity")  -- 14
    bodyVelocity.Velocity = Vector3.new(0, 2, 0)    -- 15 Upward
                                                    -- velocity
    bodyVelocity.Parent = part          -- 16 Attaching the
                          -- BodyVelocity object to the part
    print("Part Moved Up: " .. "[ " .. part.Name .. " ]")
    end
    end
end
-- Connect the function to the Heartbeat event
runService.Heartbeat:Connect(movePartsUp)           -- 17
```

1) This line of code sets the minimum bounds for a Region3 object by creating a new Vector3 object with coordinates (5, 5, 5). This defines the lowest extents along the region's X, Y, and Z axes.

2) This line of code sets the maximum bounds for the Region3 object by creating a new Vector3 object with coordinates (15, 15, 15). This defines the highest extents along the region's X, Y, and Z axes.

3) This line of code creates the actual Region3 object by combining the previously defined minBound and maxBound. This Region3 object represents a three-dimensional space in the game world.

4) This line of code initializes an empty table named parts, which will be used to store references to the parts created within the Region 3 bounds.

5) This line of code creates a table named meshTypes containing strings representing different types of mesh. These will be used later to define the shape of the parts.

6) In the context of creating parts, this line of code sets the position of a part within the Region3 bounds. The randomInRange function is called for each dimension to ensure the part is randomly placed within the defined region.

7) This line of code creates a new "SpecialMesh" object. SpecialMesh is a type of object in Roblox used to customize the appearance of parts, and this object will be used to give the part a specific shape.

8) This line of code sets the MeshType property of the mesh, choosing one of the mesh types from the meshTypes table. It uses the loop's index i to select the type, so each part gets a different mesh type.

9) This line of code sets the newly created mesh as a child of the part, connecting it to the part so that the part takes on the shape defined by the mesh.

10) This line of code defines a new function named movePartsUp(), which will apply custom upward movement to the parts.

11) Inside the movePartsUp() function, this line of code uses the FindPartsInRegion3() method to find all the parts within the defined region, storing them in the partsInRegion variable.

12) This line of code starts a "for" loop that will iterate over each part found within the region.

13) This line of code checks whether the current part in the loop is a BasePart (a general type of object that represents 3D shapes in Roblox) and whether it's not anchored, ensuring that it can be moved.

14) This line of code creates a new BodyVelocity object, which is used in Roblox to control the velocity of a part. BodyVelocity is a physical object that can be parented to a part to give it constant velocity, meaning it will continuously move in a specific direction at a specific speed. This is often used in Roblox to create complex and precise movement patterns without manually calculating and updating the part's position in every frame.

15) This line of code sets the velocity of the BodyVelocity object in an upward direction. The part will move in this direction when the BodyVelocity object is added to it.

16) This line of code attaches the BodyVelocity object to the part, making it a child of the part. This applies the velocity to the part, causing it to move.

17) Finally, this line of code connects the movePartsUp() function to the Heartbeat event of the runService. This means the function will be called on every frame update, repeatedly applying the upward movement to the parts.

BodyVelocity is highly useful in various game scenarios, such as simulating wind, controlling projectiles, or creating custom movement behaviors for characters and objects. By tweaking its properties, developers can achieve various movement patterns and effects, providing greater flexibility and precision in designing game mechanics.

The BodyVelocity properties have been explained as follows:

1) Velocity: This is a Vector3 value that defines the direction and speed of the part's movement. This vector's X, Y, and Z components represent the speed of movement along each axis in studs per second. For example, Vector3.new(0, 10, 0) would move the part upward at ten studs per second.

2) MaxForce: This is a Vector3 value that allows you to control how strong the velocity effect is. It's essentially a constraint on how much force can be applied to achieve the desired velocity. If set to a low value, other physical forces (like gravity or collisions) may overcome the BodyVelocity, whereas a high value will make the velocity effect more dominant. If you want the BodyVelocity to control the part's movement fully, you can set MaxForce to Vector3.new(math.huge, math.huge, math.huge).

3) P: This property controls the power of the BodyVelocity, representing how aggressively it tries to reach the target velocity. Higher values will make the part reach the target velocity faster, while lower values will result in a softer, more gradual change in speed.

4) D: This property controls damping, which can be considered resistance or friction against the velocity. Higher values will make the part more resistant to changes in velocity, while lower values will allow it to respond more quickly.

Summary

In this comprehensive exploration of key Roblox Services, this chapter illuminated the multifaceted aspects of game development within the Roblox environment. The Workspace is the primary container for all objects in a game, while ReplicatedStorage allows for data synchronization across Servers and clients. Players service manages user information, whereas UserInputService handles user interactions. TweenService animates properties smoothly, and ProximityPromptService assists in creating interactive prompts. RunService drives the game loop, and SoundService manages in-game audio. Lighting service manipulates the environment's visual appearance, while ContextActionService handles contextual user inputs. TeamsService administers team-based gameplay, TeleportService controls inter-place navigation, and PhysicsService governs the physical behaviors within the game. Additionally, the chapter delved into BodyVelocity, an object that applies a continuous force or velocity to a BasePart, offering developers the power to control the motion of parts with finesse and accuracy. Together, these services and functionalities enable developers to craft rich and engaging experiences, contributing to the versatility and popularity of Roblox as a game development platform.

CHAPTER 8

Task Library and Module Scripts

In Roblox game development, efficiency and code reusability are pillars for creating engaging and responsive games. The Roblox Task Library is an essential part of the Lua scripting environment, offering a robust set of functions for managing time-based actions, allowing developers to create fluid and interactive experiences. Module Scripts also serve as the building blocks for maintainable and scalable code. These specialized scripts enable developers to write reusable code modules that can be efficiently leveraged across various parts of a game, reducing redundancy and complexity. This chapter will delve into the intricacies of the Task Library and Module Scripts, exploring their roles, functionalities, and applications in creating immersive Roblox experiences. Whether you're a seasoned developer or just starting on your Roblox journey, the insights offered in this chapter provide invaluable tools for your development toolkit.

Threading in Roblox Luau

Threading in Roblox is pivotal in executing multiple tasks simultaneously or concurrently within the game environment. This approach is crucial for managing time-consuming operations without freezing or slowing gameplay. Threading allows asynchronous execution, meaning that different parts of a program can operate simultaneously, ensuring that one action doesn't hinder others, thereby keeping the game responsive. The concept of concurrency in Roblox focuses on making progress on multiple tasks simultaneously but not necessarily at the same time. True parallelism, where tasks run at the exact same time, is rarer since Roblox Luau is generally single-threaded. In Roblox Luau, threading often manifests as concurrency, where tasks appear to run together by yielding to one another.

C. Coutinho, *Roblox Lua Scripting Essentials*, https://doi.org/10.1007/979-8-8688-0026-9_8

Task Library and Threading

Roblox's Task Library is a robust collection of functions and methods to handle tasks like scheduling and managing function execution. These tools are vital in game development, contributing to the optimization and functionality of a game. The task Library offers a simplified approach to threading, incorporating methods like task. spawn, task.delay, and task.wait to manage threading efficiently. Threading in Roblox Luau, primarily handled through the Task Library, allows for the concurrent execution of tasks to maintain fluid gameplay. It is particularly valuable for animations, timed events, and other scenarios where specific functions must proceed without halting the rest of the game code. By offering powerful methods for concurrent execution, the Task Library becomes an essential component in managing multiple operations and enhancing the player's experience.

Let's dive into some of the essential methods the task library provides and see how they can be used.

The Task.delay(time, function) Method

This method allows you to delay the execution of a specific function by a given amount of time (in seconds). It can be used to create timed events or animations in a game. Listing 8-1 demonstrates the Task.Delay() method, which you could attach to a server-side script.

Listing 8-1. task.delay() method

```
task.delay(5, function()
    print("This message will be printed after 5 seconds")
end)
print("This message will print immediately")
```

The anonymous function passed to Task.Delay will be executed asynchronously, meaning that the rest of the code following the Task.Delay() method will continue to execute immediately without waiting for the 5-second delay to elapse. The second print statement will be executed right away, while the delayed function will execute after five seconds, demonstrating the asynchronous nature of the Task.Delay function.

The Task.spawn(function) Method

This method creates a new thread to run the function passed in as an argument, which will be run asynchronously. It can load game assets (e.g., textures, models) asynchronously, ensuring the game remains responsive while loading. It can be used for running animations or special effects independently of the main game loop, allowing for smoother gameplay, as these elements won't slow down the rest of the game's logic.

Listing 8-2. task.spawn() method

```
local assetId = 1369659165 -- Replace with actual assetID
local InsertService = game:GetService("InsertService") -- 1
task.spawn(function()
-- Load a model from the catalog
local model = InsertService:LoadAsset(assetId):GetChildren()[1]     -- 2
-- Add the loaded model to the game
model.Parent = game.Workspace
print("Model Asset has  now been loaded.")
end)
print("Game continues running while Asset is loading.")
```

This code in Listing 8-2 demonstrates how a potentially time-consuming asset-loading operation is handled in a separate thread, allowing the main game logic to continue uninterrupted.

1) This line of code references the InsertService, a Roblox service used to load assets, such as models, from the Roblox catalog. The game:GetService("InsertService") call retrieves this service, and the reference is stored in the local variable InsertService.

2) This line is doing several things at once. InsertService:LoadAsset (assetId) calls the LoadAsset method on the previously obtained InsertService, passing in the assetId defined earlier. This function call loads the asset (such as a model) with the given ID from the Roblox catalog. The :GetChildren() method retrieves all the children of the loaded asset, which could include multiple objects if the asset is a complex model. In this context, the desired model

is assumed to be the first child, so [1] is used to access the first element in the returned list. The result, expected to be the desired model, is then stored in the local variable model.

The Task.wait(seconds) Method

The task.wait() function is used to pause the current thread of execution for a specified number of seconds. Unlike the global wait function, task.wait is more accurate regarding the delay time and is favored for precise timing needs. The number of seconds the current thread should pause, if not specified, defaults to yielding until the next frame, which is typically 1/60th of a second. It returns the actual time waited, which might vary slightly from the requested time.

The code in Listing 8-3 demonstrates how to activate and deactivate a special powerup for players that lasts five seconds. The code provides a visual cue of starting this powerup by changing the player's head color and then reverts it to another color after the powerup duration has elapsed.

Listing 8-3. task.wait() method

```
local Players = game:GetService("Players")
local function activatePowerUp(character)          -- 1
if character and character:FindFirstChild("Head") then
-- Change the appearance to signify powerup activation (e.g., change color)
character.Head.BrickColor = BrickColor.new("Bright blue")
print("Powerup activated for", character.Name)
-- Use task.wait to pause the current thread for 5 seconds (powerup
duration)
task.wait(5)
-- Revert the appearance to normal
character.Head.BrickColor = BrickColor.new("Bright yellow")
print("Powerup deactivated for", character.Name)
end
end
-- Function to handle new players joining
local function onPlayerJoin(player)                -- 2
    player.CharacterAdded:Connect(function(character)
```

```
            activatePowerUp(character)
      end)
end
-- Connect the function to all current and future players
Players.PlayerAdded:Connect(onPlayerJoin)            -- 3
for _, player in pairs(Players:GetPlayers()) do
      onPlayerJoin(player)
end
```

1) The activatePowerUp function accepts a character object and performs the powerup effect on that character.

2) The onPlayerJoin function connects the activatePowerUp function to the CharacterAdded event of each player, so the powerup effect is triggered when a player's character is added to the game.

3) Finally, the code connects the onPlayerJoin function to the PlayerAdded event of the Players service and calls it for any players already in the game when the script starts running.

The Task.defer(function) Method

This method is used to schedule a function to be run as soon as the current task has finished. It's handy for tasks you want to run immediately after something else but without stopping the current task. In Chapter 6, you learned how to create a Screen GUI and set it up with a TextButton object. You will now use this same ScreenGui object and set it up with a TextLabel to help demonstrate the task.defer() function.

Within the "Explorer" window, locate and expand the StarteGui folder. Select the ScreenGui object that you created in Chapter 6. The Roblox Studio editor will display the UI tab for you. From within the UI tab ribbon, select the TextLabel button and position the newly created TextLabel object somewhere at the top-left of the screen. Select the TextLabel object in the "Explorer" window and click the plus icon beside it. From the list that shows up, select the item LocalScript and ensure that it has been added as a child of the TextLabel object. Type in the code provided in Listing 8-4 into this LocalScript. The script that needs to be placed on the server side within the ServerScriptService has been provided as part of Listing 8-5.

You will also need to create a RemoteEvent object in the ReplicatedStorage. You can do this manually using the Roblox Studio editor:

- Select ReplicatedStorage and click the plus icon beside it.

- From the list that shows up, select RemoteEvent.

- Name the RemoteEvent "PlayerJoined."

Listing 8-4. task.defer() method – client-side script

```
--client-side code attached to a LocalScript within StarterGui
local textLabel = script.Parent
-- Function to update the GUI
local function updateGUI(playerName)
print("3. Updating GUI for joined player: " .. playerName)
-- Update the text property when a player joins
textLabel.Text = "4. " .. playerName .. " has joined!"
end
-- Function to handle player joining
local function onPlayerJoin(playerName)
-- 1 Schedule the updateGUI() function to run immediately
-- after  the onPlayerJoin() function completes execution.
task.defer(updateGUI, playerName)
print("1. " .. playerName .. " has joined the game.")
print("2. joined game - Exiting function onPlayerJoin()")
end
-- Connect the remote event to the onPlayerJoin function
game.ReplicatedStorage.PlayerJoined.OnClientEvent
:Connect(onPlayerJoin)                              -- 2
```

1) This line of code schedules the updateGUI() function to run after the current function (onPlayerJoin()) completes execution. The playerName argument is passed to the updateGUI function. The use of task.defer() here ensures that the GUI update is precisely timed to run as soon as the player joining event has been handled. When you run this code, you will note that the print() function

statements display in the order they have been numbered, an indicator of the fact that the updateGUI() function will only be run once this onPlayerJoin() function completes.

2) This line of code sets up an event listener for the PlayerJoined remote event that resides in ReplicatedStorage. When the event is fired from the server, the connected function onPlayerJoin() is called on the client side, passing along the player's name as an argument. This enables the server to communicate with the client and inform it of a player joining the game.

Listing 8-5. task.defer() method – server-side script

```
-- cache the RemoteEvent 'PlayerJoined' for notifying clients
-- of players joining
local playerJoinedEvent = game.ReplicatedStorage.PlayerJoined
local function onPlayerJoin(player)
print("[Server-Script]: " .. player.Name .. " has joined the game.")
-- Fire the PlayerJoined remote event to all clients, passing
-- the player's name
playerJoinedEvent:FireAllClients(player.Name)
end
game.Players.PlayerAdded:Connect(onPlayerJoin)
```

Listings 8-4 and 8-5 demonstrate a complete example where the server notifies all clients when a new player joins, and the clients update their GUI using task.defer() in response.

The Task.cancel( ) Method

This method cancels a scheduled task created using either task.spawn() or task.defer() before it has a chance to run. This is useful for stopping tasks that are no longer needed. Let's say you have a game where players can press a button to summon a powerup, but you want to have a delay before the powerup is activated. You want players to cancel the activation if they press the button again within a specific time frame. Listings 8-6 and 8-7 will demonstrate how to implement this game mechanic.

You must create a Clickable object like the ClickablePart object with a ClickDetector component you created in Chapter 6. You could select this ClickablePart object within the workspace, duplicate it, and rename it to PowerUp. Give it a new BrickColor should you want to. Expand this new PowerUp object and delete the Script child object within it.

You must also create a RemoteEvent within ReplicatedStorage, as this event will be shared between the server-side and client-side scripts in this example. You can do this manually using the Roblox Studio editor:

- Select ReplicatedStorage and click the plus icon beside it.

- From the list that shows up, select RemoteEvent.

- Name the RemoteEvent "PowerUpEvent."

Listing 8-6. task.cancel() method – server-side script

```
-- Reference to the RemoteEvent 'PowerUpEvent' for triggering
-- powerups
local powerUpEvent = game.ReplicatedStorage.PowerUpEvent
-- Table to store the powerup activation status for each player
local playerTasks = {}                              -- 1
-- Function to activate the powerup
local function activatePowerUp(player)              -- 2
if playerTasks[player] then
print(player.Name .. " power-up! - Activated after waiting 5 seconds")
playerTasks[player] = nil -- Remove the entry for the player
                         -- from the table
end
end
-- Function to handle the powerup button press
local function onPowerUpButtonPress(player)         -- 3
if playerTasks[player] then                        -- 4
print(player.Name .. " has cancelled the power-up.")
playerTasks[player] = nil                    -- 5 Remove the entry
                         -- for the player from the table
return
end
print(player.Name .. " has activated the power-up button.")
```

```
-- Mark the powerup as pending for this player
playerTasks[player] = true                              -- 6
-- Schedule the powerup activation with a 5-second delay
    task.delay(5, function()                            -- 7
        activatePowerUp(player)                         -- 8
    end)
end
powerUpEvent.OnServerEvent:Connect(onPowerUpButtonPress)    -- 9
```

The script in Listing 8-6 defines the server-side logic for a powerup activation system in a Roblox game. When a player presses the powerup button, a 5-second delay is initiated. During this delay, the player can press the button again to cancel the activation. If not canceled, the powerup is activated after the delay. This script utilizes a table to keep track of individual player's activation statuses and a Remote Event to communicate between client and server.

1) Creates an empty table and assigns it to the variable playerTasks. This table tracks the status of powerup activations for individual players, with the player object as the key.

2) Defines the function that will handle the activation of the powerup. It takes the player who triggered the powerup as a parameter. If there is an entry in the playerTasks table for the player, a message is printed, and the entry for the player is removed from the table. The value associated with the player in the playerTasks table is set to nil, effectively removing the entry. This line is executed if the player has an existing entry in the table, indicating that the activation of the powerup was pending, as stated in the print() statement. Once activated playerTasks[player] is set to nil, ensuring that it's too late to cancel it now, as five seconds have elapsed.

3) Begins the definition of the function that will handle the powerup button press. This function is responsible for both activating and canceling the powerup.

4) Check if there is an existing entry for the player in the playerTasks table. If the entry exists (value is true), the player has previously activated the powerup and is now canceling it.

5) playerTasks[player] = nil removes the entry for the player from the table. This effectively cancels the activation of the powerup for that player.

6) Adds an entry to the playerTasks table with the value true, indicating that the powerup activation is pending for the given player.

7) Schedules an anonymous function to be executed after a 5-second delay. This introduces the waiting period between pressing the powerup button and activating the powerup.

8) Invokes the previously defined activatePowerUp(player) function, passing in the player who triggered the powerup. If the player hasn't canceled the activation, this function activates the powerup after the 5-second delay.

9) Connects the onPowerUpButtonPress() function to the powerUpEvent (Remote Event). When this event is fired from the client-side (e.g., when a player clicks on the PowerUp button in the game world), the connected function will be called, allowing the server-side code to respond.

Listing 8-7. task.cancel() method – client-side script

```
-- Reference to the Powerup with the ClickDetector
-- 1
local powerUp = workspace:WaitForChild("PowerUp").ClickDetector
-- Reference to the RemoteEvent - 'PowerUpEvent'
local powerUpEvent = game.ReplicatedStorage.PowerUpEvent    -- 2
-- Function to call when the button is clicked
local function onPowerUpButtonPressed()                     -- 3
powerUpEvent:FireServer(game.Players.LocalPlayer)          -- 4 Trigger
                                                           -- the server event

end
```

```
-- Connect the ClickDetector's MouseClick event to the function
powerUp.MouseClick:Connect(onPowerUpButtonPressed)          -- 5
```

The code provided in Listing 8-7 needs to be typed into a LocalScript that resides within StarterPlayerScripts, as this is the client-side code. This code provides a mechanism for a player to activate a powerup by clicking on an object. When clicked, a RemoteEvent is fired, informing the server-side script of the action, enabling the server to handle the logic of granting the powerup to the player.

1) This line of code looks for a child object named "PowerUp" within the workspace and then accesses its ClickDetector component. It assigns this reference to the variable powerUp. This ClickDetector detects when the player clicks on the "PowerUp" within the game world.

2) This line of code accesses the RemoteEvent named "PowerUpEvent" stored in the ReplicatedStorage and assigns it to the variable powerUpEvent. This event is triggered when the player clicks on the "PowerUp."

3) Defines the function onPowerUpButtonPressed(), executed when the player clicks on the "PowerUp" (detected by the ClickDetector). This function contains the logic for what happens on the client side when the "PowerUp" is activated.

4) A signal is sent to the server-side script by firing the previously defined RemoteEvent (powerUpEvent). It also passes the local player (who clicked the "PowerUp") as a parameter. This allows the server-side script to know who activated the "PowerUp" and respond accordingly.

5) This line of code connects the MouseClick event of the ClickDetector (stored in the variable powerUp) to the function onPowerUpButtonPressed. Whenever the "PowerUp" object is clicked, the ClickDetector's MouseClick event is triggered, and the connected function onPowerUpButtonPressed() is invoked.

These five methods of the Roblox task library offer robust control over task scheduling and execution. They can help optimize and manage tasks in various real-world game scenarios, such as updating GUI, tracking schedulers, and canceling unnecessary tasks. Always consider the specific requirements of your game to determine which methods will best suit your needs.

Module Scripts

ModuleScripts in Roblox is a specialized script object designed to create reusable and maintainable code modules. Distinct from conventional scripts, ModuleScripts execute only once for each required call, allowing functions and variables to be shared across multiple game areas without redundancy. Whether defining a single function or an entire library of functions, ModuleScripts enables these to be written once and invoked from different scripts, thereby minimizing code duplication.

With ModuleScripts, developers can create centralized repositories for essential game components such as gold pickups, monster statistics, button behaviors, and more. Instead of dealing with multiple scripts that require individual updates for each change, you can manage everything through a single ModuleScript. While regular scripts and LocalScripts are still needed to access the ModuleScript, they can be simplified significantly, as most of the logic can be housed within the ModuleScript.

The intended usage determines the location of the ModuleScripts within your game hierarchy. For ModuleScripts accessed exclusively by server-side scripts, placement in ServerStorage is recommended, as this provides an additional layer of protection. Conversely, if client-side LocalScripts are also intended to utilize the ModuleScripts, placement in ReplicatedStorage is appropriate.

The distinction between ServerStorage and ReplicatedStorage is essential to understand. ModuleScripts stored in ServerStorage are restricted to access only by server-side scripts, ensuring security and control over essential game logic. On the other hand, ModuleScripts placed in ReplicatedStorage can be accessed by both server-side scripts and client-side LocalScripts, allowing for broader utilization while maintaining organized and efficient code management.

In summary, ModuleScripts are a powerful tool in Roblox, promoting better code organization, reusability, and maintainability. Their implementation allows for efficient updates and collaboration, and their strategic placement within the game environment enables precise control over access and execution, depending on the specific requirements of the game.

Every ModuleScript in Roblox begins with the bare-bones code structure in Listing 8-8.

Listing 8-8. ModuleScript skeleton code structure

```
local module = {}
-- Code that the module needs to share comes here.
return module
```

The two lines of code provided in Listing 8-8 should always encapsulate the content of a ModuleScript, serving as the opening and closing lines, respectively. The curly brackets {} denote a table in Lua, and within this table, all the shared functions and variables of the module are stored.

1) The line of code local module = {} declares a local table named "module." This table will serve as a container for all the functions and variables you want the ModuleScript to share.

2) Between the two lines of uncommented code, in Listing 8-8, you will place all the code that the module needs to share. This can include function declarations, variable assignments, and other relevant code constructs. They are all placed inside the table, making them part of the module.

3) The final line, return module, ensures that the entire table, containing all the shared functions and variables, is returned when other scripts require the ModuleScript. This makes everything inside the table accessible to those scripts that need the ModuleScript.

These two lines define a structure for ModuleScripts where all shared components are neatly packaged within a table, facilitating reuse and maintainability across different parts of a Roblox game. The encapsulation within the table ensures that the ModuleScript acts as a single, coherent unit that can be easily managed and utilized.

Let's use ModuleScript to manage the behavior of NPCs (Non-Playable Characters) that a player can engage in combat. Here, we will have the player approach the NPC (a humanoid), and each time the player clicks on the NPC, the NPC's health will decrease by a value of 25. Upon the NPC's health reaching zero, the NPC is destroyed and disappears from the game world.

Begin by creating a RemoteEvent within ReplicatedStorage, as this event will be shared between the server-side and client-side scripts in this example. You can do this manually using the Roblox Studio editor:

- Select ReplicatedStorage and click the plus icon beside it.

- From the list that shows up, select RemoteEvent.

- Name the RemoteEvent "PlayerAttacksNPC."

You must now create a ModuleScript within ServerStorage and rename it to NPCModule. Type in the code provided in Listing 8-8 into this newly created NPCModule script.

Listing 8-9. ModuleScript (NPCModule) created within ServerStorage

```
-- NPCModule
local module = {}                                    -- 1
function module.CreateNPC(model, health)             -- 2
    local NPC = {                                    -- 3
        Model = model,
        Health = health,
    }
    return NPC                                       -- 4
end
function module.TakeDamage(npc, damage)              -- 5
    npc.Health -= damage                            -- 6
    if npc.Health <= 0 then                         -- 7
        npc.Model:Destroy()                         -- 8
    else
        npc.Model.Humanoid.Health = npc.Health      -- 9
        print("NPC-Health: " .. npc.Health)
    end
end
return module                                        -- 10
```

1) This line of code initializes a local table named module. This table will be used to store functions and could store variables that are part of this module. Since it's local, it's only accessible within this script unless returned at the end (which is what we do).

2) This line defines a function named CreateNPC within the module table. This function will be used to create an NPC object. The parameters passed into this function are model (the model of the NPC) and health (the initial health value of the NPC). In this case, you would have noticed that within a ModuleScript the function name needs to be preceded by the table name – "module."

3) This code block creates a local dictionary (table) named NPC with two key-value pairs. The model is assigned the model of the NPC, and Health is assigned the initial health value.

4) This line of code returns the NPC dictionary (table) to the invoker of the CreateNPC function. This allows the invoker access to the NPC object, including its model and health properties.

5) This line of code defines a function named TakeDamage() within the module table. This function will be used to deal damage to an NPC. It takes two parameters: npc (the NPC object being damaged) and damage (the amount of damage to apply).

6) This line of code subtracts the damage value from the Health property of the npc object, effectively reducing the NPC's health by the damage amount.

7) This line of code checks if the Health property of the npc object is less than or equal to 0. If true, it means the NPC's health has been completely depleted and should be destroyed.

8) This line of code destroys the npc object's model property (i.e., the NPC's model in the game). Removing the Model from the game indicates that the NPC has been defeated.

9) If the NPC's health is greater than 0, the code within the else block is executed, wherein the Health property of the Humanoid within the NPC's model is set to be equal to the Health property of the npc object. This syncs the NPC's in-game visual representation of its health bar with the NPC's logical health value and also displays the NPC's current health value.

10) This line of code returns the module table, making it accessible to other scripts that require this ModuleScript. By returning the module, other scripts can utilize the CreateNPC() and TakeDamage() functions defined within.

Overall, this script provides functionality for creating NPC objects and handling damage to those NPCs. It's designed as a reusable module that could be part of a more extensive system for managing NPCs within a game.

You must create a new server-side script to manage NPCs. This Script needs to be created within the ServerScriptService. You can rename it to ManageNPCs. It will require access to the ModuleScript provided in Listing 8-9. It will also utilize the RemoteEvent you created, namely, PlayerAttacksNPC.

Listing 8-10. Server-side script to manage NPCs created within ServerScriptService

```
--ManageNPCs
local NPCModule = require(game.ServerStorage.NPCModule)              -- 1
local playerAttacksNPC = game.ReplicatedStorage:WaitForChild("PlayerAttacks
NPC")                                                               -- 2
-- An example NPC Humanoid model existing in the Workspace
local npcModel = workspace.NPC
local npc = NPCModule.CreateNPC(npcModel, 100)                      -- 3
playerAttacksNPC.OnServerEvent:Connect(function(player, damage)     -- 4
    NPCModule.TakeDamage(npc, damage)
end)
```

1) This line of code imports a ModuleScript named "NPCModule" (Listing 8-9) from ServerStorage into the local variable NPCModule. The require() method is used to load the module, allowing this script to access functions and variables defined within the NPCModule (like CreateNPC() and TakeDamage()).

2) This line of code gets a reference to the RemoteEvent named "PlayerAttacksNPC" from ReplicatedStorage and stores it in the local variable playerAttacksNPC. The WaitForChild method ensures that the script waits for the RemoteEvent to be loaded if it's not immediately available, which helps prevent potential runtime errors.

3) This line of code calls the CreateNPC() function from the NPCModule, passing in a model from the Workspace (an NPC model) and an initial health value of 100. This results in an NPC object being stored in the local variable npc.

4) This line creates an event handler (anonymous function) for the "PlayerAttacksNPC" RemoteEvent. When this event is fired from a client-side script, the anonymous function provided will be invoked with two parameters being passed into it: player (the player who initiated the event of attacking the NPC) and damage (the damage value sent from the client-side script, which will be applied to the NPC). Within this anonymous function, the TakeDamage() function from NPCModule is called, passing in the npc object and the damage value. This results in the NPC taking the specified amount of damage.

In summary, this script provides functionality for managing an NPC using an imported module and handling a RemoteEvent representing player attacks on the NPC. It's a good example of using ModuleScripts to organize code and RemoteEvents to manage client and server interactions.

You now need to create a client-side LocalScript within StarterPlayerScripts. You can rename this LocalScript to PlayerDamageNPC. This script allows the player to attack the NPC, where the attack takes the form of clicking on the NPC to decrement its health.

Listing 8-11. The client-side script within StarterPlayerScripts enables players to attack NPCs

```
--PlayerDamageNPC
local mouse = game.Players.LocalPlayer:GetMouse()          -- 1
local playerAttacksNPC = game.ReplicatedStorage:WaitForChild("Player
AttacksNPC")
mouse.Button1Down:Connect(function()                       -- 2
if mouse.Target and mouse.Target.Parent.Name == "NPC" then -- 3
playerAttacksNPC:FireServer(25) -- Example damage value    -- 4
end
end)
```

1) This line retrieves the mouse object for the local player (the player on whose client this LocalScript is running) and stores it in the local variable mouse. This object can detect various mouse actions and properties, such as button clicks and the current target under the mouse cursor.

2) This line of code sets up an anonymous event handler function that will be triggered when the player clicks the left mouse button (Button1). The :Connect method links the provided anonymous function to the Button1Down event, part of the mouse object.

3) This line of code checks two conditions:

   - mouse.Target: Whether there's an object under the mouse cursor (e.g., the player is hovering over something in the game).

   - mouse.Target.Parent.Name == "NPC": Whether the parent of the object under the mouse cursor has a name property equal to "NPC."

   - If both conditions are true, the code inside the if block will execute. This could be used to determine if the player is clicking on a specific object in the game, such as an NPC.

4) This line of code calls the :FireServer() method on the playerAttacksNPC RemoteEvent, sending the value 25 to the server. This value represents the amount of damage dealt to the NPC by the player's attack. In the context of a game, this line of code notifies the server that the player has attacked an NPC, with the server then handling the result of that attack (i.e., reducing the NPC's health).

In summary, this script represents a client-side action where a player can click on an NPC with the mouse to attack it, and the attack information is sent to the server. It's a typical pattern for handling player interactions with objects in a networked multiplayer game.

Before testing the code provided as part of Listings 8-9, 8-10, and 8-11, you must create a humanoid NPC object that the player can click on. To create this new humanoid NPC object within your game world, follow the steps listed as follows:

1) Select the "AVATAR" tab within the Roblox Studio editor, and click the Rig Builder button, as shown in Figure 8-1.

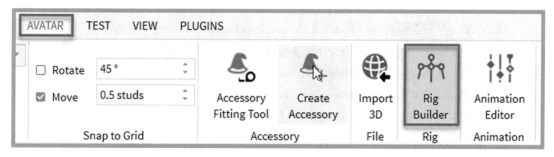

Figure 8-1. *The Rig Builder button available within the AVATAR tab's ribbon*

2) Upon clicking on the Rig Builder button, a "Generate Rig" dialog opens with options for different types of characters (like R6 or R15), body shapes, and avatars. Select the one you want to use, which will be added to your Workspace (Figure 8-2).

Figure 8-2. *Generate Rig Dialog*

3) In the "Explorer" window within the Workspace, you will notice
    that a "Rig" object has been added. Rename this "Rig" object to
    NPC, as this is the object name used in code within Listing 8-10.
    Also, ensure that you have your Humanoid at floor level so the
    player can approach it and easily click on it.

4) You can customize this Character by changing its appearance,
    clicking different body parts (head, torso, etc.), and modifying
    their properties in the properties window. You can also apply
    clothing, hair, and other accessories.

5) To make the character move realistically, you can assign or create
    animations. This can be done by selecting the Humanoid object
    inside the character model and setting up the Animator properties
    or using the Animation Editor.

6) If you need the character to have specific behaviors (like following
    paths, reacting to players, etc.), you must write and attach scripts
    using Lua.

7) This avatar rig has a Humanoid object, which makes it behave like a character. Select the Humanoid object, and you'll see various properties in the properties window that you can change, such as health, name, etc. Customize these as needed.

Creating NPCs with specific behaviors can become quite complex, especially if you want them to interact with the environment and the players in sophisticated ways. It involves not only the visual design but also potentially complex scripting.

Now that you have an NPC in the game world, you can test out the functionality of your Module script.

Summary

In this comprehensive exploration of Roblox's Task Library and Module Script, we delved into essential methods that enable efficient game development and interaction. The task. cancel() method, vital for terminating ongoing tasks, affords control over time-bound actions within the game. With the task.defer(function) method, we examined how to schedule functions for future execution, offering nuanced timing control. The task. wait(seconds) method enlightened us on creating deliberate pauses, an essential aspect of game pacing and player experience. We further explored the task.spawn(function) method, instrumental in concurrently executing functions, and the task.delay(time, function) method adds finesse to game timing by triggering functions after a specified delay. Together, these functions provide an intricate toolkit for developers, allowing for precise timing and sequencing within Roblox games, fostering a seamless and engaging gaming experience.

We also delved into the essential role of Module Scripts within Roblox development. Serving as reusable components, Module Scripts enable developers to write functions and variables in one place, which can be efficiently used across different parts of a game. This facilitates the creation of centralized sources for various in-game elements, from character attributes to game mechanics, significantly reducing redundancy and enhancing maintainability. We explored how to write, structure, and call Module Scripts and their strategic placement within ServerStorage or ReplicatedStorage, depending on usage requirements. This chapter illuminated the immense potential of Module Scripts in building more organized, scalable, and streamlined games, emphasizing their fundamental place in modern Roblox development.

CHAPTER 9

Understanding Players, Characters, and Humanoids in Roblox

In Roblox's dynamic and ever-expanding universe, three integral components stand at the core of user interaction and gameplay experience: Players, Characters, and Humanoids. This chapter, "Understanding Players, Characters, and Humanoids," delves into the multifaceted relationships and functionalities that bind these elements together. Beginning with a comprehensive overview of the Roblox Player, we'll explore the attributes and interactions that define the user's presence within the game world. Next, we'll examine the Roblox Character, the player's visual embodiment and customizable aspect, followed by an in-depth study of the humanoid, the entity responsible for simulating human-like behaviors and interactions. These objects, Player, Character, and Humanoid, are crucial components that work together to define various aspects of a playable character within the game. The following sections will provide a cohesive understanding of how players, characters, and humanoids synergize to create a rich and immersive experience within Roblox.

The Roblox Player

In Roblox, the concept of the "Player" occupies a central and indispensable role. The Roblox Player, more than just a mere user, serves as the gateway through which real-world individuals interact, explore, and engage within the platform's myriad virtual realms. Its importance extends beyond mere identification, encapsulating personalized attributes, preferences, and the fundamental connection between the human user and their in-game avatar. This section defines the Roblox Player in detail. It delves

© Christopher Coutinho 2023
C. Coutinho, *Roblox Lua Scripting Essentials*, https://doi.org/10.1007/979-8-8688-0026-9_9

into its multifaceted role within the Roblox environment, laying the foundation for understanding how it interconnects with characters and humanoids to create a seamless and immersive gaming experience.

While some other game engines might offer modular or third-party solutions for character control, the integrated nature of Roblox's character controller provides a cohesive and streamlined approach, especially for those just starting their journey in game development. If you are a seasoned developer, this functionality might still serve as a robust foundation, allowing for extensive customization and more focus on unique gameplay mechanics and features. In contrast, engines without an in-built character controller typically require more groundwork to achieve the same level of functionality, potentially slowing down the development process.

The in-built character controller in Roblox is essentially a pre-made bundle of components that control a character's movement, appearance, and interactions. It comes with the following key elements:

1) Rigging and animation: The character is pre-rigged, allowing for easy animation and customization. Standard animations for walking, jumping, and other basic movements are included.

2) Physics and collision: The character controller handles physics interactions, including collisions with the environment, gravity, and response to forces.

3) User input: It translates player input from devices (like keyboards, mice, gamepads, or touch screens) into character actions, handling walking, jumping, and other movements.

4) Camera control: The controller also manages the camera's perspective, allowing developers to create third-person and first-person views with minimal additional code.

5) Customization: While it provides a solid default setup, the character controller can be customized and extended to suit specific game requirements.

Some of the advantages of having an in-built character controller include the following:

1) Rapid development: A built-in character controller speeds up the development process, as developers don't have to create character mechanics from scratch. This can lead to quicker prototyping and iteration.

2) Consistency across games: The standardized character controller ensures consistency across Roblox games, making it easier for players to transition between different experiences on the platform.

3) Accessibility: For beginner and hobbyist developers, the built-in character controller lowers the entry barrier to game development. It lets creators focus on game design and content rather than intricate character control and physics details.

4) Flexibility: Although it provides a ready-made solution, the character controller is not a rigid structure. Developers can customize and extend it to create unique gameplay experiences.

5) Cost-efficiency: Building a character controller from scratch requires significant time and expertise. Having one pre-built saves you resources that can be allocated to other aspects of the game.

Player Properties, Methods, and Events

The Player object in Roblox is the central representation of a user within the game and plays a vital role in managing and identifying the user's interaction within the game. A Player object represents a user playing a game on Roblox. Still, rather than being a physical object in the game world, it is an abstract entity that holds information about the player, like their username, user ID, and membership status. This object is essential as it contains various properties and events that allow developers to control or respond to the player's interactions with the game, thus forming a core component in defining user engagement and behavior within a Roblox game environment.

Properties define the characteristics or attributes of a player. Some typical properties of the Player object include

1) UserId: A unique identifier for each player

2) Username: The player's display name

3) MembershipType: The player's membership type (e.g., Premium, Regular)

4) HealthDisplayDistance: Sets the distance in studs where the player can see other humanoid's health bars

Methods are actions that can be performed with or on the player object. Some methods of the Player object include

1) :Kick(reason): Kicks the player from the game, optionally providing a reason

2) :LoadCharacter(): Forces the player's character to respawn

3) :FindFirstChildWhichIsA(): finds the first child of a specific parent object that belongs to a certain class or has that class as one of its ancestors

4) :GetRankInGroup(groupId): Returns the player's rank in a specific group

5) :GetRoleInGroup(groupId): Returns the string name of the player's role in a particular group

6) :IsInGroup(groupId): Returns whether the player is part of a specific group

Events are triggers that run specific code when something specific happens to the Player object. Some examples of Player events include

1) PlayerAdded: Triggered when a new player joins the game

2) PlayerRemoving: Triggered when a player is leaving the game

Connection to Characters

The abstract Player entity object connects to the Character object, representing the player's avatar, reflecting not just appearance but the essence of interaction within the game world. Players move, interact, and engage with the game's various elements through the character, turning abstract inputs into tangible actions. The association between the player and the character is not merely aesthetic; it's a symbiotic relationship defining how the game is experienced. Listing 9-1 illustrates how you may access a player's character within a script.

Listing 9-1. Accessing a player's Character

```
-- client-side script within StarterPlayerScripts
local player = game.Players.LocalPlayer -- 1 Get the local
                                        -- player
local character = player.Character or player.CharacterAdded:Wait() -- 2 Get
the player's character
if character then                       -- 3
print("Character's name is: " .. character.Name) -- Print the
character's name
end
```

1) game.Players.LocalPlayer is a special object representing the player running the code on their client machine. Since this is a client-side operation, it refers to the specific player's client.

2) Here, you're declaring a local variable named character and trying to obtain the player's character object. The code player. Character will directly access the character if it's already available. If the character is not yet loaded, the code player. CharacterAdded:Wait() is invoked, pausing the script until the character is added to the player object. This ensures that the character variable has a value whether or not the character is already present.

3) This conditional statement checks if the character variable has a value (i.e., it is not nil). If the character variable has a value, then the code inside the block is executed. In this case, it prints a message to the console containing the character's name. If the character variable is nil, this line will not be executed.

These lines of code are typical in Roblox Lua scripting when you want to interact with the player's character, ensuring that the character exists before proceeding with the rest of the code. It shows a good understanding of handling potential timing issues in the game environment, such as the character not being loaded immediately.

Common Use Cases

You must first access it before you can work with the Player object. You can access a specific Player object via the Players service. Listing 9-2 demonstrates this.

Listing 9-2. Accessing the Player object

```
-- client-side script within StarterPlayerScripts
local Players = game:GetService("Players")
local player = Players.LocalPlayer -- Gets the player object for
                                   -- the client
```

You can use the Player object to create and manage custom statistics for each player, such as score or level. This allows you to tailor gameplay experiences based on individual player attributes. Listing 9-3 demonstrates this.

Listing 9-3. Manage custom player statistics

```
local Players = game:GetService("Players")
local player = Players.LocalPlayer
player:SetAttribute("Score", 0) -- 1 Initialize score for the
                                -- player

                        -- 2
player:GetAttributeChangedSignal("Score"):Connect(function()
print("Player Score:" .. player:GetAttribute("Score"))   -- 3
-- Print new score whenever it changes
end)
```

```
local newScore = player:GetAttribute("Score") + 90          -- 4
player:SetAttribute("Score", newScore) -- 5 This will print the new score,
as it triggers the connected function
```

1) This line of code sets up a custom "Score" attribute for the local player object and assigns it an initial value of 0.

2) This line of code creates a connection between the attribute change signal and the anonymous function that follows. This ensures that the function will be invoked every time the signal is emitted upon changing the "Score" attribute.

3) This line of code displays the new score within the anonymous function connected to the signal.

4) Here, we are retrieving the current value of the "Score" attribute, adding 90 to it, and storing the result in the local variable newScore.

5) By calling SetAttribute, we are triggering the function connected to the attribute change signal, causing the new score to be displayed.

You can use the Player object to detect when a player joins or leaves the game, allowing you to set up or clean up resources tied to that player. Listing 9-4 demonstrates this.

Listing 9-4. Players joining and leaving events

```
-- server-side script within ServerScriptService
local Players = game:GetService("Players")
Players.PlayerAdded:Connect(function(player)          -- 1
    print(player.Name .. " has joined the game!")
    -- Initialize resources for the new player
    task.wait(3)                                       -- 2
    player:Kick("Player Dead")                         -- 3
end)
Players.PlayerRemoving:Connect(function(player)        -- 4
    print(player.Name .. " has left the game!")
    -- Clean up resources tied to the player
end)
```

1) This line of code sets up an event listener for when a player joins the game. Players.PlayerAdded is an event triggered whenever a new player enters the game. Using :Connect(), this line of code binds an anonymous function to be executed whenever the event is triggered. This function will receive the newly added player object as an argument.

2) This line of code introduces a delay of three seconds. task.wait() is a function that pauses the execution of the script for a given number of seconds. In this case, the script waits three seconds before continuing to the following line of code.

3) This line of code kicks the player out of the game with the message "Player Dead." The :Kick() method is used to disconnect a player from the game and can include an optional string that describes the reason for the kick. This is generally used to communicate to the player why they were removed from the game.

4) This line of code sets up an event listener for when a player leaves the game. Players.PlayerRemoving is triggered whenever a player disconnects or is removed from the game. Like the PlayerAdded event, this line binds an anonymous function that will execute when the event is triggered, taking the departing player's object as an argument. Inside this function, you can include any logic needed to clean up resources tied to the player.

Using the Player object, you can respond to specific player inputs, such as key presses, and trigger custom behaviors. Listing 9-5 demonstrates this.

Listing 9-5. Responding to Player Input

```
-- client-side script within StarterPlayerScripts
local player = Players.LocalPlayer                      -- 1
local uis = game:GetService("UserInputService")         -- 2
uis.InputBegan:Connect(function(input, isProcessed)     -- 3

                                                        -- 4
```

```
if not isProcessed and input.KeyCode == Enum.KeyCode.K then
        print(player.Name .. " pressed the K key!")
        -- Trigger a custom action
end
end)
```

1) Players.LocalPlayer is used to access the player instance representing the client's character. Since it's client-side scripting, this refers to the player running the script assigned to the local player variable.

2) This line of code declares another local variable uis and assigns it a reference to the UserInputService. The UserInputService is a Roblox service that handles user input like keyboard presses, mouse movement, and touch input. By obtaining this service, the script can detect and handle various forms of input.

3) This line sets up an event listener that will invoke a given function when an input begins (i.e., a key is pressed, a mouse button is clicked, etc.). The InputBegan event is part of the UserInputService. It provides two parameters to the connected function: input, which is an object containing details about the input, such as the type of input (e.g., keyboard, mouse, gamepad) and the specific key code.

    isProcessed: A boolean indicating whether the system has already processed the input (e.g., opening the Roblox menu with the Esc key). If isProcessed is true, the specific input has a special function within Roblox and shouldn't be used to trigger custom game behavior.

4) This code block contains an if-statement that checks if the input hasn't been processed (not isProcessed) and if the key code is equal to the "K" key (input.KeyCode == Enum.KeyCode.K). If both conditions are met, the code inside the block will execute. In this specific case, it will print a message to the console stating that the player pressed the "K" key, and you can add any custom actions you want within this block.

The Roblox Player object is a versatile and essential part of Roblox game development, allowing you to identify and interact with individual players within your game. From tracking player statistics and responding to specific inputs to customizing appearances and managing game events, the Player object provides the means to create personalized and dynamic gameplay experiences. You can craft engaging and responsive games that cater to each player's unique needs and preferences by leveraging these capabilities.

The Roblox Character

In Roblox, the "Character" concept brings life, identity, and immersion to the player's experience. A character in Roblox is not merely a visual representation but an embodiment of the player's persona, aspirations, and creativity. Acting as the player's avatar, the character is a customizable entity with distinct appearances and attributes that reflect individuality. Its role extends into the very fabric of gameplay, influencing how players navigate, interact, and even compete within Roblox's various games and environments. This section will define what a character constitutes within Roblox and unravel its profound impact on shaping gameplay.

Character Components and Design

The Character is a Model object representing a player's physical and visual manifestation within the game world. It's what you see and control when playing the game. The Character typically includes default parts like the head, torso, arms, legs, accessories, and clothing. The Character is parented to the Workspace and is automatically linked to the corresponding Player object through the Player.Character property. When a player joins a game, Roblox automatically creates a Character for them and links it to their Player object.

Character Properties, Methods, and Events

In Roblox, the Character object represents a player's avatar in the game world, and its properties can be manipulated using Lua to achieve various game functionalities. Below are some commonly used properties, methods, and events associated with Roblox's character model.

Some common properties/parts of the Character object include

1) Head: The head part of the character

2) UpperTorso and LowerTorso: The torso or body part of the character

3) PrimaryPart: Specifies the primary part of the character used in moving the whole character

4) Humanoid: Refers to the humanoid object that contains information about the character's health, animations, etc.

Some commonly used methods of the Character object include

1) MoveTo(Position): Used to move the character (PrimaryPart) to a specific position in the workspace

2) GetChildren(): Returns a table of all child objects of the character, useful for iterating over the different child parts

3) FindFirstChild(name): Finds the first child object within the character with the given name

4) IsA(className): Returns true if an object is of a specified class or a descendant of that class

Events are crucial in programming, and in the context of Roblox, they allow for dynamic behavior based on different event triggers. Here are some of the most commonly used events related to character objects in Roblox Lua:

1) CharacterAdded: This event is triggered when a character is added to a player. This can be when a player first joins a game, respawns, or when the character model is reloaded for any reason. This event belongs to a Player object and fires whenever that player's character is added to the game. This could happen during the initial spawn, after a respawn, or if the character is recreated for another reason. You could use the CharacterAdded event to provide every player's character with a welcome message and a specific tool when they spawn in your game.

2) DescendantAdded: This event is triggered whenever a new object (descendant) is added to a character object. This event can be beneficial if you want to monitor changes to the character's structure, such as when new parts or accessories are added. In Roblox, a character comprises several components, including parts like the head, torso, arms, and legs, and accessories like hats or tools. These individual elements are referred to as descendants of the character object. The DescendantAdded event allows you to execute specific code whenever a new descendant is added to the character object. This can be useful for various purposes, such as initializing properties of newly added parts, applying special effects, or triggering game mechanics based on the character's composition. For example, when a character is given a special tool when they spawn, you can play a sound effect whenever this tool is added to the character. You can use the DescendantAdded event to achieve this. For example, you could create a bulletproof mechanic based on the character's vest. You can use the CharacterAppearanceLoaded event to ensure that you only attempt to check the character object vest once it has fully loaded.

3) DescendantRemoving: This event is triggered whenever an object (descendant) is removed from a character. This can include parts, accessories, tools, or any other objects that are children of the character. Utilizing this event can allow you to perform actions like cleaning up resources or triggering specific game mechanics when something is removed from the character. Sometimes, objects may be removed from the character during the game, whether through gameplay mechanics or other actions. This event allows you to detect when this happens and respond appropriately. This might be important for various reasons, such as deallocating resources related to the removed object, updating the game's UI, or triggering specific gameplay mechanics. For example, in a game where players can equip special accessories that grant abilities, you may want to remove the ability when the accessory is removed from the character. You can use the DescendantRemoving event to handle this situation.

Character and Humanoid Relationship

In Roblox, the relationship between the Character and the humanoid is central to defining the behavior and appearance of players and NPCs (Non-Player Characters) in the game.

A Character in Roblox is a container with all the parts and components that collectively define a player's or NPC's avatar. This includes things like the head, arms, legs, and torso, as well as other accessories or objects that can be attached to the avatar. The Character is essentially a model that contains all these parts, which scripts can reference, to control avatar appearance.

The humanoid is a special Character model object defining certain human-like properties and behaviors. This includes health, animations, and various states such as jumping, swimming, or climbing. The Humanoid object is critical for controlling how the character interacts with the environment and other characters within the game. It can trigger events and respond to environmental changes, such as taking damage or initiating specific animations.

The relationship between the Character and Humanoid can be summarized as follows:

1) Containment: The Humanoid is contained within the Character model. It's a child of the Character, which means that scripts and other components that want to interact with the humanoid must reference it through the Character.

2) Control and interaction: The Humanoid is responsible for managing various states and behaviors of the Character. This means you would interact with the Humanoid object if you want to change something related to the character's health, animations, or other human-like behavior.

3) Dependency: Without a Humanoid object, the Character would lack many essential human-like features, such as health and animations. While you could theoretically have a Character without a Humanoid, it would be static and lifeless.

4) Customization: By manipulating the properties and methods of the humanoid, you can achieve a wide range of behaviors and appearances for your Character. This includes setting custom animations, changing the health, or controlling various states like jumping or swimming.

5) Events: The Humanoid object can trigger and respond to various events, like taking damage or changing state. This allows for more complex interactions and behaviors within the game.

The relationship between the Character and the Humanoid in Roblox is deeply intertwined. The Character serves as the container and visual representation of the avatar, while the humanoid provides the functionality and behavior that make the character feel alive and human-like. Understanding and manipulating this relationship is key to creating engaging and dynamic characters within Roblox, allowing for a more immersive gaming experience. Whether you're controlling player characters or NPCs, this relationship is central to character design and interaction within the Roblox platform.

Common Use Cases

You must first access it before you can work with the Character object. You can access the Player Character object via the Player object. Listing 9-6 demonstrates how to achieve this, as well as how to list all child objects within the Character object.

Listing 9-6. Accessing the Character object and listing all its child objects

```
-- client-side script within StarterPlayerScripts
local Players = game:GetService("Players")
local player = Players.LocalPlayer
local character = player.Character or player.CharacterAdded:Wait() -- Waits
for the character if not
                        -- available
wait(3) -- Allows 3 seconds for the characters parts to be added
        -- to the character's body.
if character then
-- Loop through all objects within the character
for _, obj in pairs(character:GetChildren()) do            -- 1
print("Object Name:", obj.Name) -- Outputs the objects name
end
end
```

1) This line of code initiates a loop that will iterate through each child object within the character. The character:GetChildren() function returns a table containing all the child objects of the character.

Listing 9-7 showcases how various properties, methods, and events can be combined to respond to various aspects of a character's life cycle within a Roblox game.

Listing 9-7. Character properties, methods, and events in action

```
-- Function to handle a new character added
local function onCharacterAdded(character)
print("Character Added: " .. character.Name)
-- Utilizing the 'Humanoid' and 'PrimaryPart' properties
local humanoid = character:FindFirstChild("Humanoid")        -- 1
local primaryPart = character.PrimaryPart                     -- 2
if humanoid and primaryPart and humanoid:IsA("Humanoid") then -- 3
-- Utilizing the 'MoveTo()' method
character:MoveTo(Vector3.new(10, 0.5, 10))                    -- 4
-- Event handling for 'DescendantAdded'
character.DescendantAdded:Connect(function(descendant)        -- 5
print("Character Descendant Added: " .. descendant.Name)
end)
-- Event handling for 'DescendantRemoving'
character.DescendantRemoving:Connect(function(descendant)     -- 6
print("Character Descendant Removing: " .. descendant.Name)
end)
else
warn("Humanoid or PrimaryPart not found in Character!")       -- 7
end
end
local Players = game:GetService("Players")
local player = Players.LocalPlayer
-- 8 Waits for the character if not available
local character = player.Character or player.CharacterAdded:Wait()
wait(3) -- 9 Allows 3 seconds for character parts to be added
        -- to the character's body.
```

```
if character then                                          -- 10
    onCharacterAdded(character)
end
```

1) This method FindFirstChild() is called on the character object.
   It searches through the immediate children of the character for
   an object with the name "Humanoid." In the context of a Roblox
   character, the "Humanoid" object is typically a child of the
   character model and contains various properties related to the
   character's appearance, animation, health, etc.

2) This line of code assigns the PrimaryPart property of the character
   object to the local variable primaryPart. The PrimaryPart is
   generally the main part of a model to which other parts are
   anchored, and in the context of a character, it is set to the part
   HumanoidRootPart. The MoveTo() method uses the PrimaryPart
   to move the Character.

3) This line of code checks if humanoid and primaryPart are not
   nil and if humanoid is an instance of the Humanoid class.
   This ensures that the code block inside this if statement is only
   executed if these conditions are met.

4) This line calls the MoveTo() method on the character, causing
   the character to move to the specified position (10, 0.5, 10) in the
   game world.

5) This line of code connects a function to the DescendantAdded
   event of the character. Whenever a new descendant (child
   object) is added to the character, this function will be called,
   and the descendant's name will be printed. When you run
   the code provided in Listing 9-7, you should see the message
   "Character Descendant Added: BodyVelocity" displayed in the
   "Output" window.

6) This line of code connects to the DescendantRemoving
   event of the character. This function will be called when
   a descendant is about to be removed from the character.
   When you run the code provided in Listing 9-7, you should

see the message "Character Descendant Removing: Climbing...Running...Landing...Jumping...," etc. displayed in the "Output" window.

7) This line of code prints a warning message to the "Output" window if either humanoid or primaryPart is not found within the Character. This can be helpful for debugging.

8) This line of code attempts to get the character of the local player. If the character is unavailable (e.g., it hasn't loaded yet), it waits for the CharacterAdded event and retrieves the character.

9) This line of code introduces a delay of three seconds. This can be used to ensure that all parts are added to the Character's body before proceeding.

10) This line of code checks if the character variable is not nil, meaning that the character has been successfully retrieved or loaded. If the Character exists, the onCharacterAdded() function is called with the character as an argument.

Overall, this code handles the addition of a new Character and responds to various events related to that Character. It includes a safety check to ensure that the relevant objects exist before proceeding and demonstrates several key concepts related to Character handling in Roblox.

The Roblox Humanoid

In Roblox, the "Humanoid" is an integral component that breathes life into characters by simulating human-like behavior and interactions. A humanoid in Roblox is not merely a set of properties; it's a dynamic aspect that imparts physicality, movement, and nuanced reactions to the character, rendering them more realistic and responsive. Its role within Roblox transcends mere aesthetics, embedding itself into the functionality of characters, dictating how they move, respond to stimuli, and interact within the game's environment. This section will explore the definition of a humanoid in Roblox and illustrate its vital role as a linchpin in character functionality, enhancing the immersive experience for developers and players alike.

Humanoid Properties, Methods, and Events

The humanoid is an object within the Character model that controls various human-like attributes and behaviors. It includes properties like Health, WalkSpeed, and JumpPower, which can be modified to control how the character moves and interacts with the environment. The humanoid is crucial for applying animations and controlling how the Character responds to input from the player. Without a Humanoid object, the Character would be a static model without any dynamic, responsive behavior.

Some typical properties of the Humanoid object include

1) Health: Represents the current health of the humanoid. It is a value between 0 and the value of MaxHealth. When Health reaches 0, the humanoid dies.

2) MaxHealth: Defines the maximum amount of health a humanoid can have. By default, it's 100, but you can change it according to your requirements.

3) AutoRotate: If true, the character will automatically rotate to face the direction it moves.

4) WalkSpeed: This represents the speed at which the humanoid can move. You can adjust this to create effects like slowing down or speeding up the player.

5) JumpPower: Defines how high the character can jump. Modifying this value allows for higher or lower jumps.

6) DisplayName: The name displayed over the humanoid in the game, usually the player's username.

7) RigType: This describes the type of rig used, either R6 (a 6-part rig) or R15 (a 15-part rig), to determine how the character's body parts are connected.

8) BreakJointsOnDeath: This property determines whether humanoid joints break when they enter the dead state. By default, this value is set to true.

9) CameraOffset: In Roblox, the Camera object represents the virtual camera through which the player sees the game world. The CameraOffset property lets you shift or offset this camera relative to a Humanoid object, such as the player's avatar. You could use the CameraOffset property to create unique camera angles or perspectives in your game, like an over-the-shoulder or aerial perspective. It allows for a more dynamic and immersive experience, as the camera's position can be fine-tuned to suit the needs of your particular game design. The CameraOffset property lets you move the camera to a different position relative to the player's avatar, and this shift will move along with the avatar, maintaining the same relative position even if the avatar turns or moves.

Some standard methods of the Humanoid object include

1) TakeDamage(amount): Reduces the Health of the Humanoid by the specified amount.

2) GetState(): Returns the current state of the humanoid, such as running, jumping, swimming, etc.

3) ChangeState(newState): You can use this method to change the state of the humanoid, forcing it into a specific state like jumping.

Some common events of the Humanoid object include

1) Died: Triggered when the Health property reaches 0. This is often used to handle actions that should occur upon a character's death, like respawning or updating game statistics.

2) HealthChanged: Triggered whenever the Humanoid's Health property changes. This can be used to update health bars or other HUD elements.

3) StateChanged: This event is triggered when the humanoid's state changes, for instance, when transitioning from running to jumping. It can be used to synchronize animations or other aspects of character behavior.

4) Jumping: Triggered when the humanoid starts to jump, allowing you to customize the jump behavior or add special effects.

5) Touched: Triggered when any of the humanoid's limbs makes contact with a base part.

6) Swimming: Triggered when the speed at which a humanoid is swimming within a water terrain changes.

7) Running: Triggered when the speed at which a humanoid is running changes.

8) Climbing: Triggered when the speed at which a humanoid is climbing changes.

Integration with the Character and Player

The integration between Humanoids, Characters, and Players in Roblox is an intricate relationship that forms the core of user engagement and interaction. Humanoids infuse life-like qualities into characters, characters act as the virtual representation of players, and players control and interact with their characters through Humanoids. This synergy creates a dynamic and interactive environment where each element's role complements the other, providing an engaging and immersive experience for the players.

Understanding this synergy is crucial for developers who wish to create engaging content within the Roblox platform. It helps design intuitive control mechanisms realistic characters, and enhancing the overall player experience within the game. By manipulating and building upon these foundational elements, one can create unique and compelling gameplay experiences in Roblox.

Synergy and interaction:

1) Player-to-Character relationship:

- Control: The player's inputs are mapped to their corresponding character's actions, allowing them to control their character's movements and interactions within the game.

- Customization: Players can often customize their characters' appearance and abilities, enhancing the immersion and personal connection to the game.

2) Character to Humanoid relationship:

- Animation and behavior: The Humanoid object within the character controls the animations, making characters walk, jump, run, and more. This helps in creating a life-like experience.

- Health management: Humanoids handle the life attribute of a character, including taking damage, healing, or even dying.

3) Player to Humanoid synergy:

- Direct interaction: The player's input directly affects the humanoid's behavior, thus shaping the character's actions. This synergy allows for real-time control and feedback, which is vital for an immersive gaming experience.

Common Use Cases

Listing 9-8 demonstrates a head bobbing effect by moving the camera up, down, left, and right while the player is moving.

Listing 9-8. Camera head bobbing effect

```
-- should be parented inside the StarterCharacterScripts
local RunService = game:GetService("RunService")       -- 1
local playerModel = script.Parent                      -- 2
local humanoid = playerModel:WaitForChild("Humanoid")  -- 3

local function updateBobbingEffect()                   -- 4
    local now = tick()                                 -- 5
-- Is the character walking?
if humanoid.MoveDirection.Magnitude > 0 then            --6
local velocity = humanoid.RootPart.Velocity            -- 7
local bobble_X = math.cos(now * 9) / 5                 -- 8
local bobble_Y = math.abs(math.sin(now * 12)) / 5      -- 9
local bobble = Vector3.new(bobble_X, bobble_Y, 0) * math.min(1, velocity.
Magnitude / humanoid.WalkSpeed)                -- 10
humanoid.CameraOffset = humanoid.CameraOffset:lerp(bobble, 0.25)     -- 11
print("Head Bobbing in action")
```

```
else
-- Scale down the CameraOffset so that it shifts back to its
-- regular position.
humanoid.CameraOffset = humanoid.CameraOffset * 0.75        -- 12
end
end
RunService.RenderStepped:Connect(updateBobbingEffect)        -- 13
```

1) This line of code retrieves the RunService from the game, which manages functions related to rendering and stepping through the game loop. It's stored in a local variable for easy access later.

2) This line of code gets the parent of the current script, the player's model or character, and stores it in a local variable called playerModel.

3) This line waits until the "Humanoid" child inside the player model is available. The humanoid is an object that controls various aspects of a character's appearance and movement properties.

4) Here, the definition of the function updateBobbingEffect begins. This function will update the head bobbing effect based on the character's movement.

5) The tick() function retrieves the current time in seconds. This is stored in the local variable and is used in trigonometric calculations to achieve the oscillating bobbing effect.

6) This line of code within the if condition checks to see whether the character is moving. If the magnitude of the MoveDirection is greater than 0, it means that the character has a direction of movement and isn't standing still. If this condition is true, the code within the if statement will run, triggering the bobbing effect for the camera. If the character is stationary (magnitude equals 0), the code inside the if statement will be skipped, and the camera bobbing effect will not be applied.

7) This line of code retrieves the current velocity of the character's RootPart and stores it in the local variable velocity.

8) This calculates the bobbing effect on the X-axis using the cosine function. It creates a smooth, periodic oscillation for the left-right motion of the camera.

9) Similar to point 8 above, but for the Y-axis using the sine function. The absolute value ensures a bouncing effect for the up-down motion of the camera.

10) This creates a Vector3 object from the bobble_X and bobble_Y values and scales it based on the character's current velocity and walking speed. This represents the complete bobbing effect.

11) This line of code smoothly transitions the camera's offset to the calculated bobbing effect using linear interpolation.

12) Here, the character isn't moving. This line gradually reduces the CameraOffset to return it to its regular position.

13) This line connects the updateBobbingEffect() function to the RenderStepped event. This ensures that the function is called every time a frame is rendered, allowing the bobbling effect to update in real-time.

The code achieves a bobbing camera effect that responds to the character's movement, giving a more immersive feel to the walking or running motion within a Roblox game.

Cosine function: Let's delve into the visual effect created using the cos() function in this context. The cosine function ($\cos(x)$) is a trigonometric function that produces a wave-like pattern. It returns values between -1 and 1, repeating every 2π radians or 360 degrees. In this code, the expression math.cos(now * 9) / 5 generates these wave-like values. The wave's frequency increases by multiplying the time now by 9, meaning it oscillates more often over the same period, further dividing by 5 scales down the wave's amplitude so it doesn't bob too excessively.

A periodic effect means that the effect repeats at regular intervals. In the case of the X-axis in this code, it will cause the camera to move left and right rhythmically and smoothly. As the cosine function oscillates between -1 and 1, it will cause the camera's X position to shift positively and negatively, creating the left and right bobbing effect. Here's what the effect will look like visually on the X-axis:

1) At the Peak of the Wave (cosine = 1): The camera will be at its farthest right position.

2) At the Zero Crossing (cosine = 0): The camera will be at the center.

3) At the Trough of the Wave (cosine = -1): The camera will be at its farthest left position.

This pattern repeats smoothly and continuously as long as the character moves, giving the sensation of natural, rhythmic swaying or bobbing, like a person's view might sway when they walk or run. Using the cosine function in this way introduces a natural and repetitive left-right swaying motion to the camera's X position, giving a more immersive feel to the character's movement. It mimics the human-like sway we experience when walking or running, making the gameplay more realistic and engaging.

Sine function: Let's delve into the visual effect created using the cos() function in this context. The sine function creates a periodic effect on the Y-axis, combined with the absolute value function, to ensure that the result is always positive.

The sine function, sin(x), is another trigonometric function that produces a wave-like pattern similar to the cosine function. It returns values between -1 and 1; its wave repeats every 2π radians or 360 degrees. In this specific code, the time is multiplied by 12, increasing the sine wave's frequency and causing it to oscillate more quickly. The division by 5 scales down the amplitude, limiting the vertical bobbing effect. By applying math.abs() function to the sine function, the negative values of the sine wave are flipped to become positive. This means that instead of oscillating between -1 and 1, the sine wave only oscillates between 0 and 1. Here's how the combination of sine and absolute value functions, used in conjunction, will look like visually on the Y-axis:

1) At the Peak of the original Sine Wave (sine = 1): The camera will be at its highest position on the Y-axis.

2) At the Zero Crossing (sine = 0): The camera will be at the center of the Y-axis.

3) At the Trough of the Original Sine Wave (sine = -1): Since the absolute value is taken, this will also be treated as the wave's peak, and the camera will again be at its highest position on the Y-axis.

On account of the absolute value, the camera's motion on the Y-axis resembles a bouncing effect instead of a full up-and-down wave. It smoothly moves upward, briefly returns to the center, and then moves upward again, creating a rhythmic and repetitive bobbing motion along the Y-axis.

Using the sine function with the absolute value function creates a periodic bouncing effect on the Y-axis. This can be visually interpreted as the natural up-and-down movement of a person's viewpoint as they walk or run. The bouncing effect complements the left-right swaying on the X-axis, creating a more immersive and natural camera movement that simulates how a person's viewpoint might shift as they move. It adds depth to the experience and makes the game feel more lifelike and engaging.

Listing 9-9. Humanoid properties, methods, and events in action (1)

```
-- Get the Humanoid object
local Players = game:GetService("Players")
local player = Players.LocalPlayer
local character = player.Character or player.CharacterAdded:Wait()
wait(3)
local humanoid = character:FindFirstChild("Humanoid")
-- Setting properties
humanoid.Health = 100                                    -- 1
humanoid.MaxHealth = 200                                 -- 2
humanoid.AutoRotate = true                               -- 3
humanoid.WalkSpeed = 24                                  -- 4
humanoid.JumpPower = 70                                  -- 5
humanoid.DisplayName = "Bob"                             -- 6
humanoid.RigType = Enum.HumanoidRigType.R15             -- 7
humanoid.BreakJointsOnDeath = true                       -- 8

-- Using Events
humanoid.HealthChanged:Connect(function(health)         -- 9
print("Player Health has changed to: " .. health)
end)
humanoid.Died:Connect(function()                         -- 10
    print("Player has died")
end)
-- Using Methods
humanoid:TakeDamage(50)                                  -- 11
wait(3)
humanoid:TakeDamage(100)                                 -- 12 Kill the Player
```

1) This line of code sets the Humanoid object's Health property to 100. Health represents the current health of the character.

2) This line of code sets the MaxHealth property of the Humanoid object to 200. MaxHealth defines the maximum health the humanoid can have.

3) This line of code sets the AutoRotate property to true. When AutoRotate is true, the character will automatically face the direction in which it moves.

4) This line of code sets the WalkSpeed property to 24. WalkSpeed controls how fast the character can move in studs per second.

5) This line of code sets the JumpPower property to 70. JumpPower controls how high the character can jump.

6) This line of code sets the DisplayName property to "Bob." DisplayName is a property that can specify a name different from the username.

7) This line of code sets the RigType property to R15. RigType determines the type of rig, which in this case is R15 (15 joints), a more recent and detailed rig compared to R6.

8) This line of code sets the BreakJointsOnDeath property to true. When set to true, it causes the character's joints to break apart upon death.

9) This line of code connects a function to the HealthChanged event. When the Health property changes, the provided function will be called, and the new health value will be displayed.

10) This line of code connects a function to the Died event. The provided function will be called when the humanoid dies, and the message "Player has died" will be displayed.

11) This line calls the TakeDamage() method, dealing 50 damage to the humanoid. The humanoid's health will be reduced by 50.

12) This line calls the TakeDamage method, dealing 100 damage to the humanoid, which results in the health becoming negative, as a result of which the player is killed and crumbles to the ground, on account of the BreakJointsOnDeath property being set to true.

These lines of code set up a Humanoid object with specific properties and behaviors, connecting events that respond to changes in health or death and dealing damage to the character.

Listing 9-10. Humanoid properties, methods, and events in action (2)

```
-- Get the Humanoid object
local Players = game:GetService("Players")
local player = Players.LocalPlayer
local character = player.Character or player.CharacterAdded:Wait()
wait(3)
local humanoid = character:FindFirstChild("Humanoid")
-- Setting properties
humanoid.Health = 100
humanoid.MaxHealth = 200
humanoid.AutoRotate = true
humanoid.WalkSpeed = 24
humanoid.JumpPower = 70
humanoid.DisplayName = "Bob"
humanoid.RigType = Enum.HumanoidRigType.R15
humanoid.BreakJointsOnDeath = false
-- Using Events
humanoid.StateChanged:Connect(function(oldState, newState)-- 1
print("Player State changed from: " .. tostring(oldState) .. " to " ..
tostring(newState))
end)
humanoid.Jumping:Connect(function(isJumping)              -- 2
print("Player Jumping: " .. tostring(isJumping))
end)
humanoid.Touched:Connect(function(other)                 -- 3
    print("Player Touched: " .. other.Name)
end)
```

```
-- Using Methods
humanoid:ChangeState(Enum.HumanoidStateType.Jumping)      -- 4
                                                          -- Changes state
                                                             to Jumping
```

1) This line of code connects a function to the StateChanged event of the Humanoid object. The StateChanged event is fired whenever the character's animation state changes. The function receives two parameters: oldState, representing the previous state, and newState, representing the new state the character is entering. The function prints these states so you can see how the state has changed.

2) This line of code connects a function to the Jumping event of the Humanoid object. The Jumping event is triggered whenever the player's character starts or stops jumping. The function receives a boolean parameter, isJumping, which is true when the character starts jumping and false when it stops. The function prints this value, showing when the player jumps.

3) This line connects a function to the Touched event of the Humanoid object. The Touched event is fired when something collides with any part of the character. The function receives a parameter other, representing the object that the character has touched. The function prints the name of this object so you can see what the player's character has touched.

4) This line calls the ChangeState method on the Humanoid object, changing its state to Jumping. By calling this method, you manually set the character's animation state to a jumping state, overriding any existing animation or movement logic. Note that using this method might create an unnatural or abrupt change in animation, so it should be used with caution and understanding of how it fits into your game's logic.

Hierarchy Structure

The hierarchy structure involving these objects is as follows:

- Workspace: The main container for all physical objects in the game.

  - Character (Model): Parented to the Workspace and represents the visual manifestation of a player.

    - Humanoid: Nested within the Character model and controls human-like attributes and behaviors.

    - Other Parts (e.g., Head, Torso): Other components of the Character model.

- Players: A service containing all Player objects.

  - Player: Represents the abstract entity of a user playing the game.

Figure 9-1 provides a graphical representation of this hierarchical structure viewable via the "Explorer" window.

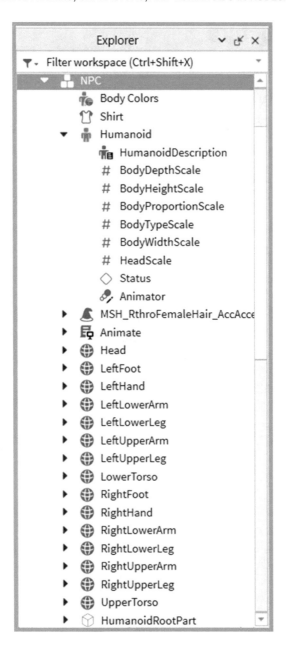

Figure 9-1. *NPC Humanoid hierarchy*

Relationships: Player, Character, and Humanoid

In Roblox, the relationship between the Player, Character, and Humanoid objects forms a hierarchical and interconnected structure that defines a player's identity, appearance, and behavior within the game. The Player object links to the Character, representing the visual manifestation of the player, while the Character contains the Humanoid object, controlling various attributes and actions.

1) Player and Character: The Player object links to the Character through the Player.Character property providing a direct connection between the abstract player and their visual representation in the game.

2) Character and Humanoid: The Character contains the Humanoid object, which controls the behavior and attributes of the Character, making it dynamic and responsive.

3) Player and Humanoid: Indirectly, the Player interacts with the humanoid through the Character, affecting how the character behaves within the game.

Together, these objects create a comprehensive system that defines who a player is within Roblox, what they look like, and how they act. It's a highly customizable system that allows for extensive creativity and control in shaping the player's experience within a Roblox game.

Summary

This chapter provided you with a comprehensive understanding of the intricacies of the Roblox Player, Character, and Humanoid, which were systematically explored. The Roblox Player section delved into the Player object's various properties, events, and methods. The Roblox Character section delved into the Character object properties, events, and methods and outlined the structure and relationship between the character and player. Finally, the Roblox Humanoid section covered health management, character behavior, related events, and the intricate hierarchy and relationship between the Player, Character, and Humanoid. Together, these components provide a comprehensive understanding of the building blocks constituting a Roblox game, setting the foundation for character development and interactive gameplay.

CHAPTER 10

Raycasting

Raycasting is a critical concept in game development, particularly in creating intricate, interactive environments. In Roblox, using Lua allows developers to create and manipulate rays, which are straight lines that extend indefinitely in a specific direction. These rays can detect collisions or intersections with physical objects within the virtual world, enabling applications such as character line of sight, shooting mechanics, or even pathfinding. Utilizing the Roblox engine's built-in workspace:Raycast() function, developers can efficiently work with rays to create complex and responsive gameplay elements. The following chapter will delve into the principles of raycasting in Roblox, exploring the Lua syntax and providing practical examples to illustrate the power and versatility of raycasting in a gaming context.

Definition and Purpose of Raycasting

Raycasting is a computational method used in computer graphics and game development to simulate the behavior of rays or light. It involves projecting a straight line or ray from a specific point in a given direction determining what objects or surfaces intersect with that ray. Raycasting aims to find information about objects in the line of sight or along the ray's path. This information can include the distance to the object, the surface's normal vector, or material properties. Raycasting is commonly used for line-of-sight calculations, collision detection, and simulating reflections or shadows.

Common Applications in Game Development

In game development, raycasting has a wide array of applications. One of its most prevalent uses is collision detection, where it can quickly determine if a bullet, gaze, or other projectile hits an object. Raycasting is also employed in artificial intelligence (AI) to simulate the vision or sensing of characters, helping them navigate environments

279

C. Coutinho, *Roblox Lua Scripting Essentials*, https://doi.org/10.1007/979-8-8688-0026-9_10

or respond to the player's actions. In rendering, raycasting can create reflections, refractions, and shadows, adding realism to virtual environments. Other applications might include generating procedural terrain, managing interaction with user interfaces, and aiding debugging by visualizing paths and interactions.

Overview of Raycasting in Roblox

Raycasting in Roblox is implemented using the workspace:Raycast() function, providing developers with a powerful tool for various applications within the platform. In Roblox, raycasting can determine whether a line segment intersects with parts within a workspace. It can be crucial in determining if an object, like a bullet, hits a target or wall. Roblox offers a specialized raycasting API that returns a RaycastResult object containing detailed information about the intersection, such as the part hit, the exact intersection position, and the surface's normal. Raycasting in Roblox enables greater interactive and responsive gameplay, enhancing the player experience.

The Ray Object

A Ray object represents a line that starts from a given point and extends infinitely in a particular direction. It is commonly used in games for various purposes like detecting intersection collisions, casting shadows, etc.

In Roblox, you can create a Ray object using the Ray.new() function. This function takes two parameters, Origin and Direction, where the Origin determines the point where the Ray begins, and Direction is a Vector that defines the direction the Ray is pointing. Listing 10-1 demonstrates how to create a Ray and visualize it in the game.

Listing 10-1. Create and Visualize a Ray

```
--Create a Ray object
local origin = Vector3.new(0, 5, 0)
local direction = Vector3.new(10, 0, 0)
local ray = Ray.new(origin, direction)                    -- 1
--Visualize Ray object in-game
local part = Instance.new("Part")
part.Name = "Ray"
```

```
part.Anchored = true
part.BrickColor =  BrickColor.new("Really red")
part.Material = Enum.Material.Neon
part.Size = Vector3.new(0.1, 0.1, direction.Magnitude)        -- 2
part.Position = origin + direction/2                          -- 3
part.Orientation = direction:Cross(Vector3.new(0, 1, 0)).unit   -- 4
part.Parent = workspace
```

1) This line of code creates a Ray object with the Ray.new()
    constructor function. It takes two parameters, origin and
    direction, which define the ray's starting point and direction,
    respectively. The created ray object is stored in the local
    variable ray.

2) Here, we set the size of the Ray part. This part will be used
    to visualize the ray. The dimensions are defined using a
    Vector3 object:

    • 0.1: Width of the part

    • 0.1: Height of the part

    • direction.Magnitude: Length of the part, equal to the magnitude
      of the direction vector, effectively making the part as long as
      the ray.

3) Here the part.Position is set to the midpoint of a line segment
    defined by the origin and the direction. By adding half the
    direction to the origin, you're positioning the part at the midpoint
    along the line segment defined by origin and direction. This
    ensures the part is positioned in the ray's center, providing a
    proper visualization.

4) This line of code sets the part's orientation to align with the ray's
    direction. The Cross() function calculates the cross product
    between two Vectors. The result of a cross-product is a Vector
    perpendicular to the plane defined by the original vectors. Here,
    the Vector direction (Vector3.new(10, 0, 0)) is crossed with the unit
    vector pointing upward along the y-axis (Vector3.new(0, 1, 0)).

The result is a vector perpendicular to both direction and the y-axis (XY plane). This resultant Z-axis Vector is normalized using ".unit," meaning it scales the vector to a unit length of 1. The orientation often requires a direction rather than a magnitude, so normalizing gives the pure direction of the resultant Vector.

Basic Raycasting

Raycasting in Roblox is the technique of extending an invisible line (ray) from a particular point in a given direction and determining what, if anything, that ray intersects within the game world. Listing 10-2 demonstrates this.

Listing 10-2. Casting out a Ray

```
--create Muzzle part
local muzzle = Instance.new("Part")
muzzle.Name = "Muzzle"
muzzle.Anchored = true
muzzle.BrickColor = BrickColor.new("Really red")
muzzle.Material = Enum.Material.Neon
muzzle.Size = Vector3.new(0.25, 0.25, 0.25)
muzzle.Position = Vector3.new(0, 5, 0)
muzzle.Parent = workspace
local function drawRay(rayOrigin,rayDir, color)          -- 1
local part = Instance.new("Part")
part.Name = "RayBeam"
part.Anchored = true
part.CanCollide = false
part.Size = Vector3.new(0.1, 0.1, rayDir.Magnitude)      -- 2
part.CFrame = CFrame.lookAt(rayOrigin, rayOrigin + rayDir) * CFrame.new(0,
0, -rayDir.Magnitude/2)                                  -- 3
part.BrickColor = BrickColor.new(color)
part.Material = Enum.Material.Neon
part.Parent = workspace
print("Ray Beam created")
end
```

```
--Cast out the ray
local origin = workspace.Muzzle.Position              -- 4
local direction = Vector3.new(0,0,-10)                -- 5
local result = workspace:Raycast(origin,direction)    -- 6
drawRay(origin,direction, "Bright blue")              -- 7
print("Ray Beam Hit: " .. tostring(result))           -- 8
```

1) This line of code defines a local function named drawRay, which takes three arguments: rayOrigin, rayDir, and color. This function will create a visual representation of a ray using a part.

2) Here, a Vector3 value is assigned to the size property of the part (that creates a visual representation of the ray beam.) The X (width) and Y (height) dimensions are set to 0.1, while the Z (depth) dimension is set to the magnitude of rayDir. The magnitude of a vector is the length of the vector.

3) This line of code sets up the CFrame (Coordinate Frame) of the part (ray beam). A CFrame describes the object's position and orientation in 3D space. Here's how the CFrame works in this line of code:

   • CFrame.lookAt(rayOrigin, rayOrigin + rayDir): This function returns a CFrame that points from the rayOrigin toward rayOrigin + rayDir. Essentially, it aligns the forward direction of the object (ray beam) with the Vector rayDir.

   • CFrame.new(0, 0, -rayDir.Magnitude/2): This creates a new CFrame that translates the object along its local Z-axis by half its negative magnitude. Since the Z-axis usually represents the forward direction, this positions the part (ray beam) to look like it originates from the Muzzle object.

   • The multiplication of the two CFrame values combines their effects, applying the rotation and translation.

4) This line of code retrieves the position of the Muzzle part in the workspace and assigns it to the variable origin.

5) This line of code creates a new Vector3 object representing the direction in which the ray will be cast and assigns it to the variable direction.

6) This line of code casts a ray from the origin in the direction using the Raycast method, the result of which is stored in the variable result. The result contains information about what the ray hit if anything.

7) This line of code calls the previously defined drawRay() function to create a visual representation of the ray in the workspace. The color is set to "Bright blue."

8) Finally, this line displays information about what the ray hit in the "output" window. If the ray didn't hit anything, the result would be nil, and the printed output would reflect that.

Combining these lines of code results in a visual representation of a ray being cast and displaying information about what the ray hit, providing a robust example for understanding ray casting within the Roblox environment.

Calculating Intersection Points

Raycasting is commonly used to detect intersections between a ray and objects in the game world. In Roblox, you can use the Workspace:FindPartOnRay() function to perform raycasting. It allows various applications, from essential collision detection to more complex tasks like shooting mechanics, line-of-sight checks, or even simulating light rays.

Listing 10-3 creates a part that acts as the origin point for the ray. When the game starts, a ray will be cast from this part in the forward direction. If the ray intersects with another part in the workspace, a marker will be placed at the intersection point. You must create a part named "Origin" in the Workspace to act as the origin point for the ray. You also need to place some obstacle parts in the Workspace for the ray to intersect with.

Listing 10-3. Lua script to perform Raycasting and mark the intersection point

```lua
-- The part that acts as the ray's origin point
local rayOriginPart = workspace:WaitForChild("Origin")
local rayLength = 55  -- The length of the ray in studs
-- Function to mark the intersection point
local function MarkIntersectionPoint(position)                    -- 1
    local marker = Instance.new("Part")
    marker.Size = Vector3.new(0.15, 0.15, 0.15)
    marker.Position = position
    marker.Anchored = true
    marker.BrickColor = BrickColor.new("Bright red")
    marker.Parent = workspace
end
-- Function to perform a raycast
local function PerformRaycast()                                   -- 2
local rayOrigin = rayOriginPart.Position   -- Start point of the
                                           -- ray
-- 3 Create a ray
local ray = Ray.new(rayOrigin, Vector3.new(0, 0, rayLength))
-- 4 Perform raycasting
local hitPart, hitPoint, normal = workspace:FindPartOnRay(ray,
rayOriginPart, false, true)
-- Check for intersection
if hitPart then                                                  -- 5
print("Ray intersected with part: " .. hitPart.Name)
print("Ray intersection hit point is: " .. tostring(hitPoint))   -- 6
print("Ray normal at the hit point is: " .. tostring(normal))    -- 7
MarkIntersectionPoint(hitPoint)              -- 8 Create a marker at the
                                             -- intersection point
else
print("Ray intersected with nothing.")
end
end
-- Call the function to perform a raycast
PerformRaycast()                                                 -- 9
```

1) This line of code defines a new local function named MarkIntersectionPoint() that takes a Vector3 argument called position. This function will be responsible for marking the point where the ray intersects with a part in the workspace.

2) This line of code defines another local function called PerformRaycast(). This function is designed to perform the actual raycasting operation to find if the ray intersects with any part within the workspace.

3) This line of code creates a new Ray object. The Ray starts at the position stored in the rayOrigin variable and has a direction and length as specified by Vector3.new(0, 0, rayLength). The direction is along the Z-axis, and the length is determined by the value in rayLength.

4) This line of code performs the actual raycasting using the FindPartOnRay() method. It casts the ray object stored in ray and ignores the part stored in rayOriginPart. The boolean false specifies not to ignore water, and true means terrain cells are treated as cubes. The method returns three values, hitPart, hitPoint, and normal, representing the part hit by the ray, the exact point of intersection, and the normal vector at the hit point.

5) This line of code checks if hitPart is not nil. If hitPart is not nil, it means the ray has intersected with a part, and the code block within this if statement will execute.

6) This line of code prints the exact point of intersection (hitPoint) to the "Output" window. The tostring() function converts the Vector3 object to a string for printing.

7) This line of code prints the normal vector (normal) at the point of intersection to the "Output" window.

8) This line of code calls the MarkIntersectionPoint() function, passing in the hitPoint as an argument. This will place a marker at the point of intersection, making it visible in the workspace.

9) This line of code calls the PerformRaycast() function, effectively initiating the raycasting operation when the script runs.

Note   The term "Normal vector at the hit point" refers to a vector perpendicular to the geometry's surface at the exact point where the ray intersects. This vector is often normalized, meaning it has a length of 1. This makes it easier to work with in mathematical calculations. The normal vector points outward from the surface. Visualizing a normal vector is relatively straightforward. Imagine a flat surface, like a plane. If you place an arrow perpendicular to that plane, pointing away from the surface, that arrow represents the normal vector. In the context of a 3D model, you can think of tiny arrows poking out perpendicularly from each point on the surface; these arrows represent the normal vectors at those points (Figure 10-1). Normal vectors are extensively used in various game mechanics like reflection (think of a ball bouncing off a surface), lighting calculations, and even advanced features like normal mapping to give textures a 3D look.

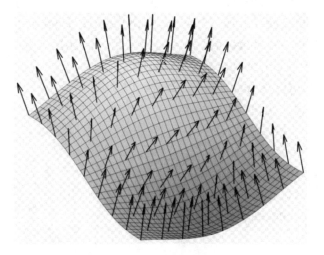

Figure 10-1. *A vector field of normals to a surface*

Raycasting with Filtering

In Roblox, raycasting is a method to find the first object along a straight path (ray). You can create a Ray object by specifying its origin and direction. Roblox also provides a set of APIs to perform raycasting with added filters. The RaycastParams.new() method, in conjunction with the FilterDescendantsInstances and FilterType properties, can be used to cast a ray through the game world and get a list of the intersecting part that is on a provided whitelist. This allows you to filter which objects you're interested in during raycasting selectively.

Imagine you are developing a game where you have multiple types of objects like enemies, allies, and obstacles. You want to cast a ray to detect only enemies and ignore everything else. You can use RaycastParams.new() to achieve this. You can use the same "Origin" part you created as part of Listing 10-3 and place obstacle and enemy objects within the line of sight of the ray cast. Ensure your obstacles are named differently than the enemies. You could name the enemy objects "enemy_1," "enemy_2," etc.

Listing 10-4. Lua script to perform Raycasting using Filtering

```
-- Define the Ray
local rayLength = 55
local rayOriginPart =  workspace:WaitForChild("Origin")
local rayOrigin = rayOriginPart.Position  -- Start point of the ray
-- Identify whitelisted Parts (Enemies) and store them in the enemies table
local enemies = {}  -- store all Enemy objects within the game world
-- Iterate through each object in the workspace
for _, obj in pairs(workspace:GetChildren()) do          -- 1
    -- Check if the object is a part
if obj:IsA("Part") then                          -- 2
    -- Check if the part's name starts with 'Enemy.'
    if string.sub(obj.Name, 1, 5) == "Enemy" then      -- 3
    -- Add the part to the enemies table
    table.insert(enemies, obj)                    -- 4
    end
end
end
-- Use RaycastParams to filter out non-enemy objects
local params = RaycastParams.new()                       -- 5
params.FilterDescendantsInstances =  enemies            -- 6
params.FilterType = Enum.RaycastFilterType.Include       -- 7
local intersectedPart = workspace:Raycast(rayOrigin, Vector3.new(0, 0,
rayLength),params)                                       -- 8
-- Process Results
```

```
if intersectedPart then                              -- 9
print("Enemy intersected: " .. tostring(intersectedPart.
Instance))                          -- 10
-- Add game logic to reduce enemy health here
end
```

1) This line of code initiates a for-loop that iterates through each object in the workspace. pairs(workspace:GetChildren()) returns a list of all child objects within the workspace. The loop variable obj will contain each object for each iteration.

2) This line of code checks whether the object (obj) is of the type "Part." "IsA" is a method that checks if an instance is or is derived from a certain class name. In this case, it checks if the object is a Part.

3) This line of code checks if the part's name (obj.Name) starts with the string "Enemy." It uses the string.sub() function to get the first five characters of the part's name and compare it to the string "Enemy."

4) If the conditions in lines 2 and 3 are met, this line of code adds the object (obj) to the enemies table. table.insert() is a standard Lua function used for inserting an element at the end of a table.

5) This line of code initializes a new RaycastParams object and assigns it to the variable params. RaycastParams is used to define various properties that control how the ray cast operation is conducted.

6) This line of code sets the FilterDescendantsInstances property of the RaycastParams object (params) to the table enemies. In the context of Roblox's raycasting system, FilterDescendantsInstances is used to specify which instances (objects) should be considered or ignored during the raycast operation. When you set this property, you provide it with a table containing the instances you want to include or exclude from the ray cast, depending on the setting of FilterType.

7) This line of code sets the FilterType property of the params object to Include. This means that the ray will only consider the instances in the enemies table for intersection. All other parts and objects in the workspace not in this table will be ignored during the raycasting process. So, the ray cast will only hit or intersect with parts whose references are stored in the enemies table. If the ray intersects with an object, not in this table, it will act as though no intersection has occurred. If the FilterType property of the params object is set to Exclude, then objects within the enemies table would be excluded from the ray cast. Setting params. FilterDescendantsInstances = enemies effectively narrow the scope of the ray cast operation to only the enemy parts, optimizing the ray cast and allowing for more controlled behavior.

8) This line performs the actual raycasting, starting from rayOrigin and extending in the direction specified by Vector3.new(0, 0, rayLength). It uses the parameters defined in the params for the ray cast. The ray cast will return the first part it hits that matches the conditions in params or nil if it hits nothing.

9) This line checks if the intersectedPart is not nil, meaning that the ray cast intersected with one of the enemy parts.

10) If the ray cast does intersect with an enemy part, this line prints a message along with the name of the intersected part to the "Output" window.

This RaycastParams.new() method, along with the FilterDescendantsInstances and FilterType properties, allows you to have granular control over what parts you're interested in when casting a ray, which can be incredibly useful in a variety of game scenarios, like shooting mechanics, line-of-sight checks, and so on.

Creating a Proximity Sensor for NPCs

Creating a proximity sensor for NPCs (Non-Player Characters) in Roblox can be done using the Raycasting functionality. Raycasting allows you to cast a ray from a starting point in a certain direction and find out what it hits, essentially simulating vision or line of sight. This is an excellent method for implementing AI vision, target acquisition, and environmental interaction. Listing 10-5 demonstrates the basics of a proximity sensor for NPCs using Roblox Raycasting. You need to create a Part within your game world that will function as an NPC and attach a script to it. The code in Listing 10-5 needs to be typed into the script attached to the NPC part. This NPC part lies in wait for the player to approach it. It will change color within the pre-defined range to indicate that it detected the player.

Listing 10-5. NPC vision system

```
local playersService = game:GetService("Players")
local npcSensor = script.Parent
local RANGE = 20                                          -- 1
local POLL_INTERVAL = 0.15                                -- 2
local COLOR_DETECTED = Color3.new(1, 0, 0)               -- 3
local COLOR_NOT_DETECTED = Color3.new(0, 1, 0)           -- 4
local function isPlayerDetected(player)                   -- 5
local char = player.Character                             -- 6
if char then
local rootPart = char:FindFirstChild("HumanoidRootPart") -- 7
if rootPart then
local rayDirection = (rootPart.Position - npcSensor.Position).unit *
RANGE                                                    -- 8
local hitInfo = workspace:Raycast(npcSensor.Position, rayDirection)
                                                         -- 9
    if hitInfo and hitInfo.Instance:IsDescendantOf(char) then
                                                         -- 10
        return true
    end
end
end
    return false
end
local function detectPlayers()                           -- 11
for _, player in ipairs(playersService:GetPlayers()) do  -- 12
        if isPlayerDetected(player) then                 -- 13
```

```
            return true
        end
end
    return false
end
npcSensor.Color = COLOR_NOT_DETECTED                    -- 14
while wait(POLL_INTERVAL) do                            -- 15
npcSensor.Color = detectPlayers() and COLOR_DETECTED or COLOR_NOT_
DETECTED                                               -- 16
end
```

1) This sets up a constant named RANGE with a value of 20. This is the distance within which the NPC sensor will detect players.

2) This sets up a constant named POLL_INTERVAL to 0.15, representing the time in seconds the script will wait before checking for players again.

3) This sets up a constant named COLOR_DETECTED to the RGB value representing red. When a player is detected, this color will be applied to the NPC sensor.

4) This sets up another constant named COLOR_NOT_DETECTED to the RGB value representing green. This color will be applied to the NPC sensor when no player is detected.

5) This is the definition of a local function called isPlayerDetected() that takes a player object as an argument.

6) Inside this function, a local variable char is defined to store the Character object of the player.

7) This line of code looks for a child named "HumanoidRootPart" within the char (Character object) and stores it in the local variable rootPart.

8) Computes the unit vector pointing from the NPC sensor toward the player's HumanoidRootPart, then scales it by the defined RANGE.

9) Performs a ray cast from the NPC sensor's position in the direction calculated, storing the first object hit in hitInfo.

10) Checks whether the ray hit something (hitInfo is not nil) and if the object hit is part of the player's character. If so, it returns true.

11) This is the definition of another local function called detectPlayers() that will check for players in the game.

12) Loops through each player in the game, using the GetPlayers() method of the playersService.

13) Calls the isPlayerDetected() function for each player. If it returns true, then detectPlayers also returns true.

14) Initially sets the color of npcSensor to COLOR_NOT_DETECTED (green), indicating that no player is currently detected.

15) It starts an infinite loop that waits for POLL_INTERVAL seconds before executing the next iteration.

16) Sets the color of the npcSensor based on the return value of detectPlayers. If a player is detected, it sets the color to COLOR_DETECTED (red); otherwise, it sets it to COLOR_NOT_DETECTED (green).

Pathfinding in Roblox

Pathfinding refers to the computational problem of finding a path from one point to another while avoiding obstacles, hazardous materials, or defined regions. In the context of Roblox, pathfinding is often used to determine the most efficient way for NPCs (Non-Player Characters) or objects to navigate the game world. The PathfindingService in Roblox provides built-in algorithms to solve these problems, particularly the A* (A-star) algorithm, known for its efficiency and accuracy. The PathfindingService is essential for any Roblox game where entities (like characters or AI) need to navigate around obstacles from one point to another.

In Roblox, the PathfindingService creates Path objects that can help you move characters from one point to another while avoiding obstacles. The primary steps involved in pathfinding in Roblox are

- Creating a path: Use the PathfindingService:CreatePath() method to create a path.

- Computing the path: Use the Path:ComputeAsync() method to determine the path.

- Getting the waypoints: Use the Path:GetWaypoints() method to retrieve waypoints.

- Moving along the path: Interpret waypoints, and move your character or object accordingly.

Firstly, you need to enable navigation visualization within Roblox Studio as follows (Figure 10-2):

1) Select File – Studio Settings.

2) From the window that shows up, select Studio from within the left pane.

3) Scroll to the bottom within the right pane until you see the Visualization section.

4) Check the check boxes for "Show Navigation Mesh" and "Show Navigation Labels."

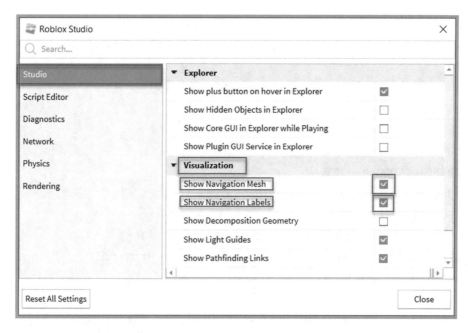

Figure 10-2. *Enabling Navigation Visualization*

Listing 10-6 provides a path-finding script using the player's character. The code in Listing 10-6 needs to be typed into a Local Script placed within StarterCharacterScripts. You would also want to create a wall obstacle part that you can move around while your experience is playing to visualize how the character avoids this obstacle while moving to its target location (Figure 10-3).

Listing 10-6. Pathfinding

```
local pathfindingService = game:GetService("PathfindingService")        -- 1
local Players = game:GetService("Players")

local pathObj = pathfindingService:CreatePath(
    {
        AgentRadius = 3,
        AgentHeight = 6,
        AgentCanJump = false,
        Costs = { Water = 20 }
    }
)                                                                       -- 2
local currentPlayer = Players.LocalPlayer
```

```
local currentPlayerCharacter = currentPlayer.Character
local currentPlayerHumanoid = currentPlayerCharacter:WaitForChild("
Humanoid")
local targetDestination = Vector3.new(100, 0, 100)          -- 3
local pathWaypoints                                          -- 4
local upcomingWaypointIdx                                    -- 5
local pathReachedConnection                                  -- 6
local pathBlockedConnection                                  -- 7
local function navigateToDestination(target)                 -- 8
    -- Compute the path
    local isPathComputed, errorMsg = pcall(function()        -- 9
    pathObj:ComputeAsync(currentPlayerCharacter.PrimaryPart.
    Position, target)
    end)
if isPathComputed and pathObj.Status == Enum.PathStatus.Success then  -- 10
        -- Obtain the path waypoints
        pathWaypoints = pathObj:GetWaypoints()               -- 11
        -- Handle path blockages
        pathBlockedConnection = pathObj.Blocked:Connect(function
        (blockedIdx)                                         -- 12
if blockedIdx >= upcomingWaypointIdx then                    -- 13
    pathBlockedConnection:Disconnect()                       -- 14
    navigateToDestination(target)                            -- 15
end
end)
-- Handle reaching waypoints
if not pathReachedConnection then                            -- 16
pathReachedConnection = currentPlayerHumanoid.MoveToFinished:Connect
(function(reached)
                                                             -- 17
if reached and upcomingWaypointIdx < #pathWaypoints then     -- 18
    upcomingWaypointIdx += 1
                    currentPlayerHumanoi
d:MoveTo(pathWaypoints[upcomingWaypointIdx].
Position)                                                    -- 19
```

```
else                                               -- 20
    pathReachedConnection:Disconnect()
    pathBlockedConnection:Disconnect()
end
end)
end
-- Initiate movement to the second waypoint (skip the first
-- waypoint, as it's the start)
upcomingWaypointIdx = 2                             -- 21
currentPlayerHumanoid:MoveTo(pathWaypoints[upcomingWaypointIdx].
Position)                                           -- 22
else
warn("Path not computed!", errorMsg)               -- 23
end
end
navigateToDestination(targetDestination)           -- 24
```

1) This line of code sets up your script to use Roblox's PathfindingService by fetching it and storing it in a local variable for easy and efficient access. It's an important step for leveraging pathfinding features in your game, such as creating paths, calculating waypoints, and listening to events that indicate whether a path is blocked or a waypoint is reached.

2) Here, we invoke the CreatePath() function from the previously obtained pathfindingService object and pass it in a table of parameters that configures the pathfinding agent. These parameters specify constraints for how the agent can move.

    - AgentRadius = 3: Specifies that the agent has a radius of 3 studs. The pathfinding algorithm will ensure the agent won't come closer than this radius to any obstacles.

    - AgentHeight = 6: Specifies that the agent has a height of 6 studs. The pathfinding will account for this when navigating through spaces.

- AgentCanJump = false: Tells the pathfinding algorithm that the agent cannot jump.

- Costs = { Water = 20 }: Specifies custom costs for traversing different types of terrain. Here, water has been assigned a cost of 20, meaning it will take 20 times the usual "effort" for the agent to pass through water.

Note   In Roblox, the Costs table allows you to specify custom traversal costs for different terrains or obstacles. This feature lets you fine-tune the pathfinding behavior according to your game's needs. For example, you might want the pathfinding agent to avoid water or certain rough terrain unless no other path is available. Setting a high traversal cost for such terrain (in this example, Water = 20) makes it less likely that the pathfinding algorithm will choose a path that leads through those areas. When the pathfinding algorithm calculates a path, it evaluates the "cost" to move from one point to another. Lower costs make a path more desirable, while higher costs make it less so. The algorithm tries to find the path with the lowest total cost. It's a way to influence the algorithm's decision-making process by adding additional "weights" to certain terrains or obstacles.

---

3) This line of code creates a local variable named targetDestination and assigns it a 3D vector with the coordinates (100, 0, 100). This vector represents a point in the game's 3D space, serving as the destination for the pathfinding algorithm.

4) This variable will store the waypoints generated by the pathfinding algorithm, indicating the path the agent should follow to reach the target destination.

5) This variable keeps track of the index of the next waypoint that the agent will move to. It helps to manage the agent's progress along the path.

6) This variable will hold a connection to the MoveToFinished event. This event fires when the agent finishes moving to a waypoint, allowing for actions like proceeding to the next waypoint.

7) This variable will hold a connection to the Blocked event. This event fires when the path to a waypoint becomes blocked, triggering a re-computation of the path.

8) The navigateToDestination(target) function orchestrates the movement of a character (or agent) from its current position to a specified target destination while avoiding obstacles. It does so by

- Calculating a path to the target

- Handling events when the path becomes blocked or a waypoint is reached

- Initiating and managing the character's movement through waypoints to reach the target

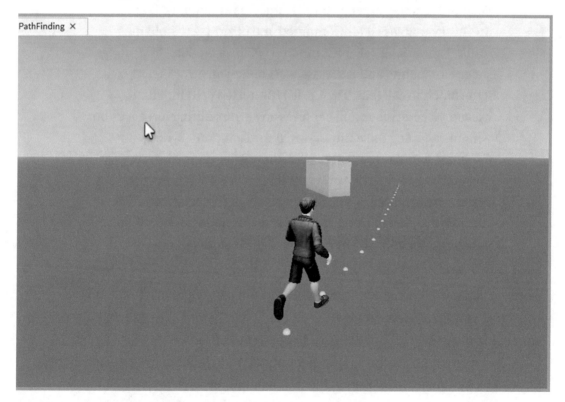

Figure 10-3. *Pathfinding in action*

This function considers any obstacles along the path, recalculating the path as needed. It also listens for events to determine when the character has reached a waypoint or the path is blocked, responding appropriately in each case.

9) This line of code attempts to compute a path to a specified target, captures the operation's success or failure, and handles any errors that may occur without crashing the entire script. It attempts to asynchronously compute a path from the current position of the player character to a target position. It uses pathObj:ComputeAsync(...) for the computation. This method computes the path asynchronously. It takes the current position of the player's character (currentPlayerCharacter.PrimaryPart. Position) and the target position (target) as arguments. It uses the local variables isPathComputed and errorMsg to hold the result. The variable isPathComputed will be a boolean indicating success or failure, and errorMsg will contain an error message if the function call fails. The pcall() (protected call) function executes a code block and captures any errors during its execution without stopping the entire script. If the ComputeAsync() function encounters an error (e.g., cannot compute the path for some reason), pcall() prevents that error from halting the entire script and returns false along with an error message. The success or failure of the ComputeAsync() function is stored in isPathComputed, and any error message is stored in errorMsg.

Note   In Lua, pcall( ) is often used for error-handling purposes. It attempts to execute its argument function in a "protected mode," which means that errors won't stop the execution of the entire program but will instead return as results from the pcall( ) function itself. This is particularly useful here to gracefully handle any issues that might arise during the path computation. If the path cannot be computed, the script can decide how to proceed, perhaps by logging a warning message, as seen later in the code.

---

10) This "if" conditional check ensures that the path was successfully computed before proceeding with the rest of the pathfinding logic. The variable isPathComputed verifies that the ComputeAsync() method executed without errors while the expression pathObj. Status == Enum.PathStatus.Success ensures that the computed path is valid and can be followed. If both conditions are met, the code within the if block will execute, which involves obtaining waypoints, handling path blockages, and managing the character's movement along the path. If either condition fails, the script will not attempt to navigate and instead log a warning.

11) This line of code fetches the array of waypoints that make up the computed path and stores them in the pathWaypoints variable. These waypoints guide the character's movement from its starting point to its destination.

12) This code block establishes a connection to the Blocked event of the pathObj. This event triggers when a waypoint on the computed path becomes obstructed. The code sets up a mechanism to handle path blockages by disconnecting the current path and recalculating a new one, ensuring the character can navigate any obstacle.

13) This "if" statement checks whether the blocked waypoint (indicated by blockedIdx) is at or lies ahead of the next waypoint the character should move to (indicated by upcomingWaypointIdx). If the blocked waypoint is the same as or ahead of the upcoming waypoint, the character will encounter the obstacle before reaching its destination. In such a case, the code will disconnect the Blocked event connection and call the function navigateToDestination(target) to recompute the path, allowing the character to navigate the obstacle. Here, "blockedIdx" is the index of the waypoint identified as blocked or obstructed, while "upcomingWaypointIdx" is the index of the next waypoint the character should move to.

14) This line of code severs the connection to the Blocked event of the pathObj. This stops the event from triggering the associated function, effectively ceasing the monitoring for blockages along the current path. This is typically done before recalculating a new path to navigate around an obstacle.

15) This line of code recursively calls the same navigateToDestination(target) function with the target destination as its argument. This effectively triggers a recalculation of the path from the character's current position to the target because an obstacle has been detected in the existing path. This allows the character to navigate around the newly found obstacle.

16) This line of code checks if a connection to the MoveToFinished event exists. If not, it establishes a new one.

17) This line of code establishes a connection to the MoveToFinished event of the currentPlayerHumanoid. This event triggers when the character finishes moving to a waypoint. The connected function will execute to handle what happens next, such as moving to the next waypoint or disconnecting the event connections if the path is complete or blocked.

18) This line of code checks if the character successfully reached the current waypoint and if there are more waypoints left to traverse. If both conditions are met, upcomingWaypointIdx += 1 increments the index to point to the next waypoint in the pathWaypoints array, preparing the character to move to that next waypoint.

19) This line of code instructs the character's humanoid component to move to the position of the next waypoint, as indicated by the upcomingWaypointIdx. This continues the character's traversal along the computed path.

20) The else section executes when the character fails to reach a waypoint, or there are no more waypoints to traverse. In either case, it disconnects the pathReachedConnection and pathBlockedConnection, ceasing the monitoring for both reaching waypoints and path blockages. This effectively cleans up the event connections and stops the path-following logic.

21) This line of code sets the index of the next waypoint to 2, effectively skipping the first waypoint. This is done because the first waypoint is the character's starting position, so there's no need to move to it. The character will begin its movement from the second waypoint in the path.

22) This line of code instructs the character's humanoid component to move to the position of the second waypoint in the path, initiating the character's traversal along the computed path.

23) This line of code executes when the path computation fails for some reason; in this case, a warning message is displayed to the "Output" window, indicating that the path could not be computed and providing the associated error message. This helps in debugging why the pathfinding operation failed.

24) This line of code initiates the pathfinding process, instructing the character to compute and follow a path to the specified targetDestination while handling any obstacles along the way.

Summary

The chapter provided an in-depth understanding of Raycasting and Pathfinding within the Roblox platform, focusing on how these concepts can be utilized for more interactive and intuitive game experiences.

This chapter began by defining raycasting as a technique to detect the intersection between a ray and 3D objects within a game environment. Its primary purpose is facilitating interactions such as shooting, collision detection, and visibility checks. The discussion then delved into Roblox-specific implementation of raycasting, highlighting the platform's unique tools and Luau API for accomplishing these tasks. You were then introduced to the Ray object in Roblox, which encapsulates the origin and direction of a ray, demonstrating how to create and manipulate it programmatically. The essentials of performing raycasting in Roblox were covered here, where you learned how to obtain and interpret the points of intersection when a ray hits a 3D object, along with relevant mathematical calculations.

You were introduced to the concept of a normal vector, a vector perpendicular to the surface of the intersected object, and how this can be used for effects like reflection and realistic impacts. You then went on to learn how to make your raycasting operations more efficient and targeted by using RaycastParams, allowing you to filter the types of objects the ray will interact with. Practical applications of raycasting were demonstrated by creating a proximity sensor to enhance NPC (Non-Player Character) behavior, giving them the ability to sense nearby players. The chapter then pivoted to pathfinding, explaining how to create efficient paths for characters to follow within the game world using Roblox's built-in PathfindingService. You learned how to set up Roblox Studio to visualize the paths and navigational meshes, offering real-time insights into how pathfinding algorithms navigate the game space. This chapter has served as a comprehensive guide for anyone looking to grasp the intricacies of raycasting and pathfinding in Roblox, replete with code samples, mathematical explanations, and practical examples.

CHAPTER 11

Tables and Object-Oriented Programming

In the intricate and diverse world of Roblox Lua programming, Tables play a pivotal role, serving as a dynamic array and a robust data structure that encapsulates key-value pairs. Coupled with Object-Oriented Programming (OOP), Tables become instrumental in organizing and structuring code in a way that models real-world entities, enabling developers to create more maintainable, scalable, and interactive gaming experiences. This chapter delves into the multifaceted usage of Tables in Roblox Lua, exploring their flexibility, performance, and integration within the OOP paradigm. Through a clear understanding of Tables and OOP, both new and seasoned developers can harness the full potential of Lua's capabilities in Roblox, paving the way for advanced game development techniques and concepts.

Tables

Lua, the scripting language behind Roblox development, is versatile and minimalistic, providing only one primary data structure: Tables. Lua is not inherently object-oriented, but its Tables offer a dynamic and powerful means to mimic Object-Oriented Programming (OOP) through tables and meta-tables. This chapter will explore the unique role that Tables play in Roblox Lua, delving into how they can be harnessed to implement OOP-like structures and paradigms from scratch. We will unfold the art of crafting classes, objects, inheritance, and more using Tables and understand how this fundamental data type opens doors to a higher level of organization and complexity in game development. By mastering the unconventional integration of Tables within an OOP framework in Roblox Lua, developers can construct more modular, maintainable, and engaging gaming experiences, utilizing Lua's flexibility to its fullest potential.

© Christopher Coutinho 2023
C. Coutinho, *Roblox Lua Scripting Essentials*, https://doi.org/10.1007/979-8-8688-0026-9_11

Object-Oriented Programming

Object-oriented programming (OOP) in the context of Lua is about structuring code through the concepts of objects and classes, although Lua itself doesn't support traditional OOP. However, the principles can still be applied creatively using tables and meta-tables.

Object-Oriented Programming (OOP) within Lua is a versatile approach that involves emulating classes and objects to create organized and reusable code structures. In this paradigm, objects are individual instances that represent elements within a game, such as a player, an enemy, or a power-up. A class, on the other hand, describes the general attributes and behaviors of these objects.

Imagine the need to create different types of animals in a game. Without OOP, each animal would require separate, repetitive code for common attributes like movement, sound, or health. With an OOP approach in Lua, you would define a general class called "Animal," specifying common properties and methods. Specific animals like a "Cat" or a "Dog" could be instances of this class, with customized attributes like color, size, and particular sounds.

This way, even though Lua lacks built-in support for OOP, the principles can be achieved through tables and meta-tables, creating complex hierarchies and relationships between different game elements. This abstraction and encapsulation streamline the coding process and make the codebase more maintainable and scalable. By defining classes for various game entities, developers can create diverse and rich gaming experiences where different objects share standard features yet maintain their unique characteristics. Whether designing various terrains, weather conditions, or interactive NPCs, implementing OOP in Lua enhances code efficiency and fosters creative game development.

Here's a brief explanation of the four foundational pillars of OOP.

Encapsulation

Encapsulation is binding or wrapping the data (variables) and the code (methods/functions) together as a single unit. Here's how it works:

- Information hiding: By making attributes private or protected, encapsulation ensures that the internal state of an object can only be changed in well-defined ways. This prevents unintended interference and misuse of the data.

- Access control: Through access modifiers like private, public, or protected, encapsulation controls which parts of an object can be accessed from outside. This maintains the integrity of the object.

- Ease of maintenance: By bundling related functionality together, encapsulation simplifies the code and makes it easier to read and maintain.

Encapsulation in Lua can be emulated by grouping related attributes and functions into tables. Since there's no native access control, all attributes are public, but convention can guide usage.

- Information grouping: By putting related data and functions into a single table, Lua enables a form of encapsulation by grouping related elements together.

- Conventional privacy: While there's no strict way to enforce private variables in Lua, developers can adhere to conventions like naming private attributes with a leading underscore to indicate intended privacy.

Inheritance

Inheritance enables a class to inherit attributes and methods from another class. The class that is being inherited from is called the parent or superclass, and the class that inherits from this parent/superclass is called the child or subclass. It allows for code reusability and the formation of hierarchical relationships. Here's how it works:

- Code reusability: By inheriting attributes and methods from a parent class, a child class can reuse existing code, reducing redundancy.

- Extensibility: Child classes can extend or override the functionalities of a parent class, enabling customization while maintaining a consistent structure.

- Hierarchical classification: Inheritance organizes classes into hierarchies, reflecting natural relationships and promoting a clear, logical structure.

Inheritance in Lua can be implemented through meta-tables, allowing one table to look up another table (the parent).

- Code reusability: By setting a parent table as a meta-table for a child, Lua enables the child to inherit attributes and methods from the parent, reducing code duplication.

- Customizable behavior: Child tables can override inherited behavior or add new attributes or methods, allowing for specialization.

Polymorphism

Polymorphism is the ability of objects to take on more than one form, depending on their context. This leads to more flexible and dynamically adaptable code:

- Method overloading: Different methods with the same name can be defined, allowing for varied behavior depending on the parameters passed.

- Method overriding: A subclass can provide a specific implementation of a method already defined in its parent class, allowing for variations in behavior while maintaining a consistent interface.

- Dynamic dispatch: At runtime, the method that needs to be executed can be determined dynamically based on the actual class of the object, promoting more adaptive and responsive code.

Lua's flexibility with tables allows for polymorphism, where different tables can define different implementations for the same method name.

- Multiple forms: Different tables can define methods with the same name but different implementations, allowing for polymorphic behavior.

- Dynamic behavior: Since Lua is dynamically typed and table keys can be accessed at runtime, polymorphic behavior can be achieved through a clever design of tables and their functions.

Abstraction

Abstraction is creating a simple model that represents more complex, real-world objects. It helps in hiding the complex reality while exposing only the necessary parts.

- Simplified view: Abstraction provides a simplified, high-level view of an object, showing only what is necessary and hiding the underlying complexity.

- Modular development: It aids modular development by abstracting functionality into clear, concise interfaces. This ensures that different parts of a system can be developed and maintained independently.

- Enhanced security: By hiding internal details, abstraction reduces the risk of unintended access or alteration of an object's state.

In Lua, abstraction can be implemented by defining clear, concise table interfaces and hiding unnecessary details within those tables.

- Simplified interface: By defining what functions a table exposes and documenting their behavior, Lua allows developers to create simplified, high-level interfaces.

- Modular design: Organizing related functionality into tables allows for independent development and maintenance of different parts of a system.

While Lua's table system doesn't natively provide all the features of traditional OOP, the flexibility of tables allows developers to emulate these principles to an extent. By following conventions and carefully designing table structures, Lua developers can achieve many benefits of encapsulation, inheritance, polymorphism, and abstraction. This approach allows for more organized, maintainable, and scalable code within Lua, fostering the creation of complex, well-structured game experiences.

Meta-Tables

In Lua, a meta-table is a specialized table that can be associated with another table to customize its behavior. Essentially, any table in Lua can become a meta-table; likewise, any table can be linked to a meta-table. This relationship is established through meta-methods, specific functions housed within the meta-table, each governing a particular operation such as addition, subtraction, or indexing. By leveraging these meta-methods, developers can define tailored behaviors for tables, including how they interact with one another or respond to certain operations. Whether defining arithmetic operations between tables or controlling access to undefined keys, meta-tables in Lua provide a powerful tool to extend and customize standard table functionality, enhancing flexibility and control within the language.

Let's say you want to add two tables together element-wise. By default, Lua doesn't know how to add tables, so you'd get an error if you try. But you can define this behavior using a meta-table. Listing 11-1 demonstrates how you could achieve this.

Listing 11-1. Creating a meta-table to add together the corresponding elements of two tables

```
local table1 = {1, 2, 3}
local table2 = {4, 5, 6}
local metaTable = {                              -- 1
    __add = function(table1, table2)             -- 2
        local result = {}
        for i = 1, #table1 do                    -- 3
            result[i] = table1[i] + table2[i]
        end
return result                                    -- 4
end
}
setmetatable(table1, metaTable)                  -- 5
setmetatable(table2, metaTable)                  -- 6
local sum = table1 + table2                      -- 7 sum will be {5, 7, 9}
```

1) Here, a meta-table called metaTable is being created. This table will contain meta-methods and special functions that define behavior for associated tables.

2) The "__add" meta-method is defined within the meta-table. This meta-method controls how two tables are added together when the + operator is used. It takes two tables as arguments and returns a new table. "__add" is a special meta-method in Lua used to define how addition (+) should be performed for tables. When

you attempt to add two tables with this meta-method defined in their associated meta-table, Lua will call the function associated with "__add," passing the two tables as arguments. The behavior of the addition operation can thus be customized based on the logic within the "__add" function.

3) A loop is initiated to iterate through the elements of table1. The # operator gets the length of the table, so this loop will run as many times as there are elements in the table1.

4) The resulting table, result, is returned from the __add function. This table contains the element-wise sum of table1 and table2.

5) The setmetatable() function associates "metaTable" with "table1." This means that "table1" now has access to the behaviors defined in "metaTable." setmetatable() is a built-in Lua function that associates a table with a meta-table. The first argument is the table you want to associate with the meta-table, and the second is the meta-table itself. Once a table has been associated with a meta-table, it can access the meta-methods defined within it, thereby altering its behavior for certain operations.

6) This line of code does the same as point 5, but for table2. Both table1 and table2 are now associated with "metaTable," and thus both have the custom addition behavior defined by __add.

7) Here, table1 and table2 are added together using the custom addition behavior defined in metaTable's __add meta-method. The result is a new table {5, 7, 9}, and it's assigned to the variable sum.

This code demonstrates how meta-tables and the __add meta-method can be used to customize the behavior of tables in Lua, showcasing the language's flexibility and extensibility.

Note   In Listing 11-1, the "__add" meta-method's word "add" has been prefixed with two underscore (__) symbols.

__index

In Lua, the __index meta-method is a key concept that provides control over how table indexing works. It's beneficial for handling attempts to access keys in a table that don't exist and the ability to inherit values from another table.

1) Default values: By using __index as a function, you can return a default value when trying to access a key that doesn't exist in the table.

2) Inheritance: It allows a table to inherit values from another table. If a key is not found in the table, Lua will use the __index meta-method to look for that key in another table, effectively allowing for a form of inheritance between tables.

Listing 11-2. __index as a function that returns a default value

```
local metaTable = {                            -- 1
  __index = function(table, key)               -- 2
    return "Key not found: " .. key            -- 3
  end
}
local myTable = setmetatable({}, metaTable)    -- 4
print(myTable["missingKey"])                   -- 5 Output: Key not found:
                                               -- missingKey.
```

1) Here, a meta-table called metaTable is being created. This table will be used as a meta-table, a table that can change the behavior of another table.

2) The __index meta-method serves a specific purpose. Whenever you attempt to access a key in a table, and that key doesn't exist, Lua looks to see if the table has an associated meta-table with an __index entry. If it does, Lua will call the __index value as a function or reference to another table. When __index is defined as a function within the meta-table (Listing 10-2), it will be called whenever a non-existing key is accessed in the associated table. The function associated with __index takes two parameters: the

table being accessed that doesn't have the key and the key that was attempted to be accessed but was not found in the table. You can define any behavior you want within the function. For example, you might return a default value or print a warning message. You can utilize the provided table and key parameters to customize this behavior.

3) If the __index function is called, it returns a string saying "Key not found:" concatenated with the key that was attempted to be accessed.

4) This line of code creates a new empty table ({}) and associates it with the previously defined metaTable using the setmetatable() function. The resulting table, with metaTable as its meta-table, is assigned to the local variable myTable. Any access to undefined keys in myTable will now call the __index function in metaTable.

5) This line of code attempts to access the key "missingKey" in myTable, which does not exist. Since myTable has metaTable as it's meta-table and metaTable has an __index function, it is called with myTable and "missingKey" as its arguments. The function returns the string "Key not found: missingKey," which gets displayed.

Listing 11-3. __index as a table that allows a table to inherit values from another table

```
local parentTable = {x = 5}                      -- 1
local metaTable = {__index = parentTable}        -- 2
local childTable = setmetatable({}, metaTable)   -- 3
print("Output is: " .. tostring(childTable.x))   -- 4
```

1) This line of code creates a table named parentTable with a single key-value pair, where the key is x and the value is 5.

2) This line of code creates another table named metaTable. Within this table, the meta-method, __index, is assigned the value of parentTable. This sets up a behavior where a key is accessed in a table (childTable in Listing 10-3) associated with metaTable as its meta-table. If that key is not found, then the key will be looked up

in parentTable instead. Essentially, it links the parentTable as a fallback for any undefined keys in any table that uses metaTable as its meta-table.

3) This line of code creates a new empty table and associates it with metaTable by calling the setmetatable() function. The resulting table, now linked with the behavior defined in metaTable, is assigned to the variable childTable.

4) This line of code attempts to print the value of childTable.x. Since childTable is an empty table, it doesn't have a key "x" defined within it. However, because childTable is associated with metaTable as its meta-table, and metaTable has an __index meta-method points to parentTable, it can inherit the value of "x" from the parentTable. Here the lookup for the key "x" will fall back to the parentTable, where "x" is defined as 5. The result is the string "Output is: 5" being displayed.

In summary, the code provided as part of Listing 11-3 demonstrates how meta-tables can be used to create a fallback mechanism for undefined keys in a table. The __index meta-method in the meta-table acts like a bridge to another table (parentTable), allowing keys to be looked up if not found in the original table (childTable).

The __index meta-method in Lua serves multiple purposes, allowing for default value handling and a form of inheritance. Whether defined as a function to handle missing keys with custom logic or as a table to enable inheritance, __index adds a robust layer of flexibility and control to Lua's table structures, making it a vital concept for more advanced programming patterns in Lua.

Note   In Listings 11-2 and 11-3, the "__index" meta-method's word "index" has been prefixed with two underscore (__) symbols.

__newindex

In Lua, tables are central constructs that allow the collection of key-value pairs. Sometimes, developers need to exert control over how tables behave, especially when keys are missing or being newly created. This is where the __newindex meta-method comes into play, complementing the __index meta-method. The __newindex meta-method specifically targets scenarios when you attempt to assign a value to a table key that doesn't exist. It allows you to specify custom behavior for this assignment, providing a way to manage how new fields are added to tables or to intercept and perform special processing during such additions.

Here's how it works:

1)   The table: The first argument is the table being operated upon, the target where the new key-value pair will be added.

2)   The missing key: The second argument represents the missing key to which you want to assign a value. Since the key doesn't already exist, the __newindex method will be triggered.

3)   The value being assigned: The third argument is the value assigned to the missing key. You want to set this new value for the specified key.

Listing 11-4. __newindex meta-method to add a new field to a table

```
local myTable = {}
local metaTable = {
__newindex = function(table, key, value)       -- 1
print("Adding key " .. key .. " with value: " .. value)
rawset(table, key, value)                          -- 2 sets the key-value
                                                      pair without
                                               -- invoking __newindex again
print("Added Key 'newKey' " .. "with value: " .. tostring(myTable.newKey)
.. " to " .. tostring(myTable))
end
}
setmetatable(myTable, metaTable)              -- 3
myTable.newKey = "newValue"                   -- 4 prints "Adding key newKey
                                              -- with value newValue"
```

1) Here, a meta-method named __newindex is being defined in the metaTable. This function is called when a new key is added to the myTable object. It accepts three parameters: the table being modified (table), the key being added (key), and the value being assigned to that key (value).

2) rawest() is a built-in Lua function used to directly set the value of a table key, bypassing any meta-methods like __newindex. In this line of code, rawest() is adding the key-value pair to the table without invoking the __newindex meta-method again. If table[key] = value were used instead, it would recursively trigger the __newindex meta-method, leading to an infinite loop.

3) setmetatable() is used to set metaTable as the metatable for myTable. By doing this, any attempts to add a new key to myTable will trigger the __newindex meta-method defined in metaTable.

4) This line of code attempts to assign the value "newValue" to a new key "newKey" in myTable. As "newKey" does not exist in myTable, the __newindex meta-method is invoked via the statement myTable.newKey = "newValue." As metaTable has been set as the metatable for myTable, Lua checks metaTable for a __newindex meta-method when a new key is being added to myTable. As metaTable has a __newindex meta-method, its associated function is called with myTable, "newKey," and "newValue" as its arguments.

The capability to intercept the addition of new keys and define custom behavior is a powerful feature in Lua. It can be used for logging, validation, synchronization, or other purposes that might be particularly relevant in complex scenarios pertinent to game development.

Classes

A class can be considered a blueprint (cookie-cutter mold) for creating objects. These objects are instances of the class and have common properties (variables) and behaviors (functions or methods) defined in the class. Although the class sets the structure, each instance of the class maintains its own state, independent of other instances. Each object (instance) will have its own copy of variables, independent of those contained within other objects (instances) of the same class.

For example, you could have a Class – NPC with essential attributes and behaviors of a typical NPC in a game. By defining an NPC this way, you can create multiple NPCs with different properties but consistent behavior. This makes it easy to manage and modify NPCs throughout the development process. If you want to add new features or behaviors, you can modify the class without changing the code that creates or manages individual NPCs. This Class concept promotes reusability, maintainability, and scalability in your game development project.

Some typical properties of the NPC Class would be

- Name: The name of the NPC, which can be used to identify or display it in the game.

- Position: The location of the NPC within the game world.

- Health: Represents the vitality or life of the NPC.

- Dialogue: The dialogue lines that the NPC can speak to the player.

- Quests: If applicable, the quests the NPC may assign to the player.

- Faction: Represents the group or allegiance of the NPC.

- State: Reflects the current state of the NPC, such as idle, walking, attacking, etc.

Some standard methods/functions of the NPC Class would be

- Speak: Allows the NPC to communicate with the player using predefined dialogues.

- AssignQuest: If applicable, assign a quest to the player.

- TakeDamage: Reduces the health of the NPC if attacked or damaged.

- Move: Directs the NPC to move to a specific location or follow a predefined path.

- Interact: Defines how the NPC responds when the player interacts with it.

- UpdateState: Allows the NPC to transition between different states, from idle to walking.

To create a Class, follow the steps listed as follows:

1) Define the Class Table: Define a table representing the NPC class.

```
local NPC = {}
NPC.__index = NPC
local self
```

- You begin by creating an empty table that will be used to represent the NPC class. You then set the __index meta-method to point at the NPC table itself. By setting NPC.__index = NPC, you're establishing a rule that if someone tries to access a field in an instance of NPC that doesn't exist in that specific instance, Lua will look in the NPC table itself to find that field. This is part of the pattern used to create class-like behavior in Lua. Here's how it works in the context of defining a method for the NPC class:

- When you create a new instance of the NPC class, you'll typically set its metatable to the NPC table.

- If you try to call a method on that instance defined in the NPC table but not in the specific instance, Lua will use the __index meta-method to look up that method in the NPC table.

- This allows all instances of the NPC class to share the same set of methods defined in the NPC table, just like objects in a class-based language share the same methods defined in the class.

These lines of code are an essential part of using tables and metatables to simulate class-based programming in Lua, providing a way to encapsulate related data and behavior in a structured way.

2) Create a constructor function: Define a constructor function to create new instances of the NPC class. This constructor function will set up properties such as name, position, health, dialogue, etc. A constructor function is a special function used to initialize new objects, or in Lua's case, tables that simulate objects. In the context of this code, NPC.new is the constructor function for the NPC class. It is responsible for creating a new table, setting up its initial state, and returning it.

```
function NPC.new(name, position, health, dialogue, quests)
    self = setmetatable({}, NPC)
    self.name = name
    self.position = position
    self.health = health
    self.dialogue = dialogue
    self.quests = quests
    self.state = "Idle"
    return self
end
```

- In the constructor function, local self = setmetatable({}, NPC) creates a new empty table and associates it with the NPC metatable. This allows the new instance access to methods and fields defined in the NPC table. The setmetatable() function associates the new empty table with the NPC metatable. This allows the new instance to access methods and fields defined in the NPC table

- self is a naming convention for the variable that refers to the newly created instance of the NPC class. It's a way to refer to the object itself within its methods.

- The lines below initialize the properties of the new NPC instance:

- self.name = name -- sets the name of the NPC.

- self.position = position -- sets the NPC's position in the game world.

- self.health = health -- sets the NPC's health value.

- self.dialogue = dialogue – sets the dialogue the NPC can speak.

- self.quests = quests -- sets the quests that the NPC can assign.

- self.state = "Idle" -- sets the initial state of the NPC to "Idle."

- Each of the above properties is stored in the table referred to by self, so they become fields of the newly created instance.

- Finally, return self returns the newly created and initialized table. This is the new instance of the NPC class, and it will have all the properties set up in the constructor function and access to the methods defined in the NPC table. When you call NPC.new(), you get back this new instance, and you can then interact with it as an object in your game code.

3) Define methods: Add functions to the NPC table to represent the methods for the NPC class. These functions can manage the NPC's behaviors like speaking, taking damage, moving, etc.

```
function NPC:Speak(dialogueIndex)
    -- Code to make the NPC speak
    print(dialogue[dialogueIndex])
end

function NPC:AssignQuest(questIndex)
    -- Code to assign a quest to the player
    print(quests[questIndex])
end

function NPC:TakeDamage(damage)
    self.health -= damage
    print("Damage: " .. damage .. "Health: " .. self.health)
end

function NPC:Move(targetPosition)
    -- Code to move the NPC to the target position
end

function NPC:Interact()
    -- Code to define interaction with the player
    print("NPC interacting with Player")
end

function NPC:UpdateState(newState)
    self.state = newState
    print("NPCs New State: " .. self.state)
end
```

Once a new NPC instance (object) has been instantiated, any of the above methods can be invoked for that instance.

4) Create instances: You can now create instances of the NPC class by calling the constructor function and passing the required parameters.

```
local npc = NPC.new("Guard", {x = 10, y = 20, z = 10}, 100,
{"Hello, adventurer!"}, {"quest1", "quest2"})
```

5) Interact with instances: You can interact with the instances using the defined methods/functions.

```
npc:Speak(1)
npc: AssignQuest(2)
npc:TakeDamage(10)
```

The steps outlined above provide a blueprint to create an NPC class in Lua, encapsulating the necessary properties and behaviors within a cohesive structure. This approach allows for more organized and maintainable code, even in a language like Lua that does not natively support classes in the traditional sense. It aligns with the concepts of Object-Oriented Programming and can be extended further to suit the particular needs of your game. Listing 11-5 illustrates the complete code to create an NPC class and test it out.

Listing 11-5. Creating the NPC Class

```
-- NPC Class Creation
local NPC = {}
NPC.__index = NPC
local self
-- Constructor
function NPC.new(name, position, health, dialogue, quests)
    self = setmetatable({}, NPC)
    self.name = name
    self.position = position
    self.health = health
    self.dialogue = dialogue
```

```lua
        self.quests = quests
        self.state = "Idle"
        return self
end
-- Class methods/functions
function NPC:Speak(dialogueIndex)
        -- Code to make the NPC speak
        self.dialogue = self.dialogue[dialogueIndex]
end
function NPC:AssignQuest(questIndex)
        -- Code to assign a quest to the player
        self.quests = self.quests[questIndex]
end
function NPC:TakeDamage(damage)
        self.health -= damage
end
function NPC:Move(targetPosition)
        -- Code to move the NPC to the target position
        self.position =  targetPosition
end
function NPC:Interact()
        -- Code to define interaction with the player
        print("NPC interacting with Player")
end
function NPC:UpdateState(newState)
        self.state = newState
end
-- Create an NPC instance
local npc = NPC.new("Guard", {x = 10, y = 20, z = 10}, 100, {"Hello,
adventurer!", "Hello World!"}, {"Quest1", "Quest2"})
-- Call methods/function of the newly created npc instance.
local damage = 30
npc:Speak(2)
npc:AssignQuest(1)
npc:TakeDamage(damage)
```

```lua
npc:Move({x = 5, y = 5, z = 5})
npc:Interact()
npc:UpdateState("Patrolling")
-- Print out the newly assigned property values
print("NPCs Name: " .. self.name)
print("NPCs New State: " .. self.state)
print("NPCs Damage: " .. damage .. " Health: " .. self.health)
print("NPCs New Quest: " .. self.quests)
print("NPCs New Dialogue: " .. self.dialogue)
```

Summary

This chapter delved into Lua's approach to Object-Oriented Programming (OOP), which is unique and mainly revolves around using tables, metatables, and specific metamethods like __index and __newindex. Tables in Lua are the only compound data type, serving as arrays and associative containers. These can be leveraged to create classes and objects. Metatables act as a higher-level construct that allows customization of table behavior. You have seen how, using the __index meta-method, you can control how a table reacts when you attempt to access an undefined key, essentially allowing inheritance behavior. The __newindex metamethod lets you define the behavior of the table when a new key is created or modified, thus offering control over properties. Using these components, Lua provides a flexible and lightweight mechanism to achieve OOP paradigms without formal class-based systems, making it highly suitable for game development.

Afterword

Dear reader,

As you conclude this journey through the essentials of Roblox Lua Scripting, I hope you've found the material enlightening and practical. Whether you've just dipped your toes into the world of game development or are looking to refine your skills, Roblox offers an invaluable platform for creativity, collaboration, and innovation.

The programming language Lua, particularly in its Roblox-specific variant, Luau, brings a unique blend of simplicity and functionality. We've delved into key concepts like variables, loops, conditional statements, functions, and tables. We have also explored the Roblox Studio environment, touching on its plethora of built-in resources. These are but the essential stepping stones to much grander projects and collaborations.

But let's not forget: The world of game development is ever-evolving. As your craft grows, so will the tools and technologies around you. Roblox, too, continually updates its features and capabilities. This means there's an ongoing opportunity – and indeed, necessity – for lifelong learning. Never be complacent; always aim to be a better version of your developer self.

One point of view that I would like to offer here is the relevance of community in your developmental journey. Roblox's thriving community of developers is a rich source of inspiration and troubleshooting. Engaging in forums, sharing your work, and even participating in collaborative projects can give you a much-needed broader perspective. It's one thing to understand the syntax and the logic behind the code; it's another to see your code breathe life into an actual game that users worldwide can experience.

Finally, stepping back and remembering why you started this journey is worthwhile. Most often, the genesis of any developer's path is a deep-rooted passion for creating something new and extraordinary. Extraordinary creations seldom occur in isolation; they are the product of consistent learning, constant questioning, and the courage to venture outside one's comfort zone.

So, here's to your next adventure in Roblox game development – may it be as thrilling as it is educational.

Warm regards,

Christopher Coutinho

C. Coutinho, *Roblox Lua Scripting Essentials*, https://doi.org/10.1007/979-8-8688-0026-9

P.S. The art of scripting in Roblox Lua is a craft as much as a skill. As you practice and create, don't just code – tell a story, create an experience, and, most importantly, have fun doing it.

Thank you for investing your time in this book. I look forward to hearing about your future endeavors in Roblox game development.

Index

A

Abstraction, 170, 306, 309
ActionText property, 192
activatePowerUp(player) function, 234
Adornee property, 195
Anchored property, 25, 36, 134, 148, 149, 152
Anonymous functions, 143, 144, 150
Arithmetic operators, 61, 80, 99
Assembly, 135
Assignment operator, 44, 50, 60, 61

B

BillboardGui object, 195
Binary operators, 60
BindableEvent, 163, 164
    bindable event, 165
    code, 165
    :Connect() method, 165
    Event property and Fire() method, 165
    limitations, 168
    local function onShootEvent, 167
    local replStorage, 167
    local shootEvent, 167
    ReplicatedStorage, 165, 166
    in Roblox, 165
    shootEvent.Event:Connect, 167
    shootEvent:Fire, 167
    shootEvent.Name, 167
    shootEvent.Parent, 167
    Weapon, 166

BindableFunction, 163, 166, 176, 177
Block comments, 38
BodyVelocity, 149, 222, 223
Boolean conditions, 70, 72, 73
Boolean literals, 45
BrickColor, 6, 108, 133, 189, 232
brick:FindFirstChildWhichIsA, 160, 161

C

calcRectangleArea, 141
CanCollide property, 35
CanWeaponReload, 176
CFrame (Coordinate Frame), 112, 120, 283
Cframe data type
    complex transformations, 113
    efficient movement, 113
    move a part, specific direction, 116, 117
    offset a part, 113, 114
    parent-child relationship, 113
    parenting a part to another part, 125
    part rotation to face another part, 121, 122, 124
    position and orientation, 112
    position and orientation information, 112
    Roblox Lua, 112
    rotate a part, 115, 116
    smooth animation, 112
    smoother rotations, 113
CFrame.lookAt() function, 121, 283
CFrame.new, 117, 120, 283

Printed in the United States
by Baker & Taylor Publisher Services